THE
MONEY DOCTOR

2013

MAKE YOUR MONEY GO FURTHER

Gill & Macmillan

Gill & Macmillan
Hume Avenue, Park West, Dublin 12
with associated companies throughout the world
www.gillmacmillanbooks.ie

Print origination by O'K Graphic Design, Dublin
Printed by Anglo Printers, Drogheda
Index compiled by Cliff Murphy

The paper used in this book is made from the wood pulp of managed forests. For every tree
felled, at least one tree is planted, thereby renewing natural resources.

A catalogue record is available for this book from the British Library.

1 3 5 4 2

The publisher would like to acknowledge the following for the use of their logos: Life Insurance
Association, The Irish Brokers Association, Professional Insurance Brokers Association, Financial
Services Ombudsman, AIB, Bank of Ireland, Permanent TSB, National Irish Bank, Ulster Bank,
the Credit Union, VHI Healthcare, Aviva Health, Laya Healthcare and GloHealth.

Photographs © Alamy and Getty.

The author and publisher have made every effort to trace all copyright holders, but if any have
been inadvertently overlooked we would be pleased to make the necessary arrangement at the
first opportunity.

Whilst every effort has been made to ensure accuracy, no legal or other liability
on the part of the author or publishers can be accepted for any information
or advice given.

CONTENTS

PREFACE

Welcome to the 2013 edition of Ireland's most comprehensive finance guide.

Ian Dury and the Blockheads' hit song 'Reasons to be Cheerful' hardly describes 2012 as the carnage continued. However bleak the situation may be though, jumping ship is not and was not an option. We are a great nation and a unique country with a culture many other countries envy, so it behoves the Irish people to stay on board and right the issues as best we can. Hope springs eternal.

Many initiatives were taken during 2012 by both the government and the EU to halt our seemingly neverending economic descent into the abyss. Some of these initiatives at least helped the plight of those who have taken a steep reduction in income, or have lost their jobs or businesses, but have also seen their properties plummet below 60% of their 2006 values. Many of these people now owe more than their property is worth – 50% of ALL mortgages are in negative equity – and with over 11% of Irish mortgage-holders in arrears of more than 3 months, steps had to be taken to ameliorate their situation. This, together with the euro stability issues, made for a very nervous 2012 – 50% of my clients this year were as worried about their savings and investments as those with debt issues.

Therefore, in this 2013 edition, I have included a special chapter – 37 – covering both the Central Bank's *MARP (Mortgage Arrears Resolution Process)* and the *Personal Insolvency Bill 2012*, launched by the government in June. The question is, of course, whether it is morally right that the lenders who so freely gave to the borrowers and saw up to 70% reductions in property values take no diminution on their debt. It is debt reality, NOT debt forgiveness. There is a difference between a family with no work who cannot afford to pay a home loan twice the value of the property and borrowers who *can* afford to repay who are simply jumping on the *forgiveness* bandwagon. Tactical delinquency is disgraceful. We need a new morality – back to core values. Slowly these values are being reinstated, albeit somewhat under duress. The government plays an important role in all of this, as do the lenders.

Also included in this year's edition is the Money Doctor's Tips for the Top – five innovative or leading edge products and services that deserve *special* mention and have the *Money Doctor* endorsement – plus the usual *Budget 2013* summary (Appendix 12), along with updates from the previous Budget and throughout 2012 across the annual, and finally, an updated 100 top money-saving tips.

During the last year, Money Doctor introduced a FREE Money Doctor App for both iPhone and Android to help track your daily spending. Simply enter every item of spending for one month via your mobile and use the simple drop-down menu categories. When you end the tracking period, you will receive a detailed report of your spending for that month within minutes, so you now have no excuse to say 'I just don't know where my money goes!' You can access the Money Doctor App from www.moneydoctor.ie or through the iTunes store or Android marketplace – type in *Money Doctor* to download.

In the updated Money Doctor Services chapter, two new services are highlighted: the fee-based 20-minute Money Doctor Consultation, and the Employee Well-being Programme, helping you to focus on your own finances.

Finally, I want to highlight the one advertisement on the inside back cover of this book: it's for the *National Treasury Management Agency's State Savings*, a suite of savings options available in post offices offering the best returns and which are a direct unconditional obligation of the Irish government. Japan is the biggest indebted nation in the world. Their national debt to GDP (Gross Domestic Product, which is all the products and services a country produces ratio) is 233.1%. Ireland has a ratio of 108%. So how does Japan stay afloat? The answer is loyalty and national pride – 95% of Japanese debt is owed to their own people. We in Ireland could do well to follow their example, and to encourage the diaspora in the year of *The Gathering* to invest back in Ireland. Supporting Ireland is top of my agenda and this sole advertisement reflects that.

I often use the following analogy to explain why financial planning is so important:

If you were driving from, say, Cork to Belfast, you wouldn't choose a road at random and hope that it would take you where you wanted to get. Rather, you would plan your journey in advance. If, as you travelled, you encountered diversions, you would get out the road map and decide on the new route. Throughout the journey you'd check your progress.

This book will act then as both a planner and a map on your journey to sound finances.

For many years I have felt that Ireland lacked an annual finance guide that offered genuinely helpful, accurate and independent money advice in language that anyone could understand. I believe that this book fills the gap. Why?

- It is **comprehensive**. Every possible subject has been covered – from getting the best deal on your mortgage to saving for retirement and from slashing your tax bill to working overseas.
- No less importantly, it is packed with **practical** advice. Whatever your circumstances, whatever questions you need answered, whatever your financial goals – you'll find the answers in the following pages.
- All the information here is presented in **plain, jargon-free English** and accompanied by **action-oriented** tips. You'll find real-life examples, checklists and a comprehensive index, too.

The book has also been written for 2013 – and so it is 'bang up to date'.

MORE THAN A BOOK

Actually, I am referring to this as a 'book' – but really it is more of a 'service', because there is also a website – www.moneydoctor.ie – with lots of extra information. So if you need personalised advice you can always email me additional questions at: jlowe@moneydoctor.ie.

THE BIGGER PICTURE

Another advantage that this book has over anything else available in Ireland is that it provides lots of guidance on financial planning. So you can use this book to resolve specific issues (such as paying off all your loans or cutting the cost of your insurance) or to create your own money plan.

WHY THE MONEY DOCTOR?

The short answer is that I aim to do for your wealth what a medical doctor will do for your health. That is to say, I will show you how to overcome any financial 'illnesses' you may be suffering from and also how to improve your financial fitness dramatically. I don't want to stretch the analogy too far but you can rely on me – as you would rely on a good doctor – to be honest, trustworthy and professional. I'm qualified and I'm experienced.

That's the short answer. Now let me give you the slightly longer answer.

At the age of 47, I resigned from my job as senior manager of an Irish bank and turned my back on 27 years of working for mainstream financial institutions. I gave up job security, a pension, a company car and five weeks a year paid holiday. This wasn't the act of a mad man, but the act of someone who had had enough of 'selling' and wanted to start 'telling'.

There is a lot that's still right with our financial services sector. It is now relatively well regulated and offers both choice and value. But it has one major flaw: it is sales driven, not *solution* driven. Banks, building societies and insurance companies always promote their own products rather than someone else's – even if their products are less appropriate and/or more expensive. This has led to a great deal of consumer cynicism and – quite frankly – suspicion. The reason why I gave up my job and changed direction was because I wanted to be above such suspicion. I wanted to be independent – free to do what was best for the 'patient'.

With my first book and this, my eighth finance annual – together with the revamped www.moneydoctor.ie website – I aim to fill what I perceive to be a real gap in the market. That is to say:

• reliable, up-to-date and accurate personal finance information
• unbiased, easy-to-understand and relevant financial advice.

In particular, I cover both the principles of better financial management and the practical aspects of taking financial decisions. *The Money Doctor* will answer all your questions about how to make the most of your money. If there is something you feel I have left out please let me know so that I can include it in future editions.

ONE FINAL POINT

Dealing with money shouldn't be a chore, but a pleasure. Whether you read this book from cover to cover or dip in and out, I hope it will inspire you in all your future financial dealings. It's not about waiting for the storm to pass, it's about learning to dance in the rain, and trust me, the storm will pass, albeit slowly.

John Lowe
Dublin, December 2012

IS THIS BOOK FOR YOU?

This book is for everyone living in Ireland who wants to better manage and structure their personal finances.

- You will find this book relevant regardless of your financial position, age or gender.
- One of the most important aspects of the guide is that it concentrates on 'how to' information, as in: how to manage your mortgage, how to get rid of your debts, how to build up savings, how to save tax and how to protect your family.
- If there is a particular subject you want to learn about, then check the detailed contents page or the index.
- The book is written in plain English and contains plenty of:
  - case histories
  - real-life examples
  - checklists
  - action-orientated advice.
- The book is divided into nine sections plus Appendices covering every aspect of personal finance. It is an annual handbook so the information it contains will be up to date, and include the latest budgetary and legislative changes.
- Each chapter begins with a summary and ends with a list of action points.
- Decision trees (Appendix 3) are designed to help you make a decision by setting out the logic process graphically and allowing you to easily retrace the steps made in coming to that decision. While they are not a substitute for proper research, they can enhance the user's ability to implement what they know.

Look out for the symbols used throughout the book:

Money Doctor Wealth Warning This symbol is used to warn you about something that may have an adverse affect on your financial wealth!

Money Doctor Wealth Check This symbol is used to highlight something that could really improve your financial fitness.

GETTING THE MOST OUT OF THIS BOOK

The Money Doctor says this book will be of relevance to you if you
- have money questions and don't know to whom to turn for an honest, accurate, unbiased answer
- want the latest financial information
- want to reduce your tax bill
- worry about money
- have, or plan to get, a mortgage
- have credit cards, store cards, hire purchase agreements, an overdraft, personal loans, a mortgage or any other borrowings, because it will show you how it is possible to pay all these debts off in a matter of years simply by following a simple, proven, logical plan
- have money on deposit or save money on a regular basis
- want to build up your capital worth and guarantee yourself a comfortable (and possibly an early) retirement
- have capital and don't know how to invest it
- have dependants and you are worried about their well-being
- have (or think you should have) any sort of life or critical illness cover
- worry about the quality of financial advice you are receiving
- are separating, or thinking of it.

THE MONEY DOCTOR WEBSITE

The Money Doctor is not just a book: it is a complete service. Visit the free Money Doctor website at www.moneydoctor.ie offering you:
- extra articles and checklists covering a huge range of personal finance topics
- the latest personal finance tips, advice and information
- jargon buster
- up-to-the-minute mortgage rates
- special calculators allowing you to see (at the press of a button) what your mortgage or other loan will cost you – as well as how much your savings will earn you
- timely information such as the current tax rates and allowances
- the chance to arrange a consultation with John Lowe, the Money Doctor, or one of the Money Doctor advisers

- podcasts on a variety of financial subjects
- an opportunity to receive the Money Doctor's free quarterly newsletter or e-zine, join on Twitter @themoneydoc, LinkedIn, plus read the weekly Money Doctor blog.

The website is updated daily and all the information it contains is available *free* – without charge and without obligation.

You should only deal with an **authorised adviser** to provide insurance, investment, pension advice and credit services.

You can be certain that any individual or firm who is authorised will not only have had to pass a stringent series of tests to qualify, but that their performance will be strictly monitored on an ongoing basis by the Central Bank.

Extra consumer protection

You should be aware that there are a number of professional bodies covering the financial services industry. My own belief is that you should only deal with members of these bodies. These are:

- The Irish Brokers Association (IBA).

- Professional Insurance Brokers Association (PIBA).

- Life Insurance Association (LIA).

Your financial adviser should ideally be a QFA (Qualified Financial Adviser) as well as having substantial financial experience. Individual membership of other professional bodies, such as the Institute of Bankers in Ireland, is also desirable.

Finally, if you are looking for advice on buying company shares then you should deal with intermediaries who are members of (or affiliated members of) the Irish Stock Exchange or an authorised agent.

Don't allow yourself to be talked into accepting advice from someone who isn't both independent and qualified. If in doubt visit my website – www.moneydoctor.ie.

ACKNOWLEDGMENTS

There are many people who deserve a clap on the back for their personal help and support to me and who have guided me throughout my career. Included are family, friends, mentors and colleagues. Special mention and special thanks go to the following for their great assistance in the production of this my tenth book:

My family who continue to support and love me. Jonathan Self (writer, novelist and mentor). George Butler (Money Doctor). John P. Carlin (friend, accountant and Co. Tyrone supporter). Simon Carty (Solicitor). Monica McInerney (best-selling novelist) for her introduction to my publishers Gill & Macmillan. Nora Mahony (proofreader), Catherine Gough (Managing Editor) and all the talented team at G&M – every one a gem. Fergal Tobin (Gill & Macmillan) for his fantastic help and for giving me the excuse to tell my friends I have lunch on a regular basis with my publisher! Special thanks to Newstalk 106FM (especially the *Lunchtime* team, Jonathan Healy, Eimear, Stephen, Emma & Aisling), RTÉ, TV3, Sunshine Radio, East Coast FM, Clare FM, Tipp FM, LMFM, Highland Radio, Waterford Local Radio FM, Midlands 103, Limerick's Live 95FM, Today FM, Ocean FM, 96FM, Cork 103 FM, MidWest Radio, South East Radio and Cliff Taylor and all the team at the *Sunday Business Post*.

PART 1

HOW TO BECOME FINANCIALLY FIT IN 2013

IT ALL COMES DOWN TO BELIEF PATTERNS

I am far too practical a person to be taken in by 'psycho-babble'. However, I do believe that *if you want to be financially better off than you are at the moment then you simply must come to grips with your own belief patterns as they relate to money*. One method of explaining what I mean is to quote some of the different things people have said to me about money:

> 'I would always shop around for a better deal on most things – but not on financial products.'
>
> 'I hate talking about money. I find it embarrassing.'
>
> 'Money seems to slip through my fingers.'
>
> 'I worry about money all the time but I don't do anything about it, because I am not sure what to do.'
>
> 'Money is boring. We have enough. Why think about it?'

In my experience almost everyone has deeply held beliefs in relation to money – usually negative beliefs. Most can be attributed to one or more of the following factors:

Formative experiences. Take, for instance, the case of someone whose family suffered financial hardship when they were growing up. Naturally, it would influence their attitude to money.

Parental influence. Some parents talk about money, others don't – but either way, children can end up being worried about there not being enough. By the same token, some parents are spendthrift while others are positively tight-fisted – again influencing their children's beliefs.

Lack of education. Though there have been recent moves to change the national curriculum, 'personal finance' is still not really taught properly in our schools.

The mystification of money. Financial institutions seem to conspire to make money as mysterious a subject as possible.

Lack of trust in personal finance professionals. Bank managers are viewed as 'fair-weather friends' and the institutions they work for as impersonal and greedy. Insurance and pensions salespeople are hardly revered in society. People are suspicious of the experts they rely on to give them advice.

Society's attitude to money. There are some societies where money is discussed openly. In Ireland, however, it is considered rude to talk about money and crass to spend too much time managing it.

THE LINK BETWEEN BELIEF AND BEHAVIOUR

There is no doubt in my mind that there is a direct link between (a) what you believe about money, (b) your behaviour in relation to money and (c) how much money you end up having. **The fact is that if you view money in a negative way, you are reducing your chances of a financially stable life. You aren't giving yourself a proper chance.**

What's more, if you think that sorting out your personal finances will take more time and effort than *not* sorting them out, think again. Not paying attention to money is likely to result in you:

- wasting a vast amount of energy worrying
- wasting a vast amount of cash
- putting yourself and your dependants at risk
- reducing your standard of living
- increasing the number of years you have to work
- suffering a shortfall in your pension fund when you reach retirement age.

If you start to *think* positively about money, I guarantee that you will begin to *behave* more positively about money. And if you behave more positively about money, I guarantee that you will find yourself able to build up much greater wealth.

What are your financial dreams?

- To own your own home without a mortgage?
- To have enough money to retire early?
- To be wealthy enough to pay for all the things you want – such as an education for your children or a second home – without going into debt?

Whatever your dreams, unless you are very, very lucky, the only way to make them come true is to make a proper plan. Such a plan – a financial plan – will help ensure that you get from where you are to where you want to be. Creating one is a lot simpler and quicker than you may imagine, as I explain in this section of the book. Furthermore, I guarantee that the process of writing a plan will – in itself – make you substantially better off. Why? Read on and you'll find out.

MONEY DOCTOR WEALTH CHECK

The section on financial planning explains:

- what a financial plan is
- why you need a financial plan
- the different stages involved in writing a financial plan
- practical tips on writing your own plan
- where to get professional financial planning help you can trust
- sample financial plans.

And more besides. Everything, in fact, you need to make financial planning easy.

1
ALL IT TAKES IS A LITTLE PLANNING

HOW YOUR FINANCIAL PLAN WILL MAKE YOU BETTER OFF

Many people are under the impression that financial planning is a complex process requiring great expertise. In fact, creating a financial plan is a remarkably straightforward activity involving three easy steps:

1   Decide what your financial or money objectives are, and prioritise them.

2   Assess what resources you have available to you now, and consider what resources you may have in the future.

3   Work out what actions you need to take to make your financial (or your 'money') objectives come true.

This short chapter explains the 'ins and outs' of writing a first-class financial plan. The next chapter explains, in greater detail, how to write your own.

WHY YOU NEED A FINANCIAL PLAN

Your financial plan should have the same qualities as the road map analogy as described in the introduction. That is to say, it should help you reach your destination; make your journey as fast as possible; and prevent you wasting time or energy.

MONEY DOCTOR WEALTH CHECK

A little planning brings big rewards

Having a financial plan will bring both *material* and *emotional* rewards. From a material perspective a financial plan will make it possible for you to meet your financial objectives. These might include some or all of the following:

- wiping out all your personal debts
- paying off your mortgage years earlier
- never having to borrow again

- having enough money to afford the things that are important to you, such as an education for your children or a second home
- having enough money to retire early
- knowing that you and your dependants are protected against financial hardships
- being wealthy enough never to have to worry about the future – whatever it may bring.

And the emotional benefits? You'll feel a tangible peace of mind once you have your financial affairs in order. In addition, a well-considered financial plan guarantees that you will never need to waste energy worrying about money again.

Some people's circumstances, of course, may be such that they will not manage to achieve any or all of these objectives. For these people, financial planning is crucial to getting the maximum advantage from limited resources even with insolvency.

SUPPOSING YOU *DON'T* PLAN?

Suppose you don't bother with a financial plan at all? Leaving something as important as your financial future to chance is risky. True, we live in a country with a relatively generous state benefit system. But would you really want to rely on it? You probably wouldn't starve, but you wouldn't have an easy time of it.

Incidentally, many people assume that the worst thing anyone can do is ignore financial planning completely. In fact, in my experience the people who are worst off are those who *compartmentalise* their money decisions. Let me give you just three examples:

1   When you want to buy a home, you look for a mortgage.
2   When you begin to think about retirement, you start a pension.
3   When you have a young family, you take out life insurance.

The trouble with a compartmentalised approach to money is that it is both wasteful and risky because you may:

- end up spending more than you have to on borrowing money
- by default, pay more tax than you need to
- end up with inferior and expensive financial products

- risk your capital, your income, and the standard of living of you and your dependants
- miss opportunities and
- make yourself unhappy worrying about your financial security.

A symptom of this approach is responding to ad hoc situations in a knee-jerk manner, for example, subscribing for newly issued shares on a whim, or paying for education fees when you hadn't expected to do so.

INSTANT SAVINGS AND MORE

Incidentally, one of the key benefits of creating a financial plan is that it will involve a review of your existing financial products. Such a review is bound to result in all sorts of savings as you identify products that are either over-priced or unnecessary. Let me give you just one real-life example:

> One of the Money Doctor's 'patients', Tony, an ex-banker, told me that he'd spent more time choosing his last car than choosing his mortgage. As a result he was, without realising it, paying 1% above the home loan market rate. He'd also allowed himself to be sold a very expensive life insurance plan. I calculated that, over the 25-year term of Tony's €210,000 mortgage, these two products alone would cost him a staggering additional €38,000 in unnecessary loan and insurance payments.

Frankly, because people pay less attention to their finances than to other areas of their lives, they tend to get 'ripped off'. With a financial plan in place, you'll know that you aren't:

- accepting lower rates of return on your savings
- paying more tax than you have to
- paying more to borrow than you have to
- taking out insurance policies that you don't need, or that don't provide you with the protection that you want, and that may well be over-priced
- making poor investment decisions
- failing to plan properly for your retirement or
- putting your money at risk.

WHAT DOES A FINANCIAL PLAN LOOK LIKE?

Your financial plan may be no more than a single piece of paper on which you've jotted down appropriate notes. You might think of it in the same way that you think of a career plan or any other sort of life plan. It is to guide you, save you time, and ensure that none of your effort is wasted. Or, if you are comfortable using spreadsheet software, you could also do it electronically. Whatever way you choose to complete a financial plan, remember it is essential for giving you a map for your financial road to the future.

HOW LONG SHOULD A FINANCIAL PLAN LAST FOR?

Obviously, there is no set period for a financial plan. My general advice is to write it so that it covers the **current** and **next phase** of your life. For instance, if you've just left university and you're starting your first job, then you might write a financial plan designed to take you through to when you own your home. Bear in mind that financial plans need to be *flexible*. You may change your own ideas about what you want or circumstances may intervene and require a change of direction.

A financial plan that only covers a specific, short-term requirement (for instance, saving for your retirement) isn't going to bring you lasting financial success.

IF YOU THINK YOU NEED HELP

You will find everything you need to write your own financial plan in this book. However, you may decide you'd like some professional help. There are any number of people who would like to help you with your personal finances, from bank managers to life insurance salespeople, from credit brokers to pension specialists.

The golden rule is: the fewer options the 'experts' can offer you, the less you should trust them.

Let me give you one pertinent example. If you go to your bank and express an interest in taking out a pension, whoever you speak to is duty-bound to offer you something from the bank's own range of products, if they have their own tied agency, even if he or she knows that you would get a better deal elsewhere. If, on the other hand, you go to an independent financial adviser he or she should recommend the best and most competitively priced product for your needs.

For more tips on getting professional help, see p. 29.

THE MONEY DOCTOR SAYS...

- There is nothing in the least bit complicated about writing a financial plan. It is simply a matter of working out what your money ambitions are, how far you have got to date, and what action you need to take to get to where you want to go.

- Unless you are very, very lucky, the only way you are going to make your financial dreams come true is by planning.

- Your plan may be a single piece of paper with a few notes.

- The process of writing a plan is likely to bring big savings as you identify financial products you have already bought that are either (a) over-priced or (b) not really necessary.

- Everything you need to write a financial plan is in this book. But if you want help, use an experienced, independent and authorised financial adviser, and be prepared to pay for that advice.

2
WRITING A FINANCIAL PLAN

EVERYTHING YOU NEED TO KNOW TO WRITE YOUR OWN FINANCIAL PLAN (OR TO GET SOMEONE ELSE TO DO IT FOR YOU)

If you've put off writing a financial plan because you thought it would be both time-consuming and tedious, then this chapter will reassure you. Not only is it possible to produce a detailed financial plan in a matter of hours but as you get involved in the process you may find it considerably more interesting than you ever imagined.

> **MONEY DOCTOR WEALTH CHECK**
>
> *First things first*
>
> Many people begin the whole financial planning process because they want to resolve a particular financial question. But you shouldn't look at financial needs in isolation. Every financial decision you make should be part of an overall plan. Thus, a particular product – such as a mortgage, loan, insurance policy or investment – should not just be judged on its own particular merits but also in terms of how it moves you closer to your financial objectives. For this reason, no financial plan can be created until you have set and prioritised your financial objectives.

HOW DO YOU DECIDE WHAT YOUR FINANCIAL OBJECTIVES SHOULD BE?

My advice is to start by dreaming. Consider what you'd like to be doing in, say, five years' time, ten years' time, and twenty years' time. Consider what work (if any) you'll be doing, where you'll be living, and how you'll be spending your leisure time. What will your family situation be? Once you have a clear picture of the future life you'd like to have, start expressing it in financial terms.

Your possible financial objectives might include:

* owning your own home, outright, without a mortgage

- making sure you have sufficient income to retire (possibly early) and live in comfort
- ensuring that you and your dependants will not suffer financial hardship regardless of any misfortunes that may befall you
- having sufficient wealth to pay for things that you consider important, whether it's charitable donations, an education for your children, or some other item such as a second home or a caravan
- having sufficient wealth to allow you to spend your time as you wish, for instance, having the money to start your own business.

PRIORITISING YOUR FINANCIAL OBJECTIVES

Having produced a list of financial objectives, your next task should be to put them in **order of priority**.

What you consider important will be determined to a great extent by your personal circumstances. For instance, if you're in third-level education, you'll have a very different view of money to someone five years away from retirement. Someone with a lot of debts will have different concerns to someone with a lump sum to invest.

Nevertheless, regardless of your age, existing wealth, health, number of dependants, or – for that matter – any other factor, I would recommend that you keep the following principles in mind when deciding what your financial priorities should be:

1 For most people, their greatest asset is their **income**. Unless you are fortunate enough to receive a windfall, it is almost certainly your income which you will use to achieve your financial objectives. Under the circumstances you don't want to risk it and you don't want to waste it. There are all sorts of relatively inexpensive insurance policies designed to protect your income. And by making sure that you don't waste a single cent (especially when buying financial services) you can ensure that it's used to optimum purpose.

2 **Personal debt** – by which I mean everything from store cards to mortgages – will be the biggest drain on your income. If you've borrowed money (and, obviously, there are many circumstances under which this makes excellent sense) then you should make it a priority to repay your loans as quickly as possible. This is easily achievable as I explain in Part 3.

3 It's vital to have a safety net or **emergency fund** to deal with those little

trials, tribulations and extra expenses that life often throws our way. In Part 6, I suggest how much this fund should be, and the best way to build it up.

4   If you've got a good, secure income, it doesn't actually matter what other assets you own. Emotionally, it's nice to have the security of owning your own home. Financially, it certainly makes sense. But, actually, the best investment that most people could ever make is in a really decent **pension plan.** With a good pension plan you can leave work early and – if you live to 100 or more – never have to worry about money again. One of the best things about modern pension plans is that they are both flexible and diverse.

5   It is not inconceivable that we will live to a very old age and in some cases suffer a reduction in our mental ability to handle money matters. Before this may arise it is worth considering setting up an **enduring power of attorney.** This is a document providing for the management of a person's affairs in the event of their becoming mentally incapacitated. The appointed person (the 'attorney') may be allowed to take a wide range of actions on your behalf in relation to property, business and social affairs. He or she may make payments from the specified accounts, make appropriate provision for any specified person's needs and make appropriate gifts to the donor's relations or friends. You can appoint anyone you wish to be your attorney, including a spouse, family member, friend, colleague, etc.

6   **Know thyself!** There's no point in setting financial objectives that you're going to find impossible to attain. Your financial objectives may involve modest changes in your behaviour, but they shouldn't require a complete change in your personality!

TEN UNIVERSAL NEEDS

Ultimately, financial planning is about tailoring a solution to meet your precise requirements. Having said this, there are a number of 'universal' needs that most of us face. To my mind they are:

1   Having an emergency fund to cover unexpected expenses.
2   Paying off any expensive personal loans and credit card debt.
3   Short-term saving for cars, holidays, and so forth.
4   Income protection, in case you are unable to work for any reason.
5   Life assurance for you (and, if relevant, your partner).

6 Starting a pension plan (in my opinion it is never too early).
7 Buying a home with the help of a mortgage.
8 Saving for major purchases.
9 Planning for education fees (if you have children), whether for private school or university.
10 Building up your personal investments.

To this, I suppose I might add long-term care planning if you're worried that your pension and/or the state may not provide for you sufficiently in retirement.

SETTING REALISTIC AIMS

If you had unlimited funds, then you could achieve all your financial ambitions without difficulty and you wouldn't need a financial plan. As it is, for most of us life is more complicated. Since we can't have everything we want instantly, we need to set realistic targets and work towards them in easy stages. To make sure we have realistic targets we must test them. Let me give you an example:

David is 40 and self-employed. His objective is to be financially independent by the age of 55. At that point he wants to be able to live comfortably without working. His current income is €40,000 a year and he feels that he'll be able to manage on much less, say €25,000 a year, once he retires. To achieve this, he'll need capital resources of between €500,000 and €600,000. At this point in time he has a pension fund worth €100,000 which, if it grows in real terms (i.e. after the effects of inflation) by 5% a year, will be worth some €208,000 in 15 years. He also has €25,000 of stocks and shares, which he expects to grow at a slightly faster rate, say 7% a year, which would mean an extra €74,000 in 15 years.

In other words, David has a shortfall of between €212,000 and €312,000. To fill this shortfall, he would have to save at least €600 a month (assuming a growth rate of at least 7%) until he reaches 55. However, €600 a month, or more, is a lot of cash to find, so he may have to adjust his expectations. Perhaps he could live on less? Or postpone his retirement an extra five years? Or earn additional money?

Note: this example is just to give you a feel for what I'm talking about. Inflation would need to be taken into account when deciding what to do. I have ignored current pension returns and low growth rates. Everything is cyclical.

Once you settle on your overall objectives, you'll have to decide which is the most important to you. For instance, would you rather pay off your mortgage ten years early, or take an annual holiday overseas? Is being able to retire early more important than putting your children through private school?

You must also weigh up other priorities. I always recommend that those with dependants take out income protection insurance before they take out life cover. Why? Anyone under retirement age is 20 times more likely to be unable to work for a prolonged period due to sickness than they are to die. Another recommendation I often make is that people with high personal debt pay it off or consolidate it before they start saving money. This is because it costs more to borrow than you can hope to earn from most forms of low-risk investment.

Anyway, the two key points I want to make are:

1   Keep your financial expectations realistic.
2   Test them to make sure.

HOW FAR HAVE YOU GOT?

If the first stage of a financial plan involves deciding what you want, then the second stage is all about working out where you've got to so far. You need to produce an honest and realistic assessment of:

* what resources you have
* what demands there are on your resources and
* what action you are already taking to meet your targets.

Once you have this information you'll know what surplus is available to you and whether you have a shortfall that needs to be made up.

If you visit my website – www.moneydoctor.ie – you'll find several aids to help you make and reach your goals. Email me directly for a Word document budget plan. Otherwise, you can use the questionnaire that follows.

YOUR MONTHLY INCOME AND OUTGOINGS

I usually suggest that people start with their income and – if relevant – their spouse/partner's income. The best way to calculate it is as follows:

Monthly income – gross	You €	Spouse/partner €
Salary or wages	_____	_____
Profits from business	_____	_____

Investment income	_____	_____
State benefits	_____	_____
Pensions	_____	_____
Other earnings	_____	_____
Anything else	_____	_____
Subtotal A	€ _____	_____
Less tax (PRSI and income tax)	_____	_____
Subtotal B	€ _____	_____

The resulting figure (Subtotal B) is your disposable income. You now need to consider how you spend it.

Monthly outgoings	You	Spouse/partner
	€	€
Rent/mortgage	_____	_____
Utilities (gas, electricity, telephone, etc.)	_____	_____
Food	_____	_____
Household items	_____	_____
Drink	_____	_____
Car(s)	_____	_____
Home insurance	_____	_____
Life insurance	_____	_____
Other insurance	_____	_____
Clothes	_____	_____
Child-related expenses	_____	_____
Credit cards	_____	_____
Other loan repayments	_____	_____
Spending money	_____	_____
Pension contribution	_____	_____
Regular saving plans	_____	_____
Anything else	_____	_____
Subtotal C	€ _____	_____

By subtracting your monthly outgoings (Subtotal C) from your disposable income (Subtotal B) you will arrive at your available surplus. Don't despair if this is a 'minus' figure. That's why you are reading this book – and, together, we are going to do something about it!

YOUR ASSETS

Working out what assets you have involves the same process as working out what your surplus income is. You need to tot up the value of everything you own and subtract any debts or other liabilities you may have.

Start with a list of the assets themselves:

Assets	You €	Spouse/partner €
Home		
Personal belongings		
Furniture and contents of home		
Car(s)		
Other property		
Other valuables		
Cash		
Savings		
Shares		
Other investments		
Subtotal D	€	

With regard to any investments you have – savings plans or a pension, for instance – you may want to work out what they will be worth at whatever point in the future you intend to cash them in. This can be a complex business. A pension fund, for instance, may grow by more or less than the predicted amount. Therefore, it could be well worth your while to get professional assistance with your calculations.

YOUR LIABILITIES

Liabilities	You €	Spouse/partner €
Mortgage		
Credit card debts		
Personal loans		
Hire purchase		
Overdraft		
Other loans		
Tax		
Other liabilities		
Subtotal E	€	

By subtracting your total liabilities (Subtotal E) from the value of your assets (Subtotal D) you will arrive at what financial experts call your 'net worth'. While it not good if this is a 'minus' figure, once again you shouldn't despair. The whole purpose of a money plan is to strengthen your finances.

THE IMPORTANCE OF MAKING ASSUMPTIONS

All financial planning requires 'assumptions'. Some of these assumptions will be personal to you, such as how much income you expect to earn in the future or how many children you anticipate supporting. Other assumptions will be related to factors only partly within your control, such as the return you can expect to receive for a particular investment. You'll also need to allow for financial factors beyond your control, such as the state of the economy.

When making assumptions, the longer the period you're planning for, the less accurate your assumptions will be. It's very hard to predict exactly what you'll be earning in, say, five or ten years, let alone what you'll be earning in twenty years.

In order to improve the quality of their assumptions, many people use historic figures for guidance. Below, I've detailed some statistics that you may find of help.

Inflation. There was a time when inflation had the single greatest influence on the economy and thus on financial planning. Although inflation has been quite low for the last few years, it still has a marked effect on the cost of borrowing and the value of your investments. An inflation rate is the general rise in prices as measured against a standard level of purchasing power. The best-known measures of inflation are the Consumer Price Index (CPI), which measures consumer prices, and the Gross Domestic Product (GDP) deflator, which measures inflation across the whole of the domestic economy. The inflation rate in Ireland was recorded at 1.90% in April of 2012. Historically, from 1976 until 2012, Ireland's inflation rate averaged 5.32%, reaching an all-time high of 23.15% in October 1981, and a record low of 6.56% in October 2009.

Interest rates. Interest rates vary enormously, especially when you are borrowing. For instance, in 2012, when a typical mortgage cost 4.05% per year, you could pay up to 21% on a typical store card. Over the last ten years the average mortgage rate has actually been c.6% a year, though in 1995 it did reach 12% a year. During the same period the average personal loan rate has been 12% a year, and the average rate for deposits in a bank or building society has been 3% a year.

Investments. Not only do the returns on different types of investment vary dramatically, so do the returns within each sort of investment vehicle. So, while investing in the stock market could bring a better average return than investing in property, an individual investor might do substantially better or worse in one or the other. In general, it is best to spread your money between different types of investment, and to assume an average return of between 4% and 7% a year in real terms. For instance, between 1997 and 2007 the average return from government bonds has been 4.7% a year, while the average return on the stock market has been 10.1%.

Money Doctor Wealth Check

How much capital will you need?

One of the hardest calculations anyone has to make is how much capital they need to provide a sufficient income for their needs. There are different factors affecting this: inflation, tax and investment performance.

On the whole, my advice is to assume a 2.5% return after inflation and tax. This means that for every €1,000 of annual income you require, you'll need €40,000 of capital. Put another way, if you want an annual income of €20,000 a year you'll need at least €800,000 worth of capital.

Money Doctor Wealth Warning

An important reminder

Do you have a will? If you do, when did you last update it? Are you taking *full* advantage of all the tax allowances and exemptions to make sure that your beneficiaries don't have to pay unnecessary inheritance tax?

If you are over 18 (or if you are younger, but married) you should draw up a will because if you don't, your money will be distributed in accordance with the Succession Act of 1965. This means that your estate could end up not going to your chosen beneficiary or beneficiaries and could even end up filling the government's coffers.

You'll find more information about using your will to save capital acquisition tax on the Money Doctor website (www.moneydoctor.ie), or through a Consultation. Don't forget, both you and your partner should draw up a will and you should also consider:

- giving a power of attorney to someone you trust should you become physically incapacitated – an enduring power of attorney
- a living will explaining anything you would like done should you become so unwell as to be unable to communicate.

WHERE DO YOU NEED TO TAKE ACTION?

Which areas of your personal finances should you be dealing with first? Answer the questions below with a 'yes', 'no', or 'maybe'. Every question you answer with a 'no' or 'maybe' suggests an area where you need to take action.

- Do you spend less than you earn each month?
- Are you satisfied with your standard of living?
- Do you pay your credit card and charge card bills in full, on time, every month?
- Have you taken out sufficient life cover to ensure that your family's lifestyle won't be adversely affected if you die?
- Are you happy with where you live? Can you afford it?
- If you had to manage without an income, would you be able to support yourself for at least three months using money you have saved?
- Do you have a clear sense of financial goals? Have you spent any time thinking about how you're going to achieve them?
- Do you have a pension? Will it be sufficient to support you in reasonable comfort?
- Do you have a will?
- Do you have other investments designed to bring you long-term capital growth?

THE MONEY DOCTOR SAYS...

- If you are not sure where to begin – begin at the beginning. Work out what you want from your money – what your priorities are.
- Although everyone's circumstances are different, we all have the same basic needs – to secure our future regardless of what happens. This is done through a combination of saving, investment and insurance.
- Take a little time to work out where you are financially – it may be the most profitable half-hour you ever spend.
- Don't be shy about asking for help. If you know you want to sort out your finances, but find it difficult, call in expert help.

3
MONEY IS A FAMILY AFFAIR

HOW FAMILIES CAN WORK TOGETHER TO ACHIEVE LONG-TERM FINANCIAL SECURITY

Anyone who has been in a settled relationship will know that money and love can be a potent combination – both good and bad. If you and your partner share the same attitude to money, then obviously you'll be able to build a secure future for yourselves faster, more efficiently and more enjoyably than if you are in conflict.

However, it would be ridiculous not to acknowledge that many relationships are blighted by arguments about money and that reaching a compromise isn't always easy. In this chapter we look at how couples – and families – can work together to reach their financial goals. And we also look at the importance of educating children about money.

PROBLEM? WHAT PROBLEM?

All relationship money problems tend to boil down to one or more of the following issues:

- how the money is earned and who is earning it
- how the money is spent and who is spending it
- how the money is being managed and who is managing it
- how the money is being saved (if it is being saved at all) and who is doing the saving
- how the money is being invested (if it is being invested at all) and who is handling the investment decisions
- what debts you have – both individually and jointly – and why they were incurred.

Of all the subjects which couples argue about – from the choice of holiday destination to who should do the washing-up – money arguments are the hardest to resolve. This is because our money beliefs tend to be (a) firmly held, (b) unconscious and (c) non-negotiable.

Couples who are serious about building a financially secure future for themselves need to keep an open mind regarding their partner's viewpoint. One of you may be a saver, the other a spender, but that doesn't mean a compromise isn't possible.

ARE YOU AND YOUR PARTNER FINANCIALLY COMPATIBLE?

When a couple disagree about money, it is almost always because they each hold different money beliefs. Which of the following categories best describes you and your partner?

Worry warts. People who worry so much that they never really enjoy money – even when they have plenty.

Big spenders. People who spend money whether or not they have it. They don't mind going into debt to fund their lifestyle.

Careful savers. People who are committed to saving. Sometimes they can be obsessive about it to the point of miserliness, however.

Optimistic dreamers. People who believe that through some miracle – perhaps an unexpected legacy or a lottery win – all their financial worries will be solved overnight.

Outright fools. People – sorry to be harsh – whose spending and borrowing is reckless.

Clever planners. People who plan for a secure financial future but still manage to enjoy a good lifestyle now.

Where a couple consists of two 'clever planners' you tend to get minimum friction. Otherwise, sooner or later, disagreements are bound to arise.

In an ideal world ...

In an ideal world, one would discuss money with a future partner before making any sort of commitment, as this would allow you to check that you are financially compatible. However, we don't live in an ideal world and so most couples will find themselves tackling financial issues after they have been together for some time. Looking on the bright side, maybe this is preferable. After all, you now know and understand each other better.

OPENING A DIALOGUE

The first and most important step for anyone in a relationship is to **open a dialogue** with their partner. If you don't communicate you won't know what they are thinking, and they won't know what you are thinking. My advice is to have a gentle discussion in which you discuss some or all of the following topics:

- Your individual values in relation to money. What do each of you think is important?
- Any assumptions either of you may have. One of you may assume that finances should always be joint, the other may have fixed ideas about keeping them separate.
- *Your* dreams and desires and *your partner's* dreams and desires. How do you both envisage the future?
- *Your* fears and *your partner's* fears. What are you both most worried about?

Both of you will have inherited traits and you need to recognise what they are before any sort of agreement can be reached between you.

ANYTHING TO DECLARE?

There are so many tricky areas when it comes to discussing personal finance with your partner that it is hard to decide which is potentially the most controversial. One subject which never fails to cause problems is that of 'secret debts' and 'secret savings'. By this I mean:

- One or both partners have borrowed money without telling the other one.
- One or both partners have tucked money away without telling the other one.

Other 'secrets' which couples keep from each other include:

- How much one or other really earns.
- Money that one or the other has given away or promised (this often arises where one or other has been married before).

If you are harbouring a money secret from your partner, my advice is come clean. The longer you leave it, the worse it will be if you are discovered. Also, it is much harder (and sometimes impossible) to tackle your joint financial position if one of you is holding out.

MONEY DOCTOR WEALTH CHECK

The gentle art of confession

You have a money secret that you need to tell your partner. How can you do it without risking a break-up? Here are some tips:

- The longer you leave it, the worse it will be and the more chance that it will cause a serious rift.

- Pick your moment. No one likes to receive bad news just when they have to go to work or do something else. Better to raise the topic when you are alone and there is a chance to talk about it.

- If appropriate, don't forget to say 'sorry'.

- A medical doctor once told me that he always prepares family members for news about the death of a loved one a day or two before it is likely to happen with the words 'I am afraid you should expect the worst' – this gives them time to get used to the idea. If you start by saying you have a confession to make and it may shock or anger them, the conversation is unlikely to be as acrimonious.

- Don't fool yourself that – say – borrowing or spending money without telling your partner won't upset them. But, equally, remember that it is only money. The important thing is that there should be honesty in your relationship.

BUILDING A JOINT APPROACH TO MONEY

Disagreements about personal finance can be very divisive – I have seen figures that suggest half of the couples who break up do so because of a disagreement about money. So when I say that you need to agree a joint financial strategy with your partner I don't say it lightly. One approach that I have found works well is to:

- **Look for common ground.** It is likely, for instance, that you both want the same thing – to be free of debt and have plenty of spare cash.
- **Communicate freely and honestly.** Assess where you are and how each of

you have contributed to the current state of affairs. Be honest. Discuss each of your strengths and weaknesses – the things you are doing right, and the things you are doing wrong.

- **Compromise.** Don't allow past behaviour and events to poison your chance of success. Put grievances behind you. Start afresh and in doing so accept that you will both have to agree to do things differently in the future.

SHARING OUT THE CHORES

There are certain basic money chores that have to be done and one of the most useful things any couple can do in relation to their personal finances is agree who is going to take on which responsibilities. My recommendation is that all major decisions are made jointly and that each partner should keep the other informed about what they are doing. The tasks that need to be divided up include:

- paying household bills
- filing and organising financial paperwork
- doing the household shopping
- checking the bank accounts and reconciling the balances
- looking after the spending money and accessing cash
- shopping for larger purchases
- saving money and arranging any loans
- investment decisions
- keeping an eye on investments
- dealing with financial institutions, banks, insurance companies and so forth.

In many relationships, one or other partner will take over management for the financial affairs. Even where this works without a hitch I feel it is not entirely a good idea. Supposing one of you should die unexpectedly – how would the other cope? Also, what happens if you go your separate ways at some point? I can't stress how important it is to share information and decisions.

MONEY DOCTOR WEALTH CHECK

How to make yourself financially compatible

Here are some valuable tips on handling joint finances – whether with your partner or with someone else, such as a flatmate or friend.

- Maintain your independence. A joint account is perfect for joint responsibilities but it is a good idea to keep an account for yourself so that you have money available to spend as you want. Decide which areas are joint expenditure and which you are each going to handle alone.

- If one half of a partnership takes over all the money management it can lead to big trouble. The person 'in charge' may end up resenting the fact that he or she is doing all the work and he or she may also become controlling. The person not involved is leaving himself or herself vulnerable and is adopting an essentially childlike position. Both of you should take decisions together – even if one of you does the day-to-day accounting.

- Be honest about how you each feel. If one of you wants to save and the other wants to spend, admit it and work out a strategy that allows each of you to do as you please. Compromise!

- Plan for a future that isn't completely dependent on staying together. I realise that this may seem pessimistic but I frequently find myself counselling people who unexpectedly find themselves having to deal with money for the first time.

THE IMPORTANCE OF INVOLVING AND EDUCATING YOUR CHILDREN

How did your parents' approach to money influence you? Now consider how your attitude will influence your own children. Regardless of your level of wealth, everything you say or do in relation to money will have an effect:

- If you don't discuss money in front of them they won't learn anything about it.
- Whatever emotions you display – such as fear, worry or indifference – will colour their own relationship with money.

- If you are mean with money or overly generous, if you never waste a penny, or if you spend like there's no tomorrow, your children will be watching and learning.

Given that they are unlikely to learn much about money from any other quarter – and given the way debt is spreading through society like some super virus – it is obviously important that you educate your children about personal finance. You need to teach them the key principles, including how to:

- save for a specific purpose
- stick to a budget
- choose competitive products
- shop around
- spend money wisely.

THE MONEY DOCTOR SAYS...

My upbringing was fairly typical for Ireland in the 1960s. There were six of us squeezed into a three-bedroom house. My father was a manager and although we never went without, money was always tight. I am reminded of the comedian Les Dawson's self-deprecating quip, 'We were so poor, the first time I saw a butcher's shop, I thought there'd been an accident!' Of course, we didn't have the luxuries that today's generation are now so used to and have come to expect. In Ireland today, our children really do not appreciate some of the hardship their parents went through and, in some respects, this is a pity, because parents' values are so much different to their children's. However, the current recession has refocused the core values of parents and their children.

Clearly, what you *don't* want to do is worry your children about money. Still, I believe there is a lot to be said for showing them where your income comes from, and what you then do with it.

When your children realise how well you manage money they can't fail to be proud of you. Naturally, they will grow up not just wanting to be debt-free and rich enough to retire when young – but actually understanding how this can be achieved. What better legacy could you leave?

If your financial circumstances have radically changed, it is far better to keep your children in the loop and ask them to help with economising. This way, the shock of change will be far less pronounced.

THE MONEY DOCTOR SAYS...

- If you are in a relationship, it is vital that you discuss your financial objectives together, sort out your differences and formulate a joint plan.
- Honesty is vital! You have to work together, not against each other.
- Remember, two heads are better than one. If you are working together you'll reach your objectives sooner – and it will be more fun, too.
- Don't forget, it is important to educate your children about finance. Don't let them leave home without good money habits and a genuine understanding of how money works.

4
GETTING HELP

Should you adopt a DIY approach to your financial planning or should you get professional help? And, if you seek help, who can you trust to give you the best advice?

Are you the sort of person who relishes the challenge of managing their own financial welfare? Or are you the sort of person who would feel happier passing the whole task to someone else?

HOW FAR SHOULD YOU GO?

You want to make the most of your money. In practical terms this means:

- keeping the cost of your borrowing (including your mortgage) to a bare minimum and making sure that you have the most suitable mortgage for your needs
- earning the highest possible return from your savings and investments without taking undue risk or paying unnecessary fees or commission
- obtaining the best possible pension plan
- taking out only the most appropriate insurance at the lowest possible price
- not paying a penny more tax than you have to
- not paying a penny more for any other financial services or products than you have to
- not being caught by any unscrupulous operators.

With the help of this book (and by visiting my website www.moneydoctor.ie) you will certainly be able to achieve all of the above by yourself. However, does the DIY approach make sense for you? The following questions may help you to decide:

Have you got the right temperament? Financial planning can be stressful and time-consuming. If you hate figure work, don't like making decisions and worry about taking risks then maybe you would be better off seeking professional assistance.

Do you have the time? Are you willing to give up a few hours a month to make sure you are optimising your finances? Do you see this as being quite good fun? If not, then maybe the DIY approach isn't best for you.

Can you access the information you need? Financial planning requires access to information. If you can't gain access to the web, and if you aren't near a good library, then it is possible you should let someone else do the legwork for you.

GETTING HELP

How to get help from someone you can trust

Whenever I do a radio phone-in as the Money Doctor I find that the question I get asked most is: 'Who can I turn to for help with my money problems?'

Consumers, understandably, want independent and expert advice. The trouble is that most people offering advice actually work for financial institutions and have products to promote. Bluntly, if you talk to a life assurance salesperson about your retirement planning you know she or he isn't going to recommend anything except one of the products her or his own company sells.

The only solution is to get your advice from someone who isn't under any pressure to *sell* anything, but is in a position to do what is best for you.

This book is designed to give you all the information you need to organise your finances, save you tax and find the most appropriate products for your needs. (If you have any questions, remember you can also take advantage of my web-based service at www.moneydoctor.ie)

However, if you want to discuss your situation through with someone – face to face – make sure you talk to a professional who is experienced in all financial areas. In other words, contact an independent financial adviser and be prepared to pay for this advice.

What can you expect from your independent professional financial adviser?

One of the key advantages to appointing an authorised adviser (someone who is independent, professional, qualified and stringently regulated) for insurances and investments is that they owe their allegiance to you and not to any particular financial institution or investment house. *Your needs* will be paramount. As a result, you can expect them to provide you with the following services:

Strategic planning. They will look at your complete financial position, agree your financial objectives with you, and advise you on how to reach your money targets. When doing this he or she should also assess your existing position and review any financial products you have in place to make sure they meet your requirements.

Competitive analysis. Having decided what products you need, your adviser should search the market for the best product offering the best value for money.

Negotiation services. When an insurance company quotes a rate, it isn't necessarily fixed in stone. In fact, it is possible to negotiate discounts on a huge range of financial products. Your adviser will know what else is available in the market and should negotiate to get you the best possible deal.

Background information. Your adviser should provide you with background information on any products or companies they recommend.

Administration. Your adviser should deal with all the paperwork on your behalf and will assist with the filling-out of any forms.

Regular reviews. Your adviser should monitor your needs without being asked. They should constantly be thinking about your situation and making sure that whatever they have recommended is performing in the desired manner.

Your adviser should also be able to look after all your financial and money needs, including:

- mortgages
- re-finance
- commercial loans
- personal loans
- asset finance and leasing
- life cover
- income protection and other insurance
- health cover
- all savings and investments
- pensions
- property and other general insurance.

Where even more specialised advice is needed (say in the selection of shares to build a portfolio, or specific tax planning), then your adviser should be able to recommend other professional experts.

Saving tax

A first-class financial adviser will be able to advise you on tax-saving products. Keep in mind though that for specialist tax advice you should always go to an accountant or qualified tax consultant. If the size of your tax bill doesn't warrant appointing an accountant, then your financial adviser should still be able to assist you. Tax is a big part of financial planning. After all, what's the point of making a better return on your investments only to lose it through poor tax advice? *Always* check that your adviser is taking your tax position into account and is properly qualified to assist you.

A very short history lesson

Prior to November 2001 there were over 9,000 'insurance brokers' offering financial advice. After that, the Central Bank took over regulation and forced them to register.

- Six thousand dropped out immediately, mainly because the scale of their operations meant they did not have the time or resources to provide the level of product research required.

- Of the two authorisations available, there are currently around 400 authorised advisers, who must give 'best advice' irrespective of agencies held.

- The balance of about 2,500 are called **multi-agency intermediaries** (originally called RAIPIs, then 'restricted intermediaries') and they can only give advice on the insurance and investment appointments held.

Then, in 2003, in order to make sure that consumers receive reliable and independent advice, the government set up the **Irish Financial Services Regulatory Authority** (IFSRA, then changed to the 'Financial Regulator'), an independent agency set up to take over the regulatory role previously filled by the Central Bank. Regulation is now back entrusted to the Central Bank of Ireland.

One of the first things to do when considering any professional adviser is to check:

- that they are regulated by the Financial Regulator, now retitled the Central Bank of Ireland
- what services they are authorised to provide and at what cost.

Financial advisers must give you a **Terms of Business** booklet, which outlines their terms of business, fees chargeable, appointments with product providers, Central Bank of Ireland authorisation and notification of the Investors' Compensation Act.

MONEY DOCTOR WEALTH WARNING

Some things are best not delegated

There is an enormous amount to be said for getting a really good professional adviser to sort out everything for you. You'll save money. You'll save time. And you will end up with the best possible products for your needs. But no matter how good your adviser, you should always take time to:

- understand what he or she is proposing, and why
- learn about the products you are committing to
- check up on the financial institutions that will be supplying those products.

THE MONEY DOCTOR SAYS...

It is possible to handle all your financial decisions without reference to anyone else. However, it requires time and commitment.

If you do decide to use a professional adviser, make sure that they are fully authorised and don't be shy about asking them questions.

Remember, it is important to have clear financial objectives.

PART 2

YOUR FINANCIAL RIGHTS

___

Are you entitled to claim any government benefits? How does the law protect you as an employee? What do you do if you buy something and are unhappy with the way you have been treated?

This section of the book will answer all your questions with regard to your financial rights. In Chapter 5 you'll discover how the Social Welfare system works and be able to assess what you may be entitled to. In Chapter 6 you'll learn about your rights as an employee. And in Chapter 7 you'll find out what your consumer rights are. I've also included useful sources of additional information and important contact information.

5
YOUR RIGHT TO SOCIAL WELFARE

HOW THE SYSTEM WORKS AND HOW TO MAKE SURE YOU RECEIVE YOUR ENTITLEMENTS

The Irish state provides its citizens with one of the most advanced, generous and comprehensive social welfare systems in the world. It isn't, however, what you would call a simple system, being made up of a bewildering array of:

- assistance payments
- benefits
- supplements
- allowances
- grants and
- pensions.

Many of the financial benefits available are 'contributory', meaning that you are only entitled to them if you have made **PRSI** (pay related social insurance) contributions in the past. Others are available to everyone, including people who have moved here from abroad.

As one would expect, the state only provides social welfare when certain conditions are met. Sometimes these conditions are very straightforward. For instance, with very few exceptions, a special grant of €6,000 is paid to widows or widowers with dependent children following the death of their spouse. In other instances you have to meet stringent requirements, often related to the size and number of your PRSI contributions. A good example of this is the invalidity pension, which is payable if you have been 'incapable of work for at least twelve months and are likely to be incapable of work for a further twelve months, or you are permanently incapable'. Furthermore, to claim this pension you must have paid PRSI at Class A, E or H for at least 260 weeks, and you must have had at least 48 weeks' PRSI paid or credited in the last tax year before you apply!

I am afraid the system is made even more confusing by the fact that the government frequently changes the nature, value, names and conditions attached to the various benefits available.

So, how can you discover exactly what you are entitled to?

In this chapter I outline, in broad terms, all the various forms of social welfare that are available, along with the more important conditions which must be fulfilled in order to claim them. Using this, you should be able to ascertain benefits to which you might be entitled.

Your next step should be to contact your local Social Welfare Office or Citizens Information Centre for further assistance. You'll find both listed in your local phone book.
Another approach is to write directly to:

> The Information Service, Department of Social Protection
> Áras Mhic Dhiarmada, Store Street, Dublin 1
> Tel. (01) 704 3000.
> or
> Retirement/Old Age Contributory & Non-Contributory Pensions
> College Road, Sligo
> Co. Sligo
> Tel. (071) 915 7100/LoCall: 1890 50 00 00.

Or, if you have access to the internet, you can go to www.welfare.ie.

THE DIFFERENCE BETWEEN CONTRIBUTORY AND NON-CONTRIBUTORY PAYMENTS

The terms 'contributory' and 'non-contributory' are bandied about a good deal in relation to social welfare benefits. The terms are slightly misleading because they imply that you have to have contributed personally to be eligible for certain payments. The contribution being referred to is generally assumed to be PRSI payments and the USC (Universal Social Charge). However, a completely different system operated prior to 1974, a third system was in place until 1953, and both may entitle you to contributory benefits.

The word 'contributory' is confusing in another respect, too. You may well be eligible to receive a contributory benefit if you are married to someone who has made contributions, or if you are the child or dependant of someone who has made contributions.

Another point to bear in mind is that you may have been in regular employment but earning so little that you were not liable to make any PRSI payments. If you are a public servant your entitlements will be linked to when you joined, and if you're self-employed a completely different set of regulations applies.

My advice, therefore, is never to assume that you won't be entitled to a particular form of social welfare until you have fully investigated each and every one of the conditions attached to it. Don't ever assume that because something is 'contributory' or 'non-contributory' it won't apply to you.

THE DIFFERENT TYPES OF SOCIAL WELFARE

I've already listed off all the different names used to describe the variety of social welfare payments. What do these various terms mean?

On the whole, social welfare **benefits** tend to be available only to those who have made PRSI contributions. Furthermore, though there are a few exceptions, social welfare benefits are not affected by your level of wealth.

Social welfare **assistance**, on the other hand, is given only to those who satisfy what's called a 'means test'.

A good example of the difference is Jobseeker's Benefit, which has PRSI conditions attached to it but for which there is no means test, and the non-contributory old age pension, which is classified as social assistance and is subject to means testing.

SO, WHAT IS MEANS TESTING?

In order that financial assistance only goes to those who are most needy, the government checks each claimant's financial circumstances first. This check is called a 'means test'.

Your means are considered to be:

- any cash income you have
- the value of your assets (your home will be excluded, but if you own a farm that would be included)
- your savings and investments.

In some cases your residential situation will be relevant. For instance, if you are unemployed but live at home with your parents and you are under the age of 24, this could reduce your entitlement.

When you apply for a means-tested form of social assistance, a 'means test officer' will consider your case. The criteria he or she uses in order to assess your entitlement will vary – of course – according to the form of social assistance you are applying to receive. You should expect, however, to be asked about your entire financial situation. This could include:

- your income
- your spouse's income
- your partner's income (if co-habiting)
- your farm income (if relevant)
- any savings, investments or other assets you may own, such as property
- your general circumstances, such as where you live, whom you live with, who is dependent on you, and so forth
- any debts you may have
- your weekly outgoings, including rent
- any other benefits you may be receiving.

Naturally, any information you provide will be treated in the strictest confidence.

There will, of course, be other conditions as well. For instance, you have to be genuinely unemployed to claim Jobseeker's Allowance. But it is your means that will be the deciding point. Note that even if you're not eligible for the maximum amount of assistance, you could still be entitled to a reduced amount.

WHAT ARE YOU ENTITLED TO? SOCIAL WELFARE PAYMENTS IN DETAIL

Below is a summary of all the main social welfare payments. You'll also find an explanation of what they could be worth to you, together with some of the more notable conditions.

Remember, the Department of Social Protection is there to help you. You shouldn't hesitate to ask their advice about what you are entitled to.

Social welfare pensions

The state makes available two different types of social welfare pension:

Contributory pension. So-called because your entitlement is linked to the amount and class of PRSI you have paid during your working life.

Non-contributory pension. Means-tested and available to those who haven't made any contributions during their working lives.

Contributory pensions in turn also fall into two categories: state pension (transition) (paid if you're aged 65 and over and have actually stopped working) and state pension (contributory) (paid from the age of 66 with no requirement that you should have stopped working).

The maximum standard amount for a contributory pension is €230.30 per week, but the actual sum you receive will be determined by the number and value of contributions you made during your working life – and your age. Additional sums are payable if you have dependent children and live alone.

The maximum standard amount payable as an old age non-contributory pension is currently €219 per week or €229 per week for those aged over 80. Again, you may be able to claim more if you have dependent children or live alone.

Regardless of whether you have made contributions or not, additional amounts may also be available if you're blind, or if you live on certain offshore islands.

Pensions for widows and widowers

If you are – or become – a widow or widower then you will also have pension entitlements. These are:

The contributory widow(er)'s pension. This – as its name implies – is available to widows or widowers where sufficient PRSI contributions have been made and is worth up to €230.30 per week for those aged 66 to 80, increasing to €240.30 for those aged over 80.

The non-contributory widow(er)'s pension. This is means-tested and could be worth as much as €188 a week.

In both instances if you have a dependent child, live alone and/or are resident on certain offshore islands you may be entitled to receive an additional sum.

Other age-related benefits

If you are aged 66 or over and you qualify for a contributory or non-contributory pension – or you satisfy a means test – you may be entitled to a number of other household benefits, including:

- free travel
- free electricity
- a natural gas allowance
- a free television licence
- a telephone line-rental allowance.

These benefits are referred to as the **Household Benefits Package Scheme**.

MONEY DOCTOR WEALTH CHECK

You don't have to be retired to claim free electricity and other benefits

The Household Benefits Package Scheme is also available to those entitled to other payments such as an invalidity pension or a carer's allowance (see below). Under these circumstances your age will not be relevant to your eligibility.

Supplementary welfare allowance

Supplementary welfare allowance provides a basic weekly allowance as a right to eligible people who have little or no income. If you have a low income, you may also qualify for a weekly supplement under the scheme to meet certain special needs. In addition, payments can be made in respect of urgent or exceptional needs.

There are four types of payments – basic payments, supplements, exceptional needs payments and urgent needs payments. To find out more about the scheme, contact the:

Supplementary Welfare Allowance Section
Department of Social Protection
Áras Mhic Dhiarmada
Store Street, Dublin 1
Tel. (01) 704 3000.

One-parent family payment

If you are bringing up a child (or children) without the support of a partner, you may be eligible to apply for the one-parent family payment, which is available to both men and women. You may earn up to €130 per week and still qualify for the full payment, while half the weekly earnings in excess of this amount will be disregarded.

Deserted wife's benefit

Deserted wife's benefit is a payment made to a woman deserted by her husband. Entitlement to payment is based on PRSI contributions paid by the wife or her husband. The deserted wife's benefit scheme was closed off to new applications with effect from 2 January 1997, when the one-parent family payment was introduced.

Guardian's payment (contributory)

This allowance is payable where both parents have died, or one parent has died and the other has abandoned the child. Being a contributory allowance, one or other of the parents must have made sufficient PRSI contributions. The payment is made up to the age of 18, or 22 if the child is in full-time education. It can be as much as €161 a week.

Guardian's payment (non-contributory)

If a child does not qualify for the contributory guardian's allowance, he or she may instead be eligible for the **non-contributory guardian's payment**. This pension is means-tested. It can be as much as €161 a week.

Invalidity pension

This is a contributory pension, so it is only available to those who meet the PRSI payment qualifications. It is payable instead of a disability benefit if you've been incapable of work for at least 12 months and are likely to be incapable of work for a further 12 months, or if you're permanently incapable of work.

As with many other pensions, the amount you receive will increase if you have dependent children, live alone, or live on certain offshore islands. If you are eligible for an invalidity pension you may also be able to claim an additional sum if you support someone else. It can be as much as €230.30 a week at age 65.

Medical cards

Medical cards entitle you to a range of free medical care. Eligibility is normally means-tested, although there are a number of exceptions including exceptions for those aged 70 or over, and anyone drawing a state pension from other EU countries. Different income limits exist for those aged under 66 and those aged between 66 and 69 and vary depending on the number of children or dependants and whether they are aged over 16 and in full-time education. Although your circumstances may not entitle you to a medical card, you could still be eligible for a **doctor visit card**, which would allow you to receive free care from your GP. If this section is relevant to you, you should seek assistance from the Department of Social Protection – see contact details on p. 35.

Treatment benefits

The state provides a range of contributory **treatment benefits** covering dental care, eye testing, glasses, contact lenses and hearing aids. In some instances, the benefits are entirely free and in others you must pay a part of the cost. There may also be upper limits on the amounts which can be claimed.

Maternity benefit

A contributory **maternity benefit** is payable to women in current employment or self-employment who have been paying PRSI. It is only payable where the mother has been making contributions – the father's contributions have no bearing on eligibility. It can be as much as €262 a week for 26 weeks.

Adoptive benefit

If you adopt a child you may still be eligible for a payment equivalent in value to the maternity benefit. This is a contributory benefit. It can be as much as €262 a week for a continuous period of 24 weeks from the date of placement of your child.

Asylum seekers

If you are applying for refugee status, you can obtain rent-free accommodation at a regional centre. Each adult is entitled to a personal allowance of €19.10 per week and €9.60 for each child. Child benefit may also be applicable. More information can be obtained from:

Reception and Integration Agency
PO Box 11487
Dublin 2
Tel. (01) 418 3200, LoCall: 1890 777 727.

> **MONEY DOCTOR WEALTH WARNING**
>
> *A tightening-up of the rules: Habitual Resident's Test*
>
> Since 2004 the government has introduced a new **Habitual Resident's Test**, which means that in order to receive a whole range of payments you must be able to prove that you are 'habitually resident in Ireland'. However, the rules do allow you to be resident in the UK, Channel Islands, and Isle of Man, too. Payments affected by this include unemployment assistance, old age contributory pension, one-parent family payment, and supplementary welfare allowance.

Child benefit

Child benefit is not means-tested, nor do you have to make any contribution in order to receive it. It is paid each month, and the amount you receive will depend on the number of qualifying children living with you and their ages. In some instances the payment may be made until the children reach the age of 18. For the first and second child it can be as much as €140 each per month and €148 for the third and €160 for subsequent children (in the 2012 Budget additional sums for additional children were stopped). It also pays to have multiple births – 1½ times the child benefit rate for twins (each) and double for triplets or greater (each).

Early childhood care & education scheme (ECCE)

This scheme provides a free year of early childhood care and education for children of pre-school age. Children are eligible for the scheme if they are aged between 3 years and 2 months and 4 years and 7 months on 1 September of the year they will be starting. The state pays a capitation fee to participating playschools and daycare centres.

Jobseeker's benefit

Jobseeker's benefit is only paid to those who satisfy the PRSI conditions. The amount you receive will be linked to your age and the amount of PRSI paid. It can be as much as €188 a week.

From January 2009 changes to income limits and the number of PRSI contributions required were introduced.

Jobseeker's allowance

This was previously known as Unemployment Assistance and is a means-tested payment available to those who are unemployed and have not made sufficient PRSI contributions or have used up their entitlement to Jobseeker's Benefit.

It can be as much as €188 per week for those aged over 25, with proportionate increases for qualified adult or child dependents.

If you want to find out why you have been turned down for a benefit, or considered ineligible, contact the:

Social Welfare Appeals Office
D'Olier House
D'Olier Street, Dublin 2
Tel. (01) 673 2800.

Back-to-work allowance and back-to-work enterprise allowance

Two different schemes exist for those who have been unemployed for a period of time and then return to work: the back-to-work allowance and the back-to-work enterprise allowance. The first is available if you move into paid employment after being unemployed; the second is given if you become self-employed. Back-to-work allowance was closed to new applicants from 1 May 2009. Note that other support is also available to those who start their own businesses, including training grants, loans, and assistance towards the cost of public liability insurance. Apply to:

Employment Support Services
Department of Social Protection
Shannon Lodge
Carrick-on-Shannon
Co. Leitrim
Lo-Call: 1890 927 999
Tel: (071) 967 2616.

Carer's benefit

If you leave work in order to look after someone in need of full-time care and attention, then you may well be eligible for the contributory carer's benefit. Additionally, you may be entitled to an annual respite care grant, which would be paid to you in June each year. This grant is, in fact, available to all carers providing full-time care, subject to certain conditions. The respite care grant is currently worth €1,700 per person cared for. The carer's benefit can be as much as €307.50 a week if you are caring for more than one person.

Disability and injury benefits

A range of disability and injury benefits – all contributory – is available to those unable to work due to a disability, injury or some form of disablement. If you are disabled, suffer an injury or have some form of disability you may also be eligible, without means testing, for a range of other benefits including **medical care**, and a **constant attendant's allowance**. If you are a public servant and have to give up work due to ill health, you will be eligible for an **early retirement pension**. These benefits have a maximum personal rate of €188 a week.

Bereavement grant

A **bereavement grant** of €850 is available subject to certain conditions based on PRSI contributions.

Widowed parent's grant

In addition to the bereavement grant mentioned above, a special grant of €6,000 is available to widows or widowers with dependent children following the death of their spouse. This is not means-tested and only minimal conditions are attached to it.

Family income supplement

The purpose of this scheme is to help families on low incomes. However, to be eligible it is necessary for one member of the family to be working at least part-time, and for the family income to be below a certain level. Although the **family income supplement** is based on the family's weekly income, once it has been set it doesn't normally fluctuate. However, if your circumstances change (for instance, if you have another child) you can apply to have it increased. The supplement is based on 60% of the difference between your net family income and the income limit that applies to your family circumstances (see Department of Social Protection leaflet **SW19**).

Drugs payments scheme

Even though you may not be eligible for a medical card, you could well be eligible to receive support under the **drugs payment scheme**. Once you are registered, no individual or family is expected to pay more than €120 a month for prescription drugs included on the list of 'essential medicines'. In order to register you should contact your GP, local pharmacy or health board.

The nursing homes support scheme

The Nursing Homes Support Scheme, also known as 'Fair Deal', provides financial support to people who need long-term nursing home care. The scheme is operated by the Health Service Executive (HSE) and replaced the Nursing Home Subvention on 27 October 2009.

Under this scheme, you make a contribution towards the cost of your care and the State pays the balance. The scheme covers approved private nursing homes, as well as voluntary and public nursing homes. Anyone who is ordinarily resident in the State and is assessed as needing long-term nursing home care can apply for the scheme.

In 2011, a total of just under €1 billion was allocated to fund the scheme and in 2012, the HSE expects to spend €994 million. In 2011, 10,671 applications were processed with a 75% approval rate. This compares to a 100% approval rate in the 2 previous years in which the scheme has operated. A number of applications were also withdrawn in 2012. Early in 2012, the Minister for Health allocated €28 million to establish a new intermediate care tier to assess and treat older people while ensuring that they do not enter into long-term care earlier than is necessary. It is not yet known how many of those who withdrew their applications are being cared for under this new programme.

Disabled persons

A host of grants and allowances exist for disabled and incapacitated persons. These include the **blind welfare allowance**, **blind person's pension**, **carer's allowance**, **disability allowance**, **motorised transport grant**, **domiciliary care allowance** and many more. Various tax credits and allowances are also available to disabled people.

Free travel

Free travel on public transport is available to almost everyone aged 66 or over. It is also available to anyone receiving an invalidity pension, a disability allowance, a blind person's pension or a carer's allowance. Note that if you are entitled to free travel, and you're married or co-habiting with someone, they may travel with you free of charge at the same time.

MONEY DOCTOR WEALTH CHECK

What you're entitled to elsewhere in the EU

As Ireland is part of the European Union, you are entitled to a wide range of benefits in other EU member states. However, since EU member states each have their own social welfare system, claiming entitlements in other countries can be fraught with problems. Keep in mind too that contributions made in one member state do not necessarily qualify you for benefits in another. For instance, if you have been working overseas and return home to Ireland, you will not automatically be eligible for unemployment benefit. However, if you have been registered as unemployed for four weeks in Ireland you are then entitled to move to another EU country to look for work and still receive the benefit for up to three months.

If you are thinking of living or working in another EU member state, then you should ask at your local Social Welfare office for a special leaflet describing the benefits which will be available to you.

Incidentally, not only are you legally entitled to look for work in any EU member state without a work permit, but you can also take advantage of each member state's national placement service. To do this, contact your local FAS Employment Services office. Details of your application will be sent overseas through the SEDOC system free of charge.

MONEY DOCTOR WEALTH WARNING

Social welfare benefits are not necessarily tax-free

Social welfare benefits are not automatically tax-free. Whether they are taxable will largely depend on the income level of the recipient. Although tax will not be deducted by the Department of Social Protection on any payments made to you, the Revenue

Commissioners will often take the tax directly from some other source of income which may be payable to the recipient. However, on the plus side, four of the 'taxable benefits' you may be entitled to will also qualify you for the PAYE tax credit. These are:

- state pension (contributory)
- state pension (transition)
- contributory survivor's pension
- guardian's payment.

A number of other benefits may also be liable to income tax. These are:

- invalidity pension
- one-parent family payment
- carer's allowance
- Jobseeker's Allowance
- blind person's pension
- non-contributory widow(er)'s pension
- non-contributory guardian's pension
- social assistance allowance for deserted or prisoners' wives.

The Revenue Commissioners do, however, make a number of useful concessions:

- If you are receiving a disability benefit the first six days will not be subject to tax.
- If you are receiving social welfare payments, child-dependent additions are not taxed (except for invalidity pensions).
- If you are a 'short-term worker' (that it is to say, you work in a trade where short-term employment is the norm) then any Jobseeker's Allowance you receive will not be taxed.

MONEY DOCTOR WEALTH CHECK

Don't forget to apply for a European Health Insurance Card

If you're travelling or staying temporarily in another EU member state (excluding the UK), then you should apply for a **European Health Insurance Card**. This will ensure that you are eligible for free health care if you become ill or have an accident when overseas. You can do this through your HSE local centre.

THE MONEY DOCTOR SAYS ...

- You may be entitled to all sorts of social welfare payments that you weren't aware of.

- Check through all the allowances, benefits and grants summarised in this chapter to see which might apply to you.

- Contact your local Department of Social Protection to find out more and to make a claim. Remember, they are there to help you.

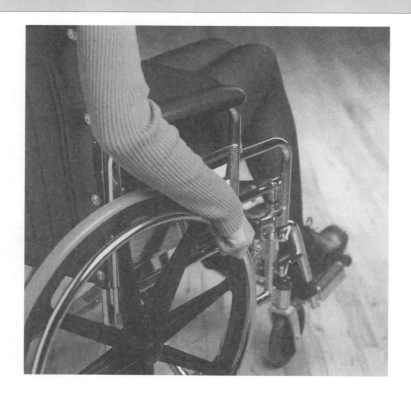

6
YOUR EMPLOYMENT RIGHTS

When most people think of 'employee rights' they think of legal rights relating to things like discrimination and redundancy. But if you are an employee you have financial rights, too. For instance, you have the right to be paid a **minimum wage** and the right to **holiday pay**. This chapter explains these rights in plain English.

You may be more protected than you imagine

In the last few years the Irish government has enacted a considerable amount of new legislation to protect employees. One reason for this was that many employers were seeking to get around the existing employment legislation by putting their workers on 'contract'. Seasonal and part-time workers were also at a disadvantage. Since 2003, however, workers on fixed-term contracts must be treated just as well as full-time employees. Furthermore, an employee cannot be expected to work on a fixed-term contract for more than four years.

MINIMUM WAGE

Since 1 April 2000 all but a tiny minority of workers over the age of 18 are entitled to be paid a minimum amount of money per hour, known as the **national minimum wage**. From 1 July 2007 the national minimum wage has been set at €8.65 per hour. However, you should note that:

- If you're in a new job you are only entitled to 80% of the minimum wage for your first year, and 90% in your second year.
- If you're under 18 you also have reduced entitlements (70% until your 18th birthday, 80% between your 18th and 19th birthdays, and 90% for the following year).
- If you are still in training or attending an educational course your employer is also entitled to reduce your wage.

ANNUAL LEAVE ENTITLEMENT

You are entitled to a minimum of four weeks **annual leave** plus **public holidays**, of which there are nine per year.

HOLIDAY PAY

If you are in paid employment, then you are legally entitled to **paid holidays**. The holiday year usually runs from 1 April–31 March. However, your employer is entitled to use an alternative 12-month period. Broadly speaking, if you're working full time, you should be entitled to a minimum of four working weeks over the year. Of course, if you switch jobs this may have the effect of reducing your entitlement.

YOUR WORKING WEEK

Under something called the 'Organisation of Working Time Act', employees cannot be expected to work more than 48 hours a week. However, there are innumerable exceptions to this. For instance, the Act does not apply to junior hospital doctors, transport employees, fishermen, and family members working on a farm or in a private house, or to the Gardaí.

There are also rules regarding rest periods. You're legally entitled to an 11-hour rest period every 24 hours; one period of 24 hours rest per week preceded by a daily rest period – in other words a total of 35 hours in a single block; and rest breaks of 15 minutes where up to four and a half hours have been worked, or 30 minutes where up to six hours have been worked. Slightly different arrangements apply to night workers.

ON-CALL WORKERS

If you are expected to be **on call** for work, then you should be paid for it. The rule is that you are entitled to receive pay for at least a **quarter** of your on-call hours even if you don't end up working. The maximum amount your employer has to pay you is for 15 on-call hours a week.

DISMISSAL RIGHTS

Your employer can only dismiss you if he or she can prove that you aren't capable, competent or qualified to do the work you were employed to do. Alternatively, your employer must show that your conduct was in some way unacceptable; or that by continuing to employ you he or she would contravene another statutory requirement. The only other reason an employer may dismiss you is if he or she is making you redundant (see over, p. 52). This said, unfair dismissal normally only applies to those who have been employed for at least a year's continuous service with the same employer. Furthermore, there are many exclusions, including those who are aged 65 and over.

If you feel that you've been unfairly dismissed then you must make your complaint within six months.

Note that once you've completed at least 13 weeks with the same employer you are entitled to pre-set periods of notice. This ranges from one week's notice if you've been working for 13 weeks to two years, to eight weeks' notice if you've been working for over 15 years.

TIME OFF WORK

There are various other reasons why you can legitimately claim time off work. For instance, you can take:

- **Emergency time** off in order to deal with family emergencies resulting from an accident or illness. You are entitled to up to five days over a period of 36 months, and such leave is paid.

- Up to 26 weeks' **maternity leave** if you become pregnant, during which time you can claim maternity benefit. Your employer is not obliged to give you any additional income over and above this maternity benefit. When the maternity benefit period ends, you're entitled to take up to a further 16 weeks of unpaid leave.

- Up to 14 weeks' parental leave especially if you are a **new father**, but this is unpaid and without any social welfare entitlement.

- Time off if you are an **expectant mother**, **parent** or **carer** with a special need. For instance, expectant mothers can take time off without loss of pay to go to medical examinations.

WHAT TO DO IF YOU ARE UNHAPPY WITH YOUR EMPLOYER ...

If you feel that your employment rights are being abused, you can obtain further information from:

National Employment Rights Authority
O'Brien Road, Carlow
LoCall: 1890 80 80 90.
Tel: (059) 917 8990

The Labour Relations Commission will also assist you. Their address details are:

Rights Commissioner Service
Labour Relations Commission
Tom Johnson House, Haddington Road, Dublin 4
Tel. (01) 613 6700.
LoCall 1890 220 227 (outside the 01 area)

REDUNDANCY

If you have worked for the same employer for at least two years – even if it is part-time – and you are made redundant, then you may well be eligible for a **redundancy payment**. Various conditions apply. For instance, you must be aged between 16 and 66, and you must have normally worked at least eight hours a week. Also, 'redundancy' only covers the situation where you've been dismissed because – essentially – your employer no longer needs your services. This could be for a variety of reasons, including a change in location, or a decision by the employer to carry on the business with fewer employees. The amount you receive will be based on the number of years you've worked. You should receive two weeks' pay for every year of service to a maximum of €600 a week, topped up with one additional week's pay. If you receive a large lump-sum redundancy payment then you may be liable to pay tax on it. For further information about this, turn to Chapter 31.

THE MONEY DOCTOR SAYS...

- Know your financial rights as an employee and don't let your employer bully or cajole you into accepting anything less.
- Remember, there are lots of circumstances where your employer must pay you. And lots of circumstances where your employer must let you have time off.

7
YOUR RIGHTS AS A 'FINANCIAL' CONSUMER

Do you suspect your bank of over-charging you? Have you felt that an insurance salesperson has sold you a product you don't need? Are you worried about personal financial information being used for marketing purposes?

If you have any concerns about the way you've been treated by a financial institution, then this chapter is for you. In it you'll learn how the law protects you and what you can do if there's something you are unhappy about.

Your basic rights

As the customer of a financial institution you have a wide range of rights. You don't need to suffer poor service, over-charging, mis-selling or fraud. If you're unhappy, there are dedicated, independent organisations which will assist you. Furthermore, if you have lost money you may also be entitled to compensation.

HOW TO COMPLAIN

If you are unhappy and wish to complain, then, in the first instance, you should write to the financial institution concerned and offer them an opportunity to redress the situation. If you are not satisfied with the response you receive, follow the appropriate course of action outlined in the relevant section below.

If you're unhappy with your bank, building society, credit union or insurance company

If you're unhappy with your bank, building society or credit union, you can appeal to the Financial Services Ombudsman. This body also covers insurance complaints and is authorised to make awards of up to a limit of €250,000.

All the banks in Ireland now offer a wide range of financial services including insurance and pensions, so this body will cover all that area should you have a complaint to make.

The finding of the Financial Services Ombudsman is legally binding on both parties, subject only to appeal by either party to the High Court. A party has 21 calendar days from the date of the finding in which to appeal.

The details are:

Financial Services Ombudsman's Bureau
Third Floor
Lincoln House
Lincoln Place
Dublin 2
Lo-Call: 1890 88 20 90
Tel. (01) 662 0899
Fax (01) 662 0890
Email: enquiries@financialombudsman.ie

Financial Services
Ombudsman

If you're unhappy with your financial advisers

In order to make sure that consumers receive reliable and independent advice, the government set up the Financial Regulator, now operating within the Central Bank of Ireland. Before you even consider dealing with any professional adviser, you should check that they are regulated by the Central Bank of Ireland and what services they are authorised to provide. They must give you a Terms of Business letter, which outlines their terms of business, fees chargeable, appointments with product providers, Central Bank of Ireland authorisation, and notification of the Investors' Compensation Act. You'll find more information about choosing a professional adviser in Chapter 4.

There are, in fact, three different bodies to which your adviser may belong:

1   The Irish Brokers Association (IBA).
2   Professional Insurance Brokers Association (PIBA).
3   Life Insurance Association (LIA).

If you're unhappy with your pension company

If you feel that you have been given poor pension advice, then you should contact the Financial Services Ombudsman's Bureau and you should also get in touch with the Ombudsman in charge of pensions. The latter can be contacted at:

The Office of the Pensions Ombudsman
PO Box 9324
36 Upper Mount Street, Dublin 2
Tel. (01) 647 1650

HAVE YOU BEEN TURNED DOWN FOR A LOAN OR CREDIT CARD FOR NO APPARENT REASON?

If you have been turned down for a loan or credit card, it is probably because of your **credit rating**. Almost all the lenders in Ireland rely on credit bureaux to provide them with information about their potential customers. If the information that any particular credit bureau holds is incorrect, it can result in you being turned down for credit. The two bureaux which operate in Ireland are legally obliged to advise you of the information they hold about you. Their details are:

The Irish Credit Bureau (ICB)
Newstead House, Newstead,
Clonskeagh, Dublin 14.
www.icb.ie

and

Experian Ireland
Newenham House, Northern Cross,
Malahide Road, Dublin 17.

You will pay a small charge for this service. For instance, ICB will charge €6. Do note that they respond only to written or on-line requests and the service usually takes no more than three days. You should get in touch with the Ombudsman for Credit Institutions and the Ombudsman for the Financial Services if you're not satisfied with the response you get.

If you're worried about Big Brother

Many of us, with a certain amount of justification, worry that large organisations – such as banks and insurance companies – hold incorrect and unnecessary information about us on their files. Under the Data Protection Act you have the right of access to any personal file relating to yourself held by either a company or other type of organisation. To discover what data a company or organisation holds about you, you simply have to write to them saying that you're making your request under the Data Protection Act. If you encounter any resistance, then you should contact the Data Protection Commissioner at:

The Data Protection Commissioner
Canal House
Station Road
Portarlington, Co. Laois
Tel. (057) 868 4800.
LoCall 1890 252 231

If you discover that an organisation has incorrect information about you, you are entitled to have it corrected.

MONEY DOCTOR WEALTH CHECK

The Deposit Protection scheme

With the level of uncertainty about the future of some of our financial institutions it should be reassuring to know the details of this scheme. This has been in place since 1995 and guarantees individual deposits of up to €100,000 held in any bank, building society or credit union regulated by the Central Bank of Ireland. This consists of 14 Irish and non-Irish deposit-taking institutions operating in the Irish market.

Other institutions such as Rabobank and Investec are covered by similar guarantees, the former from Dutch bank Rabo Group and the latter through the UK Financial Regulatory Authority (from January 2011 and covers up to €100,000 per person).

THE MONEY DOCTOR SAYS...

- If you are unhappy with the service you have received from a financial institution you should, in the first instance, offer them the opportunity to put things right. The best way to do this is to put your complaint in writing.

- If you aren't satisfied with the response you receive – take it further. Complain to the relevant Ombudsman.

- Legal action is always an option – but remember, it will cost you money, whereas there is no charge involved in asking an Ombudsman.

PART 3

BANKING, BORROWING AND GETTING OUT OF DEBT

This section deals with three extremely important topics. Firstly, it offers a comprehensive guide to modern banking services in Ireland, together with tips on getting the most from your bank at the lowest possible cost. Secondly, it explains how you can pay off all your debts – including your credit cards, loans, overdrafts and even your mortgage – quickly and easily. Thirdly, it looks at the different ways in which you can borrow money and suggests the most inexpensive ways to do so.

8
BANKING

HOW TO ENJOY THE BEST BANKING IN IRELAND

What do you demand from your bank? A first-class service? Free banking? Total security? A range of competitively priced financial products? With a little careful planning, as I will explain in this chapter, you can enjoy the best banking in Ireland.

UNDERSTANDING THE BANKING SYSTEM

The first step to enjoying better banking is to understand how the banks themselves operate.

To begin with, despite the charges they make, banks don't make their profits from providing day-to-day banking services. This is because it is incredibly expensive running a branch network, handling millions of transactions, dealing with vast quantities of cash and providing customers with all the other services we (rightly) demand.

So, how *do* banks make their profits? The answer is by selling their customers a wide range of other financial services – everything from mortgages to credit cards, and from insurance to stockbroking.

Every time you use your bank, whether you are withdrawing cash from a machine, paying a bill, or ordering a statement, you present your bank with another opportunity to sell you something. Much in the same way as supermarkets use 'loss leaders' (popular products sold at below-cost price in order to attract customers), banks offer banking services – especially current accounts – as a way of attracting and keeping customers.

In fact, *operated properly* a current account is one of the greatest financial bargains of all time.

Why have I put the words 'operated properly' in italics? Because in order to recoup some of their expenses, banks stipulate that you must follow the terms and conditions relating to your account. If you don't, they hit you with all sorts of extra charges.

Loyalty doesn't pay

Don't imagine for a moment that by being loyal to a bank you'll get a better service. The era of 'relationship banking' is long gone. For instance, the decision over whether to lend you money is no longer made at branch level but by a centralised team. Of course, no bank wants to lose its customers, but the threat to take your business elsewhere is no longer as powerful as it once was.

Making the banking system work for you

How, then, can you get the most from your bank? I would offer you four straightforward and easy-to-follow rules:

1   Only buy the services and products you need from your bank. Don't allow them to persuade you into buying something you don't really require.

2   Make sure the services and products you buy are competitively priced. Buying a financial product from your bank may be more convenient – but it could cost you a lot of money.

3   Don't hesitate to shop around or move your business. Banks rely on customer inertia. In other words, they know that many people can't be bothered to ring around for a better price, let alone move their account elsewhere for a better deal.

4   Avoid breaking the terms and conditions attached to any product you purchase from your bank, as the consequences will undoubtedly be expensive.

You may imagine from what I am saying that I am 'anti-bank'. Far from it. Today's modern banks offer customers a fantastic choice and – if you buy wisely – a chance to pay little or nothing for your day-to-day banking.

WHAT BANKS DO BEST

At the heart of all banking lies the **current account.** This basic bank account should provide you with the following facilities:

- a safe and secure place to deposit cheques or cash
- somewhere convenient to keep your money in the short to medium term, until you need to spend it
- access to your cash via branches and cash machines
- a simple and easy way to pay your bills
- a comprehensive record of all your day-to-day financial transactions.

In order to provide all this, the typical current account will offer you some or all of the following services:

- a cheque book
- an ATM (this stands for automated teller machine) card allowing you to get cash 24 hours a day
- a direct debit facility so that you can pay your bills automatically
- a standing order facility allowing you to make regular payments
- a Visa debit (Laser) card so that you can arrange direct payments without having to write a cheque in-branch, buying in shops, on-line and even overseas
- regular statements
- overdraft facilities.

Your current account should also give you access to a telephone banking facility and – if you use the internet – on-line banking. Both should allow you to access your account – and arrange for other transactions – without having to go into a branch.

Although you can obtain some of the services listed above from An Post, one building society and credit unions, only five banks in Ireland offer you full current account banking facilities. These are:

 Bank of Ireland

 National Irish Bank

✻ Ulster Bank

 permanent tsb

BASIC BANKING SERVICES EXPLAINED

There are various banking terms that regularly cause customer confusion. I know, because I used to be a banker. Below, I explain them in plain English.

Standing orders

A **standing order** is exactly that – a regular ('standing') instruction ('order') to your bank to make the same payment to the same person or organisation on an agreed date. For instance, you might order your bank to pay €200 a month to me because you appreciate this book so much. Or, for that matter, you might instruct them to pay me a much larger amount every other month or every quarter, six months or year. You can instruct them to do this until further notice or until a date you specify.

Direct debits

A **direct debit** is basically an authorisation to your bank to pay a regular bill on your behalf. For instance, you might sign a direct debit instructing them to pay your ESB bill when it's presented. With a direct debit you don't specify the amount that is going to be paid and because of this there are some very strict safeguards in place to protect you. One of these is that only reputable organisations are allowed to use the direct debit system.

Laser cards (debit cards)

A **Laser card/Visa debit card** works exactly like a cheque book – but using plastic instead of paper. When you pay someone with a Laser card they apply to your bank for the money, which is then transferred to their account. The upper limit for a single payment is €1,500.

You should only make a payment by debit card if you have sufficient funds in your account or if your overdraft credit is large enough to meet the payment. There is an annual €5 stamp duty charge on debit cards. All debit cards also double as ATM cards. Thanks to debit cards you no longer need to take cash when shopping or wait for a cheque to clear before collecting goods. However, Laser cards are now phased out in favour of Visa Debit Cards.

Overdrafts

An **overdraft** is a short-term loan offered by your bank as part of your current account facility. There are two types:

An **authorised overdraft** is one that has been arranged in advance – though you don't, necessarily, have to use it. The bank normally charges for agreeing this facility, usually €25.

An **unauthorised overdraft** is where the bank decides that despite the fact that you have no agreement to borrow from them, they will still make some payment on your behalf. Unauthorised overdrafts attract penalties and high rates of interest called surcharges. With one bank, it can amount to over double the normal overdraft rate!

What many bank customers do not realise is that banks expect your current account to be in credit for 30 days a year and will charge you extra if it isn't.

WHAT PRICE BANKING?

So, what can you expect to **pay** for your current account banking? There isn't an easy answer. All banks have different pricing structures so that what one bank offers for free, another will charge for.

In 2004 the Irish Financial Services Regulatory Authority (now known as the Central Bank of Ireland) surveyed bank customers and found that on average they were being charged between €50 and €137 for current account transactions. The level of charges was linked to the customer's choice of bank and level of usage. Today these charges are greater.

A direct comparison of current account charges isn't possible because all five banks offer different products and make different charges, plus they change endlessly. Check out the National Consumer Association website (www.nca.ie) for a snapshot comparison of different accounts. If you want to save money on your own current account fees, the best way is to follow the money-saving tips detailed below.

CUTTING THE COST OF YOUR CURRENT ACCOUNT

There are a number of ways in which you can dramatically reduce the cost of your current account banking. These include:

1   With competition hotting up, all the banks now offer free banking, subject to various conditions. Shop around for the best package to suit your individual circumstances.

2   Don't use a bank overdraft facility. Banks will charge you for setting it up. They'll charge you interest on it, and if you exceed the overdraft, a surcharge and an additional cost on top of this interest! Also, they'll use it as an excuse to charge you for other facilities.

3   Don't, whatever you do, go overdrawn without formal agreement. An unauthorised overdraft will result in you being charged an extremely high rate of interest plus huge additional fees. Even going overdrawn for a couple of days could result in you paying anything from €20 upwards for the privilege.

4   Don't allow your cheques to 'bounce', referred to as being 'Returned Unpaid'. All five banks make heavy charges if your cheque or direct debit has to be returned unpaid. This happens, of course, if you haven't sufficient money in your account or you don't have a large enough overdraft limit. '**Refer to Drawer**' or '**Payment Stopped**' are stamped on the cheque. With the former, your credibility is shot, and there is a question mark on your ability to honour a debt. With the latter, you might wish to stop payments to a supplier of faulty goods if it is outside the cheque card guarantee (capped at €130).

5   Don't bank a cheque that might not clear. A cheque which is lodged to your account, but not honoured, could cost you as much as €17.14 including unpaid charges and referral fees per transaction.

6   Consider using An Post (their BillPay service or online service at www.mybills.ie are excellent, with over 120 bills payable through any of the *c.*1,250 post offices throughout Ireland, six days a week and completely free of charge) or credit union account for limited banking facilities – a far more economical way to do one's banking, see pp 67–8.

7   Consider using a credit card to pay all your bills. If you settle your credit card statement in full every month, this won't cost you anything. See the section on credit cards below for more information about this.

8   Internet and telephone banking eliminate cheque costs and other bank charges by enabling you to make payments and transfers between accounts on-line or over the telephone with a secure password.

Money Doctor Wealth Check

The advantage of a joint account

If I am advising someone who is married, co-habiting or has other dependants I often recommend that they open a joint account and keep a bit of emergency cash in it. Why? When someone dies, it often takes months before his or her affairs can be wound up. During this time all bank accounts and other assets will be frozen. This frequently leaves the bereaved worrying about money. If you have a joint account, however, no such problem arises. Joint accounts are useful in other circumstances too, as everyone named on the account has the right to operate it, subject to the signing authority given.

Note: Joint accounts do not automatically escape inheritance tax.

OTHER TYPES OF BANK ACCOUNT

In addition to offering current accounts, all five banks offer a range of **deposit** and **saving accounts**. The usual rule with these is that the longer you leave your money, and the more money you deposit, the better the rate of interest you will receive.

In the current climate of low interest rates, many bank deposit accounts offer an extremely poor return.

To put this in perspective, if you deposited €1,000 with your average high street bank for one year you would earn €10 before tax. Unless you are not liable to income tax, you would have to pay Deposit Interest Retention Tax (DIRT tax) on this at 27%, meaning you would be left with a rather modest €7.30 for your trouble.

I examine the whole question of what to do with your savings in Part 6. In the meantime, my only comment would be that you should not leave your short-term savings in a current account, where it's unlikely to be earning any interest at all, but instead you should shop around and put any spare money where it gets the best rate.

Other bank services to consider

As already mentioned, all five banks offer a wide range of other services, from credit cards to personal loans, and from pensions to mortgages. There is a great temptation if you have your current account with a particular bank to use them for one or more of these other services. I would advise you to resist this temptation. Let me give you two examples of why it's such a bad idea.

At the time of writing I checked the market for the best and worst mortgage rates.

- The best 92% mortgage for a first time buyer is at 3.74% (standard variable rate).
- The worst 92% mortgage for a first time buyer on a standard variable rate (no interest-only facility) is at 4.45%. Some existing borrowers can pay up to 5.9%.

At the same time I also checked credit card interest rates:

- Best credit card interest (after the 'loss leader' rates) is 9.14%.
- Worst credit card is a store card in the range of 19.1–22.6%.

As you can see, it definitely pays to shop around.

MONEY DOCTOR WEALTH CHECK

Switching is easy!

All five banks have adopted a code of practice to make it easier to move from one bank to another. Under this code, it should take you less than ten days to get a new account up and running, and all your standing orders and direct debits should be transferred from your old account within one week after that. If you have any trouble changing your bank you should contact the Financial Services Ombudsman's Bureau. You'll find their address on p. 54.

THE BUILDING SOCIETY OPTION

Building societies were owned by their members or – in plain English – their customers. However, since summer 2011, the two remaining building societies have effectively disappeared. EBS has merged with AIB to form one of the pillar banks but keeping their own identity, and the lending business of Irish

Nationwide has been handed over to Irish Bank Resolution Corporation. The INBS deposits were transferred over to Permanent TSB.

STATE SAVINGS: ACCOUNTS FROM THE NATIONAL TREASURY MANAGEMENT AGENCY (NTMA)

State savings products from the NTMA are sold in all post offices. Although post offices do not have any ATMs, there are about 1,150 branches and, of course, they're open 6 days per week. You can also use post offices – without cost – to pay a range of up to 120 household bills, and to buy money drafts at minimal cost.

THE CREDIT UNION OPTION

Credit unions, like building societies, are owned by their members. There are 490 credit unions in Ireland – each one serving a local community. Their original role was to help people to save and also to provide inexpensive loans. In the last few years, though, many have expanded the range of financial services they offer dramatically. For instance, many credit unions now offer budget accounts, which are perfectly suitable for paying regular bills. The main drawback to using a credit union for your day-to-day banking is that you can't take advantage of a national branch network or ATM machines. Plus, very few credit unions offer interest or dividends following the Financial Regulator's advice. However, for some people they do offer an acceptable option.

BANKING ON HOLIDAY

You're going abroad, what should you do about money? Here are a few useful tips:

1   Since Ireland is one of the 17 countries that comprise the eurozone, you can pay with **euro** when visiting Austria, Belgium, Cyprus, Finland, France, Germany, Greece, Italy, Luxembourg, Malta, The Netherlands, Portugal, Slovakia, Slovenia, Estonia and Spain. Like the American dollar, the euro is widely accepted in many other countries, while not legal tender. Unfortunately, euro cheques from Ireland cannot, yet, be used for payments when visiting another eurozone country.

2 Wherever you're travelling in the world – whether it's in the eurozone or not – a **credit card** is probably the least expensive, most secure and most convenient way of paying. Visa and MasterCard are the most widely accepted credit cards overseas. However, I would not recommend credit cards as a means of obtaining cash when overseas as all the credit card companies charge a fee for cash advances plus a high rate of interest from the day of withdrawal. You will also find the exchange rate is not to your advantage!

3 If you have an **ATM card** from one of the five Irish banks you'll find that you can use it extensively all over the world. The advantage of this is that you need not carry a great deal of cash with you, providing you have sufficient funds in your current account. Note, however, that you may not get the best rate of exchange and there could be special charges. Check with your bank before you head off.

4 The practical option is to ask for the minimum credit limit on your current credit card and pre-lodge all the funds you expect to spend on your holiday. Simple, but sensible.

THE MONEY DOCTOR SAYS...

- It is possible to enjoy free or very low-cost banking if you take advantage of the system.
- Unauthorised overdrafts are very expensive and should be avoided if at all possible.
- Bank loyalty doesn't pay. Always shop around for the best deal.
- If you settle up each month in full, a credit card can be a very inexpensive way to manage much of your banking.
- There are alternatives to the banks – An Post and credit unions.

9
GETTING OUT OF DEBT

HOW TO PAY OFF ALL YOUR LOANS – INCLUDING YOUR MORTGAGE – QUICKLY AND EASILY

The greatest threat to your financial well-being is borrowing. I am not talking about reckless borrowing, either, but ordinary borrowing in the form of personal loans, overdrafts and credit cards. This is because the cost of borrowing money is a huge drain on your most valuable asset – your income.

What's more, the cost of borrowing can't just be measured in terms of the interest you are paying. You must also factor in the opportunity cost – the money you would otherwise be making if you were investing your income instead of spending it on servicing your debts. Let me give you one simple example:

> €10,000 repaid over seven years at an interest rate of 10% will require monthly repayments of €166. Total interest cost €3,945.

> Invest €166 a month into – say – the stock market for the same period and assuming the same sort of growth as we have seen over the last ten years bar the last few – you'll have a lump sum of almost €20,000 in seven years.

Which is why, in this chapter, I explain the benefits of being debt-free, together with two proven methods to make paying off all your loans fast and painless. For those who are beyond the point of being able to get out of debt, see Chapter 35, Personal Insolvency and Bankruptcy.

YOU MAY NOT EVEN REALISE YOU HAVE A PROBLEM

Most people borrow money but fail to think of themselves as being in debt. The fact is:

- You don't have to be in any sort of financial difficulty to be in debt.
- When you add up the cost of servicing your debt – including your mortgage – it may come to more than you imagine.

- Debt is the single greatest threat to your financial freedom and security. It is sucking away your most valuable asset: your income.

- The first benefit of being debt-free is that your money becomes your own to spend or invest as you prefer.

- Not having any debt will make you less vulnerable. You won't need so much insurance, for instance.

SIZING UP THE PROBLEM

Over the last twenty to thirty years consumer debt has increased at a frightening pace. Why should this be? Some borrowing is unavoidable – for instance, loans taken out when ill or unemployed. Some can be attributed to other factors such as changing social values, lack of education at school, our consumer society and 'impulse' spending. However, I believe the main reason for the borrowing boom is that debt has become a hugely profitable business. Bluntly, lenders use clever marketing tricks to 'push' debt onto innocent consumers. They are doing this because the returns are irresistible. Look at how much money they can make:

- If you leave money on deposit at a bank you'll typically earn less than 1% (€1 for every €100) a year by way of interest.

- That bank, however, can lend your money to someone else at anything up to 24% (€24 for every €100) a year.

Under the circumstances, is it any wonder that financial institutions are falling over themselves to lend money? Or that they devote themselves to coming up with new ways to sell loans to their customers?

DEBT COMES IN MANY DISGUISES

The trouble with the word 'debt' is that it has all sorts of negative connotations. Many people believe that providing they are never behind on their repayments they are not in debt. This isn't true. A debt is when you owe someone money. It could be:

- an unpaid balance on a credit card

- an overdraft

- a personal loan

- a car loan or loan for some other specific purchase
- a mortgage on your home
- a secured loan
- a hire-purchase agreement
- an unpaid balance on a store charge card
- a business loan
- a loan made by a friend or family member.

It is important to remember that just because you are never in arrears and have an excellent credit rating, it doesn't mean you are debt-free.

MONEY DOCTOR WEALTH WARNING

It is compound interest that makes debt so expensive

When you are earning it, it has the power to make you very rich. When you are paying it, it has the power to make you very poor. Albert Einstein described it as 'the greatest mathematical discovery of all time'. It is the reason why banks, building societies, credit card companies and other financial institutions make so much profit from lending money. And it is the reason why ordinary investors can make themselves rich simply by doing nothing. It is a fiendishly simple concept called **compound interest.**

Perhaps the easiest way to understand compound interest is to look at two hypothetical examples:

Imagine that you borrow €1,000 at a rate of 10% a year. At the end of one year – assuming you have made no repayments – you will owe €100 in interest (10% of €1,000) or a total of €1,100. If you wait another year then you will owe an additional €110 in interest (10% of €1,100) or a total of €1,210. In other words you are paying interest on the interest.

Now imagine that you have €1,000 to invest and you deposit it in a savings account, which pays interest at a rate of 10% per year. At the end of one year you will be entitled to €100 interest. If you withdraw this interest but leave your capital, at the end of the second year you will be entitled to another €100 interest.

Supposing, however, that you don't withdraw the interest but leave it to 'compound'. At the end of your first year your €1,000 is worth €1,100. At the end of your second year you will have earned €110 interest, meaning that your original €1,000 is worth €1,210. Put another way, your interest is earning you more interest.

When you borrow money, compound interest is working against you. Supposing, for instance, you borrow €5,000 on a credit card at an interest rate of 15% – which isn't high by today's standards. The credit card company allows you to make a minimum payment of 1.5% each month. After two years you will still owe approximately €4,700, having made repayments of €1,750, of which €1,450 has been swallowed up in interest.

Compound interest is your greatest enemy and your greatest ally. When you are in debt, it works against you. But when you have money to invest you can make compound interest really work for you.

'Compounding is man's greatest invention as it allows the reliable systematic accumulation of wealth.' – Albert Einstein

BEWARE THE MINIMUM PAYMENT TRAP

You make your lender happy when you:

- borrow as much as possible
- pay it back over as long a period as possible
- borrow at the highest possible interest rate
- make the minimum monthly payment.

You should be particularly wary of the **minimum payment trap** – where the lender allows you to pay back very little of the debt each month. This is particularly prevalent in the credit card and store card sector. When you opt for the minimum monthly repayment your repayment will be made up almost completely of interest so that the debt itself hardly ever gets reduced. Another thing to watch for is 'revolving credit' – where the lender keeps upping your credit limit or offering you new loans. It can take up to 20 years to repay some credit card debt if you only make the minimum payment each month!

DEBT THREATENS YOUR FUTURE FREEDOM

I certainly wouldn't go so far as to say all debt is bad. There are plenty of instances where borrowing money makes financial sense – in order to buy your own home, for example, or to pay for education. *It is when you are borrowing money to finance your lifestyle that you are getting into dangerous territory.* Living beyond your means threatens your future financial freedom. Let me give you an example:

> Cathal is the manager of a supermarket and earns a good income. However, it isn't enough to cover all the things he and his family like to enjoy, so he borrows frequently. In a typical year he might borrow to pay for Christmas presents, a holiday or just to cover other shortfalls in his monthly expenditure such as clothes or eating out. He views this as 'short-term' debt but the reality is that every year between the ages of 35 and 55 he borrows an average of €4,000 more than he earns. Because this is short-term, unsecured debt he pays an average of 12% a year in interest. His monthly debt repayments (excluding his mortgage) are €360.
>
> Cathal's twin brother, Ray, is also a supermarket manager and earns exactly the same income. However, he lives within his means. He doesn't eat out as often, go on holiday as frequently or drive such a nice car. He saves the €360 his brother spends each month on servicing his debts and instead he invests the money. He manages a return of 6% a year on average between the ages of 35 and 55 and so he builds up a tax-free lump sum of €160,000.

The fact is, your most valuable asset is your income and there is only so much that each of us will ever earn during our lifetimes. By spending a large portion of it on servicing debt you are – basically – giving it away to your lenders. Surely your need is greater than theirs?

SEVEN EXCELLENT REASONS TO BECOME DEBT-FREE

Here are seven reasons why you should pay off all your debts – including, perhaps, your mortgage.

1   It will make you less vulnerable. If you are in debt and for some reason your income is reduced or stops altogether (suppose, for instance, you fall seriously ill and don't have permanent health insurance), then not being able to repay your loans could have serious consequences.

2   It will make your family less vulnerable. I don't want to depress you but when you die your debts won't die with you – your estate will have to pay them all.

3   You won't have to worry about inflation. If you owe money and interest rates rise (as recently as 1981 interest rates were as high as 20%) then you could easily find yourself struggling to make your monthly payments.

4   You won't have the stress which comes with debt. The fact is that owing money is stressful.

5   You'll enjoy a genuine sense of satisfaction. There is a real peace of mind which comes with not owing money and with owning your home outright.

6   It will open up new choices. Suddenly all the money you are spending on servicing your debts will be available for you to spend or save as you prefer.

7   It will ensure you have a comfortable retirement. Furthermore, it may allow you to retire early. Why should you have to wait until you are 60 or 65 to give up work?

MONEY DOCTOR WEALTH WARNING

How lenders will try to trick you

With so much profit at stake lenders put a lot of effort into persuading consumers to borrow. There is a catch to every offer! Let me give you just one example:

Josephine goes to buy a new bed in the local store sale. It is marked down from €1,300 to €1,100 and as she goes to pay the shop assistant persuades her to take out a store card as it will give her an extra 10% saving. So instead of €1,100 she pays just €990. However, Josephine doesn't pay off her store card at the end of the month but instead takes 36 months to do so. The result? Because she is being charged 15% interest, the bed ends up costing her €1,548. Not so much of a saving, after all!

> A couple of other things to watch out for. Firstly, **loan consolidation**. When used properly – as I will explain in a moment – loan consolidation can be an excellent way to speed yourself out of debt. However, unscrupulous lenders often lure borrowers into taking out expensive consolidation loans – even encouraging them to borrow extra for a holiday or other luxury item. Secondly, if **transferring credit card debt** to save money, only too often a low interest or zero interest period is followed by a much higher rate. Check the conditions carefully and don't be taken in by lenders.

THE FIRST STEP TO GETTING OUT OF DEBT

There is one thing you must do before you set out to eradicate all your debt: stop borrowing. After all, you can't get yourself out of a hole if you keep digging. Take a once-and-for-all decision to:

- not just to pay off your debts, but to stay out of debt
- not to borrow any more money unless it is absolutely unavoidable (or there is a very reasonable chance that you can invest the money you borrow to make more than the loan is going to cost you to repay)
- not to live beyond your means
- avoid 'bargains'. In my book a genuine bargain is something you need to buy but which you manage to get at a lower price than you expected to pay for it. Something that you don't need but you buy because it seems to be cheap is definitely not a bargain.

There are various actions you can take to make this easier on yourself. You can:

- Cut up all your credit cards and store cards.
- Cancel your overdraft limit. But remember, most banks will allow a 'shadow' overdraft on your account. This means that informally they may allow your account to overdraw by say €500 before you are contacted. This is costly and may eventually have to be formalised, so you are back in the overdraft trap again. Keep track of all transactions on your account.
- Use a charge card where the balance has to be paid in full at the end of each month or take the prepaid card option.

- Avoid buying any unnecessary items.
- Do not take out any new loans, including hire-purchase agreements and overdrafts.
- Do not increase the size of any existing loans.
- Pay with cash whenever possible (nothing reduces one's tendency to spend money as paying with cash).

American money expert Alvin Hall (you may have seen him on television) suggests that anyone with trouble curbing his or her expenditure should keep what he calls a **money diary**. The basic idea is that you carry a small notebook with you wherever you go and write down details of every single penny you spend. You should include everything – from your daily newspaper to your mortgage repayments. After a couple of weeks you'll have a precise picture of where your money is going and this, in turn, will help you avoid spending money on things you don't really want or need. If you are prone to impulse spending or if you always spend more than your income I can see the good sense in this approach. Download a **free** Money Doctor App that will track your spending. Simply type 'Money Doctor' into your iPhone or Android appstore to download.

TAKING STOCK OF YOUR SITUATION

Once you have stopped making the situation any worse you need to take stock of your situation. In particular, you want to gather together full details of your debts. The information you require about each of your debts is:

- to whom you owe the money
- how big the debt is
- how long you have to pay it back (the term), if relevant
- what the rate of interest is and whether it is fixed or variable
- whether you will be penalised for paying back the debt early (and if so what the penalties are)
- what the minimum monthly payment is (if this is relevant)
- whether the interest is calculated daily, monthly or annually.

Obviously, it is important not to overlook any possible debts, so here is a quick checklist to remind you. Don't forget to include any money that your spouse or partner may owe, too!

- mortgages
- secured loans
- credit cards
- store cards
- overdrafts
- personal loans
- car loans
- hire- or lease-purchase
- catalogue company loans
- family or friends who may have lent you money
- student loans.

Most of the information you need should be supplied to you each month by your lenders. However, if it isn't, then you should telephone or write to them asking for full details.

MONEY DOCTOR WEALTH CHECK

The 'savings' conundrum

The Money Doctor often encounters 'patients' who have debts but who are saving money at the same time. If you cannot make a greater return on your capital than the deposit interest rate on your savings, it may well be to your advantage to reduce debt where the interest rate chargeable is far higher than that of the deposit interest rate.

In most cases, it makes sense to stop saving money and to use any existing savings to pay off some or all of your debts. Why? Because usually what you are earning from your savings will be substantially less than what you are paying out to borrow.

€100 in a savings account may be earning you as little as €1 after tax.

€100 owed on – say – a credit card may be costing you as much as €24 or even more a year.

So if you had savings of €1,000 and used it to pay off €1,000 of credit card debt you could be saving yourself as much as €240 a year. More if you have borrowed on a store card.

Note, however, it does not make sense to cash in your savings if, for example, you have an endowment policy where you may need to leave it mature. You would be well advised to take professional advice since some are worth more than others.

Overall, however, it does not make financial sense to be investing a small amount of money each month if – at the same time – you are spending a small fortune on servicing a debt.

THE ART OF DEBT ELIMINATION

You've taken the decision not to incur any extra debt. You've got a real grip on the size and nature of your problem. What next? You have two options:

- the **consolidation** approach
- the **sniper** approach.

Option 1: The consolidation approach

The idea behind 'consolidation' is to reduce the cost of your debt dramatically. Instead of having lots of different loans – all at different rates – you have a single loan at one, much lower rate. It works particularly well if you own your own home. What you do is:

- Add up all the money you currently spend making your debt repayments.
- Consolidate all your debts into a single, much cheaper loan.
- Keep on making the same monthly payments.

This is best explained with an example. Below I have listed off all the debts that Brian and Sheila have along with the interest rate they are paying on each one:

Type of debt	Monthly cost	Interest rate (%)
Mortgage	€900	5.5
Home improvement loan	€16	10
Credit card 1	€45	16
Credit card 2	€30	16
Store card	€71	17
Car loan	€225	10

The total amount Brian and Sheila are spending on their debts is €1,287 a month. Since they own their own home they can consolidate all their debts in with their mortgage. At the moment their mortgage is for €128,000 and has 19 years to run. Although consolidating their loans increases their mortgage to €152,000, by continuing to pay €1,300 a month they can shorten the length of their mortgage to just 14 years. At the same time they will save themselves €27,000 in interest! Incidentally, to optimise the benefit of consolidation it may be preferable to take out something called a **current account mortgage**. The full benefits of these mortgages are explained on p. 117.

Please remember, debt consolidation is a once-in-a-lifetime course of action. It only works to your advantage if you carry on making the same monthly payments, otherwise all you are doing is spreading the cost of your short-term debt over the longer term. I believe one should never borrow money for a longer period than the life of the asset you are buying.

Currently it is virtually impossible to obtain such a consolidation loan with any of the lenders in Ireland. I would strongly advise using professional help.

Option 2: The sniper approach

If you don't own your own home – or if you don't have sufficient capital tied up in your property to consolidate your debts in with your mortgage – you'll need to take what I call the 'sniper' approach. This involves 'picking off' your debts one at a time starting with the most expensive. What you do is:

- Find some extra money. Just because you don't have a mortgage doesn't mean that you can't consolidate your debt. Move your borrowing to where it is costing you the least.
- Use the money you are saving each month to pay off your most expensive debt – in other words, the one with the highest rate of interest.

Do you sometimes pay more than the minimum amount required each month? If you do then make sure you pay it to whichever of your debts is costing you the most. Incidentally, you may find that one or more of your existing lenders will be open to negotiation.

To use a typical example, imagine that Neil has the following debts:

Type of debt	Monthly/minimum cost	Interest rate (%)
Credit card €4,000	€60	16
Store card €5,000	€75	17
Car loan €8,000	€258	10

Every month he usually pays about €100 more off one or other of the debts – on a purely random basis. Also, he is able to find €100 from other sources (see below) to help speed himself out of debt. In other words, Neil has €200 extra to apply to getting himself out of debt. Therefore, what he needs to do is pay off his most expensive debt first – his store card. By paying an extra €200 a month he can do this within 20 months. This frees up the store card minimum payment of €75 to help pay off his next most expensive debt – which is his credit card.

MONEY DOCTOR WEALTH CHECK

Put your money to the best possible use...

The secret to getting rid of your debts is in putting your money to the best possible use. Your objective is to get your loans onto the lowest possible rate of interest and then to use the saving to speed up the process of paying off your debt.

Of course, if you could find some extra money each month, then you could get out of debt even faster. One way to find extra money is to look at the way you spend your income and see if you couldn't make some basic savings without necessarily cutting back. For example:

- Many people pay more than they have to for their banking. Review your arrangements. Could you be earning extra interest? Saving interest? Avoiding unnecessary costs?

- Don't pay for anything you neither need nor use. For instance, membership fees, internet charges and magazines.

- Double check you aren't overpaying your tax. Are your tax credits correct?

- Review all your insurance costs. This is a fiercely competitive market and you may be able to save a substantial amount.

In general, it isn't what you earn but how you spend it that will make the difference to your finances. You could be on an enormous salary but if you are up to your neck in debt (as many high-income earners are) it is useless to you.

THE MONEY DOCTOR SAYS...

- If you only take action on one aspect of your finances make it your priority to get yourself out of debt.
- The first step is to stop borrowing and to get a realistic position of what you owe and how much it is costing you.
- Consider consolidating your debt in with your mortgage, if you can.
- Remember, if you save money or have any spare cash you should put it towards paying off your debts, providing you still maintain a Rainy Day Fund or Emergency Fund.
- Pay your most expensive debts off first.

10
BORROWING

IF YOU DO HAVE TO BORROW I WILL SHOW YOU HOW TO BORROW SENSIBLY

HOW TO BORROW SENSIBLY AND INEXPENSIVELY

There are times when it makes sense to borrow. And times when borrowing is unavoidable. Either way, you want to make sure that you don't pay a cent more than you have to. If there is one area of personal finance where consumers get 'ripped off' regularly, then it is when they borrow.

Look at the difference!

Nothing better illustrates the way in which consumers can overpay for a loan than a quick comparison of rates:

Secured loan from one of the specialist lenders	6%+
Personal loan (unsecured) from any high street bank	10%+
Credit card from any of the main providers	17%+
Store card from any of the major retail outlets	19%+

As a consumer it is not impossible that you might simultaneously be paying anything from 6% to 20% to borrow money – which is ridiculous.

MONEY DOCTOR WEALTH CHECK

How to compare loan rates

In order that consumers can compare interest rates, the government insists that the cost of loans is expressed in terms of an **annual percentage rate** (APR).

Confusingly, there is more than one way to calculate the APR – but broadly speaking it is an accurate way of assessing how much a loan is going to cost you including all the hidden costs such as up-front fees.

> Clearly, the lower the APR, the cheaper the loan, the better it is for
> you.
> Remember, financial institutions make enormous profits from
> lending money. You should never, ever be shy about shopping
> around or asking for a lower rate.

SO, WHAT IS 'SENSIBLE BORROWING'?

There are times when it makes excellent sense to borrow. For instance, if you
want to:

- buy, build or improve your home
- finance a property investment
- pay for education
- pay for a car or other necessary item
- start a business.

There are also times when it is impossible not to borrow money – if you are
temporarily unable to earn an income, for instance, for some reason beyond
your control.

There is no intrinsic harm, either, in genuine short-term borrowing for
some luxury item. What is really dangerous, however, is short-term borrowing
that becomes long-term borrowing without you meaning it to do so. This is not
only extremely expensive but makes you more vulnerable to financial
problems. I can't emphasise enough how bad it is for your financial well-being
to borrow money to pay for living expenses. In particular, you should
definitely avoid long-term credit card and store card debt.

If you have succumbed to the temptation of credit card or store card debt –
and you want to pay it off – read Chapter 9 on getting out of debt.

NEVER BORROW FOR LONGER THAN YOU HAVE TO

Making sure that you pay the lowest rate of interest is one way to keep the
cost of borrowing down. Paying your debts back quickly is another. Compound
interest (see Appendix 2) really works against you when borrowing money.
The difference between paying back €1,000 at 15% APR over one year and –
say – three years is a staggering €300 in interest!

BUILD UP A GOOD FINANCIAL/CREDIT RATING HISTORY

It is vital at all times to be aware that defaulting on loans or credit cards is registered with the Irish Credit Bureau (ICB) and will greatly affect your ability to borrow or borrow at attractive interest rates. Never let unauthorised arrears build up on any loan. If your circumstances change during the term of a loan, inform the lender and come to an agreed and realistic repayment schedule. (See Chapter 14, 'If I have trouble making my mortgage repayments, what should I do?' for details of whom to contact to avoid money lenders if you are in dire circumstances.) Even negotiating an extension to an interest-only repayment will be recorded in the ICB.

WHY RATES DIFFER SO WIDELY

Financial institutions set their charges according to the level of risk involved and prevailing market conditions.

As far as they are concerned, loans fall into two categories:

Secured loans. Where, if the borrower fails to make the repayments, there is a physical asset – such as a house or even an insurance policy – that can be 'seized' and sold to meet the outstanding debt. Because of this secured loans should cost considerably less.

Unsecured loans. Where, if the borrower fails to make the repayments, the lender has no security and thus risks never getting paid (though this is rare). Such loans cost considerably more.

THE FIRST RULE OF BORROWING

The first rule of borrowing for less is, therefore, to take out a secured rather than an unsecured loan. This isn't always practicable – but where it is, you'll save a substantial amount of money.

Secured loans

Secured loans include:

- mortgage on your property
- secured loan (which is like a second or extra mortgage) on your property
- asset-backed finance (used, for instance, for major purchases such as cars).

Unsecured loans

Unsecured loans include:

- bank overdrafts
- credit union loans
- personal or term loans – including car loans
- credit cards
- store cards
- hire-purchase
- money lenders.

> **MONEY DOCTOR WEALTH WARNING**
>
> ### Interest rates have not always been so low
>
> We have enjoyed relatively low interest rate stability up to recently. Things were very different less than a decade ago. Indeed, in the early 1990s mortgage rates went up to 15% at one point, and some people were paying over 30% a year on their credit card debt.
>
> We saw in 2008 that interest rates rose by nearly 2%. Therefore, don't borrow so much that a change in interest rates (or a change in your personal circumstances) would leave you in crisis.
>
> Rates plummeted to 1% ECB rate during 2009 and remained there for 18 months, and while they increased up to 1.5% in 2011, the likelihood is that they will revert to less than 1% until 2013. Nevertheless, consider carefully further borrowings.

CHOOSING THE BEST LOAN FOR YOUR NEEDS

With the possible exception of borrowing to fund a major holiday or a special event such as a wedding, you should try to make sure that the useful life of whatever you're using your loan for will be longer than the time it takes you to repay it. Remember, the rate of interest you're charged is only part of the equation. The other part is the length of time it will take you to repay the loan. For instance, you might think it was sensible to take out some extra money on your mortgage to buy a car since mortgages are, undoubtedly, the least expensive way to borrow. If, however, your mortgage still has 15 years to run then you'll be paying for your car over all that time. Under the circumstances, you should opt for an alternative method or else ensure that you overpay your mortgage in order to clear that part of the debt sooner.

THE MONEY DOCTOR BEST LOAN GUIDE

Here are the ten most usual ways of borrowing money ranked in order – starting with the least expensive first and ending with the most expensive last.

1   **Loans from family, friends and employers.** Often family members, friends and employers will make interest-free or low-interest loans. My advice is always to regularise such loans with a written agreement so that there is no room for misunderstanding or bad feeling at a later date.

2   **Mortgages and secured loans.** Since the demise of tracker mortgages interest rates have increased, but are still low in relative terms. However, because of funding difficulties, most lenders will no longer consider equity releases or top-up mortgages to finance other non-property purchases. If you are fortunate enough to have a sympathetic lender and have sufficient equity in your property, this can still be an inexpensive way to finance a major purchase. However, bear in mind that if you say, buy a car and add it to your mortgage what you should do is increase your monthly repayments so that that bit of your debt is paid off in less time. Otherwise, you could be paying for your car over the whole term of your mortgage. If you do this, however, ensure that your extra payments 'reduce the capital' (loan) rather than credit your repayment account.

3   **Asset finance and leasing.** I am a big believer in asset finance and leasing when available. Although not as cheap as a mortgage, this can be an economical way to fund major purchases and it has the benefit of being very tax-efficient if you are self-employed or running a business. You should ask an authorised financial adviser with access to all providers to find you the best possible rate. Leasing is also very quick and you can receive your cheque within 48 hours of your application.

4   **Overdrafts.** If you have a bank current account you can ask your manager for an overdraft facility. Once approved, you will be able to spend money up to this amount. There won't be a set re-payment period but there may well be an annual arrangement charge. Authorised overdrafts are usually fairly competitive (though you shouldn't be afraid

to negotiate). Exceeding your overdraft limit, however, can lead to heavy charges and the embarrassment of bounced cheques – for this reason unauthorised overdrafts should be avoided. Bear in mind, too, that most banks expect your current account to be in credit for 30 days a year and will charge you extra if it isn't.

5   **Credit union loans.** We are fortunate in Ireland to have a network of local credit unions willing to lend money to its members at a competitive rate of interest. To qualify for a loan you must first join the credit union and then – normally – save a regular amount with them for a set period of time. Because credit unions are non-profit making they tend to offer much better value for money. Not all credit union rates are the same and while it is worth shopping around, you can only open a credit union account in the nearest office to where you live or where you work.

6   **Personal or term loans.** The cost of personal or term loans can vary enormously. Essentially, when you borrow the money you agree to a set repayment period or 'term'. The rate of interest charged is normally variable and you should always pay close attention to your statements to check that it hasn't risen out of line with market rates. Where a rate is fixed in advance – giving you the security of knowing what your repayments will be – it is likely to be higher.

Where a loan is provided by a dealer or retailer, check the conditions closely. Sometimes you may be offered a low or zero rate for an agreed period that will rise dramatically in cost after the set term. Also, the cost of providing this credit will be built into the price of whatever you are buying.

7   **Credit cards.** Used properly, a credit card will give you as much as 45 days interest-free credit. On a certain day every month your bill will be calculated for the previous 30 days and sent to you for payment by the end of the following month. If your cut-off date is – say – the 17th of the month, all charges between 17 December and 17 January would have to be paid for by the end of February. If you can't pay the full amount then you are given the option of paying a reduced amount. This could be less than 5% of the total outstanding. The catch is that you will be charged an extremely high rate of interest – possibly 20% a year. Credit cards are an extremely expensive way to borrow and credit card

companies are very aggressive in their marketing methods. If you are going to use a credit card then don't fall into the trap of making the minimum payment each month. A relatively small balance could take you years to clear.

Note: if your income is high enough your bank may offer you a 'gold' credit card with a built-in overdraft facility at a preferential rate. Your credit card balance will be settled each month using the overdraft. This can be a cost-effective way to borrow and is worth investigating.

8   **Store cards.** I am afraid I am not at all enthusiastic about store cards. They work in the same way as credit cards except – of course – you can only use them in the store (or chain of stores) that issues the card. Their single advantage is that having such a card may entitle you to an extra discount on first purchase and again during any sales. Their huge disadvantage is that the rate of interest charged on outstanding balances almost always makes normal credit cards look cheap by comparison. My strong advice – unless you are very disciplined with money – is not to use store cards.

9   **Hire-purchase.** Hire-purchase allows you to buy specific goods over an agreed period of time. In other words, it is a bit like a personal or term loan. The difference is that the rates charged for hire-purchase are normally somewhat higher and you might be better looking at alternatives such as a personal loan or a lease. Remember, too, that with hire-purchase you don't own whatever you are buying until you have made your last payment. This is not the case with, for example, a personal loan. However, if you have paid over half the term in the HP agreement, you can return the goods (e.g. a car) with the loan scrapped at that point.

10 **Money lenders.** Whether licensed or unlicensed, money lenders are always about the most expensive way to borrow and the rates they charge are outrageous. When they are trading illegally there is the added risk of violence or intimidation if you don't pay what they say you owe them. You should avoid them like the plague! Incidentally, the definition of a money lender – and licensed at that – is an entity or someone who charges you a minimum of 23% interest a year! A list of licensed money lenders is available from The Central Bank.

(See Chapter 14 'If I have trouble making my mortgage repayments, what should I do?' for details of whom to contact to avoid money lenders if you are in dire circumstances.)

THE MONEY DOCTOR SAYS...

- Think carefully before you borrow money. Is it sensible to take out a loan for whatever you are planning to buy? Don't borrow money to pay for 'lifestyle' items. No loan should ever last for longer than the thing you are spending the money on!

- Shop around for the most competitive rate. There is a huge difference and you can save yourself – literally – thousands of euros by making sure you have the cheapest possible loan.

- Read any credit agreement very carefully and seek clarification of any sections you don't fully understand.

- Don't allow your short-term borrowing to become long term by mistake.

- Don't be blindly loyal to any particular lender. Go where the best rate is.

- If in doubt, seek expert help – consultation@moneydoctor.ie.

PART 4

COMPLETE GUIDE TO INSURANCE

Life insurance...home insurance...pet insurance...medical insurance...product warranty insurance...travel insurance...income protection insurance...there is no shortage of different insurance policies to choose from.

In principle, so much choice is a wonderful thing. It allows you to protect yourself, your family and your possessions from a whole range of risks – at one end catastrophic, at the other mildly irritating.

In practice, of course, so much choice can be confusing and can easily lead to you:

- *not taking out cover you should really have*
- *taking out cover that you don't actually need*
- *taking out the wrong amount of cover (too much or, more worryingly, too little)*
- *paying more than you have to.*

I am afraid the problem is often compounded by the fact that many people end up receiving poor or heavily biased advice.

Anyway, this section of the book has a single purpose: making sure that you have the appropriate cover for your needs and that you aren't paying more for it than is necessary. It is divided into two chapters. In the first, we will consider cover for people, and in the second, cover for things.

11
PROTECTING YOURSELF AND YOUR FAMILY

HOW TO BUY THE MEDICAL, INCOME AND LIFE INSURANCE YOU ACTUALLY NEED – AT THE LOWEST POSSIBLE PRICE

First-class medical protection, critical illness cover and life insurance are available at a relatively low price providing you know how to buy it.

In this chapter you'll discover how to:

- make sure you aren't sold cover you don't need
- decide what cover it is sensible for you to take out
- find out who you can trust to advise you
- make sure you get your cover at the lowest possible price.

American filmmaker Woody Allen quipped that his 'idea of hell is to be stuck in a lift with a life insurance salesman'. Mr Allen is by no means alone in his distrust of both life insurance and the people who sell it. Why should this be? I'm sure it is partly because no one likes to think about anything bad happening to them, and partly because – in order to draw attention to a very real need – life insurance salespeople are forced to bring up uncomfortable subjects with their prospective clients.

However, although it is not something you may rush to tackle, making certain that you have adequate life – and health – insurance will bring you *genuine* peace of mind.

YOU KNOW YOU SHOULD...

It isn't pleasant to dwell on being ill, having an accident or – worst of all – dying. Nevertheless, you owe it to yourself – and those you care for – to spend a little time making sure you are **protected** should the worst happen. This means being:

- *protected* by PHI (permanent health insurance) if you are too unwell to earn an income
- *protected* by private medical insurance if you need medical attention
- *protected* by life cover if you, or your partner, should die.

For a relatively small amount of money you can take out a range of insurance policies designed to:

- provide for you, or your dependants, if you, or your partner, should die
- give you a lump sum or a regular income if you find you have a serious illness, are incapacitated or cannot work
- meet all your private medical bills in the event of an accident or illness.

There are, of course, plenty of facts and figures available proving just how likely it is for someone of any age to fall ill or die. Sadly, such statistics are borne out by everyone's personal experience. The truth is we all know of instances where families have had to face poor medical care and/or financial hardship as the result of a tragedy. We all know, too, that spending the small sum required to purchase appropriate cover makes sound sense.

SPEND TIME, NOT MONEY

The odd thing about the different types of insurance dealt with in this chapter is that none of them is expensive when you consider the protection they offer. The secret is to identify exactly what cover you *really* need and not to get sold an inappropriate or overpriced policy. It is also important to review your needs on a regular basis. What you require today, and what you'll require in even two or three years time could differ dramatically.

The best way to start is by considering what risks you face and deciding what action you should take. Here are three questions that everyone should ask themselves, regardless of their age, gender, health or financial circumstances.

Question 1: What would your financial position be if you were unable to work – due to an accident or illness – for more than a short period of time?

Obviously, your employer and the state will both be obliged to help you out. However, if you have a mortgage, other debts and/or a family to support, your legal entitlements are unlikely to meet anything like your normal monthly outgoings. If you do have a family then your spouse will have to balance work, caring for you and – possibly – caring for children. Is this feasible or – more to the point – desirable? How long will your savings last you under these circumstances? Do you have other assets you could sell?

Unless you have substantial savings and/or low outgoings then **income protection cover** (sometimes known as permanent health insurance) and/or **critical illness insurance** could both make sound sense.

Question 2: Do you have anyone dependent on you for either financial support or care? Are you dependent on someone else financially? Do you have children – or other family members – who would have to be cared for if you were to die?

If you are single and don't have any dependants then the reason to take out **life insurance** is in order to settle your debts and/or leave a bequest. If, on the other hand, there is someone depending on you – either for money or for care – then life cover has to be a priority.

If you are supporting anyone (or if your financial contribution is necessary to the running of your household) then you need to take out cover so that you don't leave those you love facing a financial crisis.

If you are caring for anyone – children, perhaps, or an ageing relative – then you should take out cover so that there is plenty of money for someone else to take over this role.

Question 3: Does it matter to you how quickly you receive non-urgent medical treatment? If you need medical care would you rather choose who looks after you, where you are treated and in what circumstances? How important is a private room in hospital to you?

We are fortunate enough to enjoy free basic health care in Ireland. However, if you are self-employed or if you have responsibilities which mean that it is important for you to be able to choose the time and place of any medical treatment, then you should consider **private medical insurance**.

INCOME PROTECTION COVER

If you are of working age then the chances of you being off work for a prolonged period of time due to illness or an accident are substantially greater than the chances of you dying.

It is for this reason that income protection cover is so valuable. As its name suggests, it is designed to replace your income if a disability or serious illness prevents you from working. If you are in a company pension scheme – or if you have arranged your own pension – you should check to see what cover you have already since it is sometimes included.

Incidentally, most policies only pay out after the policyholder has been off work for a minimum of 13 weeks *unless* hospitalised. Also, if you want to reduce the cost you can opt for a policy that doesn't pay out until you have been off work for 26 weeks.

THE MONEY DOCTOR SAYS...

As with anything *you should shop around* for all your insurance cover. Costs vary dramatically. Remember, too, that an authorised adviser, regulated by the Central Bank of Ireland, can explain all the policies to you and can steer you to the best for your needs.

MONEY DOCTOR WEALTH WARNING

Don't be sold something you don't need

I don't believe it is advisable to buy insurance from anyone who isn't qualified to inform you about every single option available to you. Salespeople who are tied to one company – or even a small selection of companies – are clearly not going to offer you the same quality of advice as someone who has a detailed knowledge of the entire market. For further advice on this crucial area see Chapter 4.

CRITICAL OR SERIOUS ILLNESS INSURANCE

Horrible as it is to think about, imagine being diagnosed with a serious illness. I am talking about something like cancer, heart disease or multiple sclerosis. Naturally, under the circumstances, you might need special care and/or want to make life changes. This is where **critical** or **serious illness insurance** comes in. (The name of this insurance cover is changing to **specified illness cover**.) Providing you survive for two weeks after your diagnosis you will receive a lump sum of tax-free money to spend however you wish. Clearly, such a sum would allow you to seek specialist treatment, pay off your debts or in some other way ensure that you didn't have any financial problems.

It is important to remember that this cover provides you with a lump sum – not an income.

LIFE COVER

There are several different types of **life cover** – but they are all designed to do one thing. For a relatively low monthly payment they provide a lump sum if the insured person dies. The lump sum is tax-free and may go into the insured's estate or may be directly payable to a nominated person (such as his or her spouse). Some of the uses to which this lump sum might be put include:

- paying off a mortgage
- paying off other debts
- being invested to provide a replacement income
- being invested to provide money for childcare or the care of someone else such as an ageing relative.

In the case of more expensive life cover the policy can have a cash-in value after a period of time has elapsed. The cost of life cover will be determined by your age, gender, and lifestyle. If you are a non-smoker and don't drink heavily you will save quite a bit of money.

Below are details of the different types of cover available so that you can decide which is most appropriate to your requirements.

Term insurance

As its name implies, **term insurance** is available for a pre-agreed period of time – usually a minimum of ten years. It is mandatory when you take out interest-only home loans.

It is particularly useful for people with a temporary need. For instance, if you have young children you and your spouse might take out a 20-year plan giving you protection until your family has grown up and left home. By the same token, you might take out a policy that would pay off the exact amount of your mortgage.

Term insurance is the least expensive form of life cover and you can opt for:

Level term. The amount of cover remains the same (level) for the agreed period. For instance, you might take out €50,000 of cover for ten years. The cost will remain fixed for the same period, too.

Decreasing term. The amount of cover drops (decreases) every year. For instance, you might take out €50,000 of cover that drops to €48,000 in the second year, €45,000 in the third year and so forth. Such policies are almost always taken out in conjunction with mortgages in order to pay off the outstanding debt should the insured die. Note this sort of cover can't be extended or increased in value once you have taken it out.

Convertible term. Although the cover is for a set period of time, a convertible policy will allow you to extend your insurance for a further period regardless of your health. This is a very useful feature because it means that if you suffer some health problem you won't be denied life cover because of it. In fact, if you extend the policy, the insurance company will charge you the same premium as if you were perfectly healthy. Convertible term cover is normally not much more expensive than level term cover and – therefore – is usually the better option.

Whole of life assurance

There are two benefits to taking out a **whole of life** assurance plan. Firstly, providing you carry on making your monthly payments, the plan is guaranteed to pay out. In other words, you are covered for the whole of your life. Secondly, there can be an investment element to the cover. So if you decide to cancel the plan you'll receive back a lump sum.

There are various features you can opt for with whole of life cover. You can vary the balance between actual life cover and the investment element, for instance. Also you can decide to end the cover at a particular point – when you retire, for instance. Some whole of life policies are designed to meet inheritance tax liabilities.

However, whole of life cover is more expensive than term cover and in most cases, the premiums are reviewed upwards at regular intervals.

PRIVATE MEDICAL INSURANCE

This type of insurance is designed to meet some or all of your medical bills if you opt to go for private treatment.

Only four companies provide this cover in Ireland. VHI (Voluntary Health Insurance), Laya Healthcare, Aviva Health and GloHealth. Between them they offer a wide range of plans with an array of options, conditions and limits. The basic decisions you have to make are:

- Do you want a choice of consultant?
- Do you want a choice of hospital?
- Do you want private or just semi-private hospital accommodation?
- Do you want outpatient cover?

Discounts can be available if you join through a 'group' – your employer, for instance, or a credit union.

As with all insurance, it is well worth getting expert help in deciding which option is best for your needs.

WHICH TYPES OF COVER SHOULD YOU CHOOSE?

Is it better to take out income protection or critical illness insurance? Should you opt for term life or whole of life cover? If term cover – which sort? If whole of life – what investment element should you include? Do you need private medical insurance, or is it a luxury you can do without?

Although these are personal decisions that only you can make, *a professional authorised adviser will be able to guide you*.

Keep the following points in mind when making your decision:

- If you have a limited budget, I would opt – first and foremost – for either income protection or specified illness cover. Depending on your circumstances you might take out both.
- If you are on a tight budget, then take out decreasing term insurance to cover your mortgage.
- If you have joint financial responsibilities – for instance, if you are married – and you have limited resources, it is more important to cover the main income earner.
- Covering a husband and wife together on the same policy often doesn't cost that much more than covering just one person.
- If you are self-employed, private medical cover is not really a luxury but more of a necessity and the premiums are tax deductible for everyone.

MONEY DOCTOR WEALTH WARNING

Six things every life assurance company must tell you...

The sale of life assurance is strictly regulated and your life assurance company must provide you with six important items of information before you sign on the dotted line. These are:

1   The cost. Not just the monthly premium but also whether the cost will ever be subject to review. If the cost is fixed, this is referred to as level premiums. There are reasons why the cost could be increased. For instance, it could be because the benefit will be going up at some point in the future.

2   A description of the main purpose of the product. For instance, whether it's a savings or protection policy.

3   Full details of all the charges and any commission that is going to be made to a broker or salesperson.

4   If there is an investment element to the policy, you should be given examples of the expected return, together with details of any future tax liability. Any guarantees should also be explained.

5   You should be told what will happen if you cancel (or 'surrender') the policy early. What will this do to the projected value?

6   Background information about the insurer and anyone else involved such as the broker or intermediary.

Note: by law they must also give you a 'cooling-off' period. This is time in which you can change your mind about the policy you have purchased and cancel it, without cost or penalty.

MONEY DOCTOR WEALTH WARNING

You _must_ be truthful

When you complete an application for life cover – in fact, for any sort of insurance – the onus is upon you to advise the insurer of any facts which may affect the risk they are undertaking. Indeed, you'll be asked to sign a declaration to the effect that you haven't withheld any relevant information. If you lie – or even if you fail to reveal something that may be important – your policy may end up being invalid. Clearly, it would be a complete waste of your money if – when you came to claim – the insurer were not legally bound to pay up. In the case of life cover you must provide information about your medical history and also about any risks (such as dangerous sports) that might have some bearing on your life expectancy.

HOW MUCH LIFE COVER DO YOU NEED?

One of the most difficult problems regarding life cover is deciding quite how much you need. If you wanted to replace your income then you will require close to between 10 and 15 times your annual _after-tax_ earnings.

> So, if you take home €1,000 a month you should aim to have a minimum of €120,000 cover, which is €1,000 (your salary) x 12 (number of months in the year) x 10 (minimum advisable level of cover).

Remember, it is possible to keep the cost of life cover down by going for a 'term' policy. Bear in mind too that it's better to have some cover than no cover at all.

Life cover tax tip

If you're worried that you may have to pay inheritance tax (see Chapter 27 for further information about this), then one solution is to set up your life assurance policy so that it is not counted as part of your estate when you die. This is done by 'writing the policy under trust' – which is as simple as completing a form your insurer or agent will provide. Incidentally, if you do this, not only will the proceeds from your life cover escape inheritance tax, but also the money will be paid to your chosen beneficiaries relatively quickly – usually in a matter of weeks. It doesn't cost anything to put your life assurance under trust, and you can change the beneficiary (or beneficiaries) at any time.

KEEPING THE COST DOWN

There are two ways to keep the cost of your insurance down to an absolute minimum:

1   Always get independent professional assistance from someone who is authorised to look at *every option* for you. This is one purchase where shopping around and expert knowledge can save you serious money.

2   Refine your needs. By taking out the *right sort of cover* and the *right level of cover* you won't be wasting money. Quitting smoking can be beneficial both in terms of your health and your finances. If you are free of the habit for over 12 months, it could mean up to a 50% reduction in your monthly life cover premiums. Email me for details.

THE MONEY DOCTOR SAYS...

- Don't stick your head in the sand, believing that 'it won't happen to me'. Protecting yourself and your family should be one of your key financial priorities.

- Choose an independent, professional authorised adviser who you feel comfortable with to advise you.

- Don't get sold cover you don't need.

- Review your needs regularly – every two or three years – to make sure you have adequate protection.

- This is a fiercely competitive market. Having an expert shop around for you could mean big savings – email consultation@moneydoctor.ie.

12
PROTECTING YOUR POSSESSIONS

INSIDER TIPS ON HOW TO KEEP THE COST OF YOUR GENERAL INSURANCE TO A BARE MINIMUM

With the cost of general insurance only going one way it is important to make sure that you are getting value for money. In this chapter you'll discover:

- details of all the different types of cover you should consider
- how to ensure that you aren't paying more than you have to
- other buying tips.

THE IMPORTANCE OF PROPER COVER

The temptation, when insurance premiums rise, is to reduce the amount of cover you have or – where cover isn't obligatory – to cancel the policy completely.

There are two reasons why it is important to make sure that you have adequate 'general' insurance.

Firstly, if you have borrowed money in order to pay for something, you should always ensure that there is sufficient insurance to re-pay the debt in case disaster strikes. To quote just one real case history:

> Frank borrowed €15,000 to buy a car and only took out the cheapest motor insurance he could buy – third party, fire and theft . The car was involved in an accident and completely destroyed. Because Frank didn't have comprehensive insurance he is now saddled with paying off the original car loan plus paying for a replacement car.

Secondly, if you under-insure then you always risk receiving less of a pay-out when you come to claim. This is particularly true when it comes to home insurance. Again, let me quote a real case history:

> John and Moira didn't have a mortgage on their house and although they had buildings and contents protection they hadn't bothered to check the amount of cover for many years. Unfortunately, an electrical fault resulted

in the house being burned down (thankfully, no one was hurt). When they came to claim, because they were under-insured, the insurance company would only pay three-quarters of the price of re-building.

Shopping around for insurance is no one's idea of fun. On the other hand, the cost of not taking out adequate insurance can be huge. And if you invest even a small amount of time reading this chapter and acting on it, you will keep the cost to a bare minimum.

THE DIFFERENT TYPES OF 'GENERAL' INSURANCE

So what is 'general' insurance anyway? It is a catch-all expression encompassing some of the following areas:

- home and other forms of property insurance
- motor insurance
- public liability
- insurance for your other possessions such as boats, caravans and mobile telephones
- pet insurance
- travel insurance
- credit insurance
- professional indemnity insurance
- other risk insurance (e.g. Golfsure – for that round of drinks after a hole in one!)

DON'T JUST RELY ON BROKERS

General insurance is the one area where I would suggest that you shouldn't rely solely on brokers to get you the best deal. In many areas there are now 'direct' operations that can undercut brokers substantially. To find details of these direct operations look in your *Golden Pages* and keep an eye out for companies advertising in the national press. Remember, too, that some insurance companies tend to rely on customer inertia when it comes to renewal. So, having won your custom, they may push the cost of cover up in the second year hoping that you won't be bothered to check elsewhere. Telephoning around and filling in extra paperwork is a nuisance, but think of it this way: if it takes you – say – three hours work to save €200 then you are effectively paying yourself nearly €70 an hour after tax.

HOME INSURANCE

Home insurance is divided into 'buildings' cover and 'contents' cover.

Buildings cover

Buildings cover is obligatory if you have a mortgage and you may find that your lender automatically provides this protection (or at the very least a quotation) for you. The insurance will protect the structure of your home (the building itself, outbuildings, fixtures and fittings and so forth) against fire, storm damage, flood, subsidence, and other similar accidents. Most policies also include public liability cover so that if something happens to someone on your property (for instance, if they have an accident) you are protected. The main thing to watch for with buildings cover is that you have sufficient protection. The cost is worked out on the value of your home and is linked entirely to the re-building cost. So where your home is located, how old it is, its size and the materials from which it is constructed will all influence the premium. If you would like help deciding how much cover to take out then the Society of Chartered Surveyors (38 Merrion Square, Dublin 2, and their website, www.ics.ie) produces an annual guide. Not all buildings policies will cover you for the same things so you should check the small print. One way of keeping the cost down is to make sure you have smoke alarms fitted; another is to join your local neighbourhood watch scheme.

Contents cover

Contents cover is even less standard than buildings cover. The sort of protection you'll receive can vary enormously and when comparing prices you need to bear this in mind. For instance, are you being offered new for old cover, which means that if you claim you'll receive the exact cost of replacement with no reduction on account of the age of your possessions? Also, how much of the loss will you be expected to pay for yourself (known as an excess)? And to what extent are valuables – such as jewellery or cash – actually covered? You'll find that there are all sorts of 'extras' that may or may not be included – from employer's liability to theft of bicycles and from liability to third parties to personal liability. Tedious as it is, the only way to know what you are actually getting is to read the small print. Happily, there are a number of ways in which you can keep the cost of your contents cover down:

- Fit an approved alarm system.
- Fit approved locks to doors and windows.
- Join your neighbourhood watch scheme.

Do note that discounts are sometimes offered to people who are at home most of the day – for instance, if you are retired.

MOTOR INSURANCE

With such high insurance premiums you may be tempted to try and reduce the cost by any means possible. For instance, city-based car owners usually pay higher premiums than their rural counterparts and some are tempted to pretend that their car actually 'lives' in the country. Remember, if you ever come to claim, many insurance companies now send out an investigator to make independent inquiries and a false statement could result in being taken to court for fraud.

Motor insurance is more expensive if you:

- don't have a full licence
- have a history of motor offences
- are under 25 years old
- have made claims in the past
- have a criminal record.

Obviously, you can't make yourself any older than you actually are, but if you don't have a full licence it is well worth putting in the effort to pass the test. By the same token, don't rush to put in a minor claim as it may result in higher premiums. Also, remember that fines may not be the only cost of speeding.

INSIDER TIPS ON BUYING OTHER GENERAL INSURANCE

In my opinion many types of general insurance do not offer value for money. I am particularly suspicious of:

Extended warranties. These cover you against faults developing in your electrical and mechanical goods. Often the retailer makes more money from these insurance policies (by way of commission) than on the sale of the actual product. As legislation offers you 12 months' protection anyway (and as, in general, such goods are much better made nowadays) I am suspicious of such policies.

Mobile telephone insurance. This protects you against loss of or damage to your phone. This is often expensive in relation to the actual cost of replacing your telephone. Furthermore, many people end up buying this cover without meaning to because they don't pay proper attention when completing the contract.

Credit card insurance. There are two types of cover offered by credit card companies. The first protects you against fraud and the second against you being unable to make your repayments due to an accident, illness or redundancy. Both types of cover are expensive and in most cases I would advise against them.

Pet insurance. This protects you against having to pay vet bills if your pet is ill or involved in an accident. Again, I would strongly suggest examining the value for money offered by such policies.

One more point is in relation to buying **travel insurance**. This is often sold by travel agents at highly inflated prices since they earn good rates of commission on every policy sold. Travel insurance is important – but there are many different sources of cover. If you are a regular traveller, you may like to consider an annual policy. Also, if you have a credit card, a certain amount of cover may be included in with your annual fee.

THE MONEY DOCTOR SAYS...

- Check the small print! All insurance policies are not equal.
- It may not be much fun shopping around but it helps if you think of the saving in terms of effort and reward. Three hours spent saving €200 is worth virtually €70 an hour after tax to you.
- Don't get sucked into buying cover you don't really need.
- Don't be tempted to under-insure, it could leave you exposed.

PART 5

A-Z OF PROPERTY PURCHASE

I don't think it would be an overstatement to say that property – and, in particular, owning it – was something of a national obsession. It is easy to understand why: home ownership offers security and the potential to make a capital gain. Indeed, in the ten years up to 2006 residential property prices had grown at an average rate of 12% per annum. Sadly the downturn has taken hold, but there are still opportunities in the property market especially now for those with money and income.

Only the fortunate few can afford to buy a home outright. For the rest of us, saving up until we had the full cost of the apartment or house we wanted to buy would be impractical. Leave aside the fact that it would probably take decades, we would need to live somewhere else in the meantime. The solution is to take out a mortgage or home loan. Such loans are 'secured' against the value of the property being purchased and – because this means the lender faces much less risk – they are normally the least expensive type of borrowing you can undertake.

From a financial perspective, mortgages are the most important consideration when buying a property, which is why the longest chapter in this section is devoted to them. They are not, however, the only thing you need to think about if you own – or are thinking of owning – a property. Just as important are issues such as whether it is better to rent or buy, investing in property, property-related costs, tax and a host of other related topics, all subjects that are covered extensively in what follows.

13
MORTGAGES

HOW TO SECURE THE BEST-VALUE MORTGAGE IN IRELAND

The number of active lenders in the mortgage market has decreased sharply in the last two years and so has the range of products and options. This chapter explains:

- how to make sure you've got the mortgage that suits you best

- how to make sure you are paying the lowest possible price

- who to trust for mortgage advice.

In addition, we look at how mortgages work, re-mortgaging, tax relief and just about every other property-related question you can think of.

TAKING ADVANTAGE OF THE MORTGAGE REVOLUTION

Please put any pre-conceptions you have about buying a home or arranging a mortgage to one side. The truth is:

- Your home is *not* necessarily your most important investment.

- Your home is definitely *not* your most expensive purchase.

- You *don't* have to take 25 years to pay back your mortgage.

Also, and this is crucial to keeping the cost of buying your home or investment property to a bare minimum:

- The interest rate your mortgage lender charges you makes a huge difference to the cost of buying your home.

- The type of mortgage you have also makes a huge difference to the cost of buying your home.

Changes in the mortgage market in the last four years have meant that for the foreseeable future you may be tied to the lender from whom you originally got your mortgage. For this reason it is essential that you do careful research before selecting a particular lender or product. *Independent advice from an authorised adviser will stand you in good stead over the whole term of your mortgage.*

Not necessarily your most important investment. Definitely not your most expensive purchase.

Received wisdom has it that the most important investment most of us will probably ever make is in our home. There is no doubt that owning your home is a significant part of being financially secure:

- The cost is not dissimilar to renting a home – making it a good financial decision.

- You aren't at the mercy of unscrupulous, unpleasant, greedy or inefficient landlords.

- With luck you'll see the value of your property rise in the longer term – giving you a tax-free gain.

Nevertheless, although it makes sense to buy your own home, you shouldn't be fooled into thinking that it is the 'be all and end all' of investments. It is arguable, in fact, that building up your other investments – especially a pension plan – is substantially more important. Furthermore, the stock market has – traditionally – always produced a better return than property. I'm not trying to put you off buying your own home – far from it – but don't forget it is only one part of establishing your personal wealth.

It is also worth remembering that your home won't automatically be your most expensive purchase. Depending on interest rates, that honour could easily go to your mortgage. If you buy a house for €200,000 and take out a traditional, repayment mortgage for €160,000 (80% of the purchase price) and pay it back over 25 years at an average rate of 6%, the total cost of buying your home (including interest) will be €309,265.09. That's €109,265.09 more than the actual cost of your home. Which is why it is crucial you choose the least expensive mortgage option available to you.

INTEREST: ALL THE DIFFERENCE IN THE WORLD

The rate of interest you are charged on your mortgage makes a huge difference to the total cost of your home as the table opposite indicates:

Cost of €100,000 25-year repayment mortgage: interest payable

Annual interest rate (%)	Cost per month (€)	Total interest over term (€)
3.75	514.13	54,239
4	527.84	58,350
4.25	541.74	65,251
4.5	555.83	66,750
4.75	570.12	71,034
5	584.59	75,377
5.25	599.25	79,773
5.5	614.09	84,225
5.75	629.11	88,730
6	644.30	93,290
6.25	659.67	97,900
6.5	675.21	102,561
6.75	690.91	107,224
7	706.78	112,033

The difference between paying – say – 5.5% and 6.5% (which doesn't sound like much) actually equates to €18,336 of interest over the 25-year term and increases repayments by €161.12 per month. Put another way, think how much extra you would have to earn after tax to end up with €18,336 in your pocket. Paying more mortgage interest than you have to can seriously damage your wealth. Shopping around makes excellent sense.

TWO MORTGAGE OPTIONS: REPAYMENT VERSUS INTEREST-ONLY

Although there is a whole range of mortgages to choose from, they all fall into one of two categories:

- repayment (annuity) mortgages
- interest-only mortgages

Repayment/annuity mortgage

The first option is a repayment (or annuity) mortgage. With this type of mortgage your monthly repayments are divided into two parts. The first is the interest you owe on the total amount borrowed. The second is repayment of part of the capital you have borrowed. The big advantage of this mortgage is that you are guaranteed to have paid off your whole loan at the end of the term. However, in the early years almost all your monthly repayments will be in interest. Let me give you an example:

> Sheila takes out a €200,000 mortgage over 25 years at an interest rate of 5.6%. Her monthly capital and interest payments are €1,240.15. At the end of the first year she will have paid a total of €14,881.80 but will still owe over €196,000 to her lender. In year ten she will have paid €148,817 and will still owe €150,795. Put another way, in the first ten years roughly two-thirds (66%) of what she pays to her lender will be interest, and only one-third (33%) will be capital.

MONEY DOCTOR WEALTH CHECK

Save extra interest

When choosing a repayment mortgage, make sure the interest is calculated **daily** or at least **monthly** ('monthly rest'). Why? Because over the term of your mortgage this will save you a tidy sum of money. The real thing to avoid is something called the 'annual rest system', which will cost you the most. Some lenders may still have customers on their books who are on this system and it can add about 0.35% to your interest rate. If you are in this position, go back to your lender and ask them to change you to a monthly calculation.

Interest-only mortgages

The other sort of mortgage on offer is an **interest-only mortgage**. With this type of mortgage you pay only the interest for the agreed period. With **investment mortgages** you pay interest only on the amount borrowed *and* at the same time you would set up a savings plan, which – it would be hoped – will pay off the capital at the end of the term. Your monthly repayments will, therefore, consist of interest on the loan and a contribution to a savings plan. This is ideal for certain types of loans e.g. commercial loans where the interest remains constant and the tax relief can be maximised (because the capital is not being repaid, you are receiving the most tax relief on the interest in the first year right through to the end of the term).

In the case of both a home and an investment property there are certain circumstances where you might not bother with the savings element, as I'll explain in a moment.

Around 20 years ago interest-only home loans got a bad name because many borrowers were advised to take out **endowment policies** (see below for an explanation) to re-pay the capital at the end of the term. Unfortunately, some of these policies failed to produce a sufficient return to do so. In other words, borrowers found that after 25 years they still owed money to their lenders.

Despite past problems with endowment mortgages, interest-only home loans can make sound financial sense. For instance, if you are self-employed, the tax benefits of a **pension-linked interest-only** mortgage can be very substantial, in particular when taken out for commercial property.

Here is a quick summary of the three main types of interest-only mortgage options available:

Endowment mortgages. There are various types of endowment policy available: these are investments offered by life insurance companies. The money you pay to the life insurance company is partly used to provide you with **life cover** (so that if you die the mortgage itself can be repaid) and partly invested in the **stock market**. If the money is invested well, then obviously your original loan will be repaid and you might even be left with a tax-free sum. However, if the performance of the endowment policy is not good, then you could be left with insufficient cash to repay your original loan. There is no tax relief on endowment policy premiums.

Pension-linked mortgages. The difference between this and an endowment mortgage is that the life insurance company (after taking out money to pay for life cover) invests your cash into a **pension fund**. This has very definite tax benefits for anyone who is self-employed or on an extremely high income. Ordinarily, the pension fund is designed to mature on your retirement age at double the original amount being borrowed. Twenty-five per cent of this pension fund is available at maturity for encashment, tax-free, and even though you will have to pay tax on the rest of the fund you should have sufficient money to pay off the rest of the mortgage.

New rules on self-direct trusts or **SSAPs** (small self-administered pension schemes) now allow pension funds to borrow on properties. Indeed, there are all sorts of other tax benefits available to those who buy property as part of their pension fund. Some of this is covered elsewhere in the chapters on retirement planning and tax. However, as it is such a complicated area you will need to take specialist advice (consultation@moneydoctor.ie) if you wish to take advantage of the new rules.

Interest-only mortgages. It was possible to borrow money to purchase property at very competitive rates of interest without any obligation to re-pay the capital before the end of the term. For instance, if you took out a 20-year interest-only mortgage all you have to pay each month is the agreed rate of interest. The capital sum isn't due until 20 years have passed. This could suit you for all sorts of reasons. Perhaps you are expecting to receive a lump sum – such as an inheritance – before the 20 years are up. Maybe you intend to re-sell the property during this period. Possibly you have other investments that could be cashed in to repay the loan. Possibly you will win the Lotto! Do note that you will have to take out level term life cover that covers the entire amount borrowed for the full term in association with an interest-only mortgage, so that the loan can be repaid in the event of your death. While the credit crunch rages all around us at the moment, interest-only loans are virtually a thing of the past for new borrowers.

FIXED OR VARIABLE RATE?

As if you didn't have enough choice already, another decision you must make when mortgage shopping can be whether to opt for a fixed or variable rate. A **fixed rate** means that the amount of interest you pay is pre-set for an agreed period of time. This offers you the benefit of certainty. Even if interest rates rise your repayments will stay the same. On the other hand if interest rates fall you won't benefit. You incur a penalty should you wish to pay off or part pay off your mortgage while on a fixed rate of interest. Generally, this sum is set at between three and six months' interest on the amount being repaid.

A **variable rate**, on the other hand, will move with the market. This is fine while interest rates are low but if they begin to rise you could be adversely affected. There is generally no penalty if you wish to pay off all or part of the loan before the end of the mortgage term.

Tracker mortgages *were* the real deal, and today are costing Ireland's lenders a fortune to maintain. The interest rate tracked the ECB rate (currently

0.75%) and the lender agreed a margin (or profit) that had to be maintained for the entire term of the mortgage; only if the ECB rate moves does your tracker rate move. Today there are some lucky mortgagers paying 0.5% over the ECB rate (total 1.25%) as they would have negotiated their loan based on only having to borrow less than 50% of the value of their home.

> ## THE MONEY DOCTOR SAYS...
>
> Unless you are self-employed, on a high-income or have some other source of funds coming to you in the future, the Money Doctor normally recommends that you take out a repayment or annuity mortgage when buying your main home. This said, there are some interesting variations now available allowing you to combine an interest-only mortgage with a repayment mortgage, in particular pension-based mortgages.

A WORD ABOUT 'CURRENT ACCOUNT' MORTGAGES

Also known as an offset mortgage, this means that funds on current and savings accounts are offset against your mortgage balance for interest calculation purposes. This way, you save the interest on that amount which is offset. Over the course of the mortgage term, the savings can be substantial if you are disciplined.

Only one lender in Ireland offers this product and it is well worth enquiring from that lender or your financial adviser.

WHY YOU SHOULD TRY TO MAKE MORTGAGE OVERPAYMENTS

Something I have become very keen on in recent years is the idea of overpaying your mortgage each month. This can't be done with all mortgages (for instance, you can't do it where you are on a fixed rate) but where it is possible and your income allows, it brings real benefits. With interest rates low at the moment and potentially likely to stay low for the next few years, it may be also important to remember that if your return/yield is far greater than the cost of the money (the mortgage rate), then investing your surplus monies elsewhere may be more beneficial. Consider these two examples, though, where overpayment can also be beneficial:

Mary takes out a repayment mortgage for €250,000 with a term of 25 years at 5.5%. Her minimum monthly repayment is €1535.22. However, she decides that she can afford to pay an extra €235 a month. As a result, her mortgage will be paid off six years earlier and she will save €57,070 in interest.

John also takes out a repayment mortgage for €320,000 with a term of 30 years at 5.75%. His minimum monthly repayment is €1867.43. He 'overpays' by €320 a month and as a result his mortgage will be paid off nine years earlier and he will save €120,429.31 in interest!

In both instances, by taking out a current account mortgage they could save even more interest. This is because any money on deposit in their current account is offset against their mortgage debt.

> ### THE MONEY DOCTOR SAYS...
>
> With the range of mortgage choices available, many borrowers worry about whether they are making the right decision for their needs. This is where a really good independent financial adviser offering a full choice of lenders can help. He or she will be able to guide you to the least expensive, most appropriate mortgage for your needs. Email consultation@moneydoctor.ie.

HOW THE RIGHT PROFESSIONAL ADVISER WILL SAVE YOU MONEY

It goes without saying that you should shop around for the best possible mortgage deal as so much of your hard-earned cash is at stake. Two things to watch out for:

1 You may not always be comparing like with like. There is a great deal of difference between a ten-year fixed rate mortgage and a current account repayment mortgage. Each will cost a different amount and each is designed to meet different needs.

2 You may not be offered a full range of options. A bank or building society – for instance – might only have three or four types of mortgage to offer you. Many mortgage advisers deal with less than five lenders.

There are eight mortgage lenders in Ireland at this point in time, seven mainstream and one specialist. To get the best possible deal you should always deal with an adviser who is **authorised** by the Central Bank of Ireland to act on behalf of the majority of these lenders.

Please remember, too, that even if you are a customer with a particular financial institution, your authorised financial adviser may still be able to negotiate a better deal on your behalf. This is because a professional will know what the best deal available actually is, while the lender will know that the adviser has other options should the lender fall short of the client's requirement.

MONEY DOCTOR WEALTH CHECK

The latest information...

If you want the latest financial information – everything from interest rates to tax-saving tips – then log on to the Money Doctor website at www.moneydoctor.ie.

THE MONEY DOCTOR SAYS...

- Don't be complacent. Even a small difference in the rate you pay can make a huge difference to the cost of your mortgage. No lender deserves your loyalty. Go to where the best deal is.

- Don't trust any adviser who isn't authorised to act for all the financial institutions offering home loans in Ireland, or at the very least use an adviser who can tell you where the best deals can be obtained, irrespective of the agencies held. There are eight lenders and anyone who can't tell you about all of them isn't going to get you the best deal.

- Do not panic if your home is worth less than your mortgage. As long as your income can meet the monthly mortgage repayment, the loss will only crystallise upon sale of the home. Always obtain professional advice for strategies.

- Remember, authorised financial advisers should be independent and, in most cases, you will pay a fee for their services, plus they will definitely find you the best package for your needs.

14
PROPERTY QUESTIONS

ANSWERS TO YOUR PROPERTY AND MORTGAGE QUESTIONS

This chapter contains detailed answers to all your property and mortgage questions, including:

- Should I buy or rent my home?
- How much can I borrow on my income?
- What is 'APR'?
- Is it worth switching my mortgage to get a lower rate?
- Help! I'm self-employed. How do I get a mortgage?
- What will it cost for me to buy my home?
- What tax relief will I receive on my home loan?
- Does it make sense to buy a second property as an investment?
- What are the benefits of owning a home in a designated area?
- What's the story with local authority loans?
- What other state housing grants might be available to me?
- Is it worth repaying my mortgage early?
- What different types of home insurance will I need?
- If I have trouble making my mortgage repayments what should I do?

SHOULD I BUY OR RENT?

Ireland is one of the few countries in Europe where buying one's home is the norm. Broadly speaking, at present the cost of buying a home is the same as – or in many cases less than – renting the same property. This is linked to supply and demand, of course, and varies from region to region as well as from property to property. We were in a low-interest environment until 2006 – and this favoured house purchase – as did the availability of mortgage interest relief. Interest rates rose between 2006 and 2008, and while they are now back to historically low levels, consumers are more reluctant to borrow, and the relatively meagre tax relief for first-time borrowers only is not an attraction in itself. Even this tax relief ends 31 December 2012 for first-time buyers.

If a future government were to introduce greater tenant rights the situation might change, but at the moment – if you can raise the sufficient deposit – buying makes better long-term sense. After all, when you give up a rental property you receive nothing back. Whereas when you have paid off your mortgage you will own your home and may have seen a nice, tax-free capital gain as well.

House prices in Ireland rose at an unprecedented rate in the ten years to 2006 and most informed opinion then was that as long as we continued in a low-interest environment and our economy remained healthy, a sharp fall in house prices seemed unlikely. However, things have changed dramatically over the last 6 years and prices are down 50% from the 2006 peak. Renting is cheaper but as property values fall, you may pick up a bargain from foreclosures or 'distressed sales', while the introduction of more rental purchase schemes may be an interesting development over the next few years.

HOW MUCH CAN I BORROW?

You should always put down as much of a deposit as possible when buying your home. You will need a minimum of 8% of the purchase price (that is to say €24,000 if you are buying a €300,000 property) but it is preferable to have more. Why? Because it makes you less vulnerable to moves in interest rates and property values, plus your authorised mortgage intermediary will be able to negotiate a lower interest rate with a lender if you have over 20% deposit – the less the percentage you have to borrow, the better the interest rate may be.

Depending on what you earn, lenders may give you a mortgage of between three and five times your income. For example:

- If you earn €60,000 a year you may be able to borrow up to €300,000 over 35 years, though Permanent TSB capped their multiple at 3.5 times, so in this example €210,000 would be the maximum approved.

- If you and your partner earn a combined income of €80,000 you may be able to borrow between €280,000 and €360,000 over 35 years.

Your ability to repay a mortgage will be based on your net disposable income (NDI) (gross income less tax, USC, PRSI and any existing loan repayments) and will be stress-tested to allow for future rises in interest rates. The maximum percentage of your NDI that can be set aside for financial commitments, including a home loan, is 35%, so on a net income of €4,000 between two borrowers, the maximum allowable would be €1400 monthly.

WHAT IS APR?

The initials 'APR' stand for annual percentage rate and it is the way in which the cost of your loan is expressed. What makes it different from a straight interest rate is that it takes into account not just the interest rate but also the timing of any interest payments, capital repayments and other charges, arrangement fees and so forth. The APR must, by law, reflect the actual rate of interest charged over the full period of the loan.

IS IT WORTH SWITCHING MY MORTGAGE TO GET A LOWER RATE?

The short answer is: it depends if you can find a new lender willing to allow you to switch. If the loan to value of your mortgage is less than 60% there are two things to consider, apart from proof of ability to repay:

* How much can you save by switching lender?
* What is switching lender going to cost you?

The first question is relatively easy to answer. The second question will depend on a variety of factors including:

* whether you are on a fixed interest rate – in which case there may be a penalty for switching
* how much it is going to cost you by way of legal and other costs.

If you can save 0.25% a year interest – or more – it could well be worth the switch. If in doubt, consult an authorised mortgage intermediary or accountant and ask them to do the figures for you.

HELP! I'M SELF-EMPLOYED

Most financial institutions are pleased to lend to someone who is self-employed – though if you have less than three years' sets of accounts it may be harder. This is another instance where a professional authorised mortgage intermediary will help. He or she will know which lenders are keen for your business and willing to offer you the lowest rates. Remember that it is the net profit (after expenses but before tax) that lenders use for borrowing eligibility.

Note: it is no longer possible to get a mortgage in Ireland without a statement from your accountant to the effect that your tax affairs are completely up to date.

WHAT WILL IT COST FOR ME TO BUY MY HOME?

There are various expenses in buying a home:

Valuation fees. No lender will let you have a mortgage without a proper valuation. The price of this will vary but is likely to be in the region of €130. You may like to ask an architect or some other type of professional property adviser to survey the building for you to check its condition and the likely cost of repairs. The fee for this will be linked to the amount of work required and could run to several hundred euros or more for a large house.

Legal fees. This is primarily the cost of employing a solicitor to look after the whole transaction for you. The normal cost is in the region of 1% of the total price plus VAT at 21% and outlay. So for a €200,000 house you will have to find in the region of €2,400. Your lender may also charge you a certain amount to cover their legal fees if it is a commercial transaction. Negotiation over legal fees is possible and you should ask for a reduction, especially if you are a first-time buyer.

Land registry fees. On a €200,000 property these would be up to €750. The fee is to cover registering the property in your name.

Stamp duty. This is based on the purchase price of the property.

Stamp duty

The following rates of stamp duty apply to all residential properties:
On and after 8 December 2010

Property value	Rate
Up to €1,000,000	1%
Balance	2%
Commercial stamp duty rates	For any property over €80,000, stamp duty is chargeable at 6%

Search fees. This is to check that the property has planning permission, isn't located on the site of a proposed development and so forth. Usually around €150.

Arrangement fees. Some lenders charge application and arrangement fees. These could amount to between €100 and €300 but generally only apply to non-home loans.

If you would like to know exactly what your home loan is going to cost you to buy visit my website – www.moneydoctor.ie – where you'll find a calculator that will work it out for you.

To give you a typical example, for a first-time buyer purchasing a house for €200,000 with an 80% mortgage (€160,000) the total fees will be of the order of €4,000.

WHAT TAX RELIEF WILL I RECEIVE ON MY HOME LOAN?

You will be entitled to **mortgage interest relief**, which will be given to you automatically 'at source'.

Measures in Finance Act 2012

The Finance Act 2012 included the following changes to the rules on mortgage interest relief:

- First-time buyers in 2012 will get mortgage interest relief at a rate of 25% for the first 2 tax years, reducing after that, with the appropriate first-time buyer ceilings.
- Non-first-time buyers in 2012 will get mortgage interest relief at a rate of 15% from 2012 until 2017, 22.5% for the next 3 years and 20% for the final 2 years.
- A special rate of 30% for the tax years 2012 to 2017 is being introduced for first-time buyers who bought their sole residence for the first time in the years 2004 to 2008 or paid their first mortgage interest payment during this period.
- The maximum relief is €10,000 per person per annum.

With effect from 1 May 2009, the number of tax years in respect of which mortgage interest relief may be claimed is 7 years for first-time and non-first-time buyers.

- Mortgages taken out on or after 1 January 2013 will not qualify for mortgage interest relief.
- Mortgage interest relief will be abolished completely after 31 December 2017.

DOES IT MAKE SENSE TO BUY A SECOND PROPERTY AS AN INVESTMENT?

Buying property and renting it out became an increasingly popular investment in the 2000s. There were various reasons for this including:

- tax incentives – you can claim 75% of any loan interest you pay on borrowings to acquire and/or improve the property, against any rental income you receive. Plus, if you buy certain types of property or property in particular areas you will receive additional tax breaks
- potential increases in property values
- possible high yields in relation to other investments
- low cost of borrowing money.

In general, the only investors who don't make money from renting out property are those who have over-estimated the return they'll receive, haven't allowed for all the likely costs and lack the patience to wait out any market downturns. The secrets to success are undoubtedly:

- Allow for periods without tenants (known as 'voids').
- Make sure you have calculated all the costs including loan repayments, redecoration, maintenance and repair.
- Don't view it as a short-term investment.

WHAT'S THE STORY WITH LOCAL AUTHORITY LOANS?

County councils and city corporations both provide financial support to anyone on relatively low incomes so that they can afford to buy their own home, but you can be waiting a long time to be facilitated.

If you cannot get a loan from a building society or bank, you may be eligible for a local authority mortgage. The amount borrowed can be up to 97% of the cost of the house subject to a maximum loan of €165,000 and subject to repayments which cannot exceed 35% of the household net income (i.e. income after tax, USC and PRSI). Also introduced in 2012 were the mortgage –rental schemes. Email me for details.

WHAT OTHER STATE HOUSING GRANTS MIGHT BE AVAILABLE TO ME?

There are various other grants available from the state including:

Affordable housing. Many new developments now include a percentage of what is referred to as 'affordable housing'. These are houses, flats or building sites that must be sold at well below market price to people who would not otherwise be able to afford to buy their own home. The affordable housing scheme allows lower-income house buyers the chance to buy newly constructed homes and apartments in areas where property prices have created an affordability gap for lower-income house buyers. There are of course conditions that preclude the buyer from making a 'quick kill'.

Improvement grants. A range of loans will be available from your local authority so that you can improve or extend your home.

Mortgage subsidy. If you are a local authority tenant and you give up your home to buy a property on the open market, you may be entitled to financial support for up to five years. The **mortgage allowance scheme** is an allowance of up to a maximum of €11,450 payable over a five-year period to local authority tenants. The allowance is paid directly to the lender and your repayments are reduced accordingly for the first five years of the mortgage. The allowance paid in any year cannot exceed the amount of the mortgage repayments.

Shared ownership. The **shared ownership scheme** is aimed at those who cannot afford to purchase an entire home in one transaction. It allows you to buy a proportion of your home initially and to increase that proportion in steps until you own the whole house. During this stage, ownership is shared between you and the local authority and you make payments on a mortgage for the part you own and pay rent to the local authority for the other part at a rate of 4.3%.

Disabled persons grant. Given to cover the cost of adapting a private home for the needs of someone who is disabled.

Thatching grant. Available towards the cost of renewing or repairing thatched roofs on houses. Thatchers are a dying breed but it is important to reward and help those who are maintaining our heritage.

Home Energy Savings Grants. A range of grants is available to improve home insulation, install renewable energy systems and upgrade existing heating systems to become more energy-efficient. Details can be found on www.seai.ie.

IS IT WORTH REPAYING MY MORTGAGE EARLY?

Should you overpay your mortgage each month? Should you use all your available cash to reduce your mortgage? Should you use a lump sum of cash to reduce or pay off your mortgage? The answer is *probably* yes if the following applies to you:

- You don't have any other – more expensive – debts. (If you do, these should be paid off first.)
- It won't leave you without some savings tucked away against a rainy day.
- There aren't other investment opportunities that might be worth more to you in cash terms.

If you were thinking of paying off some or all of your mortgage, I would strongly advise consulting an authorised adviser or mortgage intermediary first. He or she will be able to work out the figures for you.

WHAT DIFFERENT TYPES OF HOME INSURANCE WILL I NEED?

This is covered in greater detail in Chapter 12 on insurance. In summary, homeowners should take out the following cover:

Buildings insurance. This will be compulsory if you have a mortgage. Basically, it means that if some damage is done to the fabric of your home (by a fire or flood, for instance), then money is available to repair or rebuild as necessary.

Contents insurance. This protects you against loss of or damage to your home contents.

Mortgage repayment insurance (payment protection insurance). This cover is optional but means that if you are ill or made redundant, your mortgage repayments would be paid for you. Payments usually last for up to a year. Refunds are underway from some of the providers who mis-sold this product. Email me for details.

IF I HAVE TROUBLE MAKING MY MORTGAGE REPAYMENTS, WHAT SHOULD I DO?

Contact your lender immediately. The worst thing you can do is keep them in the dark about any financial problems you may be encountering. If you need help with your finances you could contact a qualified, experienced financial adviser:

- Your local St Vincent de Paul Society, which runs a special advice scheme.

- The Department of Social Protection, which also runs a free advice scheme called MABS (Money and Budgeting Advice Service). You can obtain details from your local social welfare office or public library.

THE MONEY DOCTOR SAYS...

If you have any questions about property or mortgages not answered in this book then please do email me (jlowe@moneydoctor.ie) or book a one-to-one consultation – consultation@moneydoctor.ie.

PART 6

GUARANTEED SAVINGS AND INVESTMENT SUCCESS

My favourite quote about wealth is Ernest Hemingway's, who in response to F. Scott Fitzgerald's comment that the rich are different, replied: 'Yes, they have more money.'

And getting yourself into a position where you have 'more money' is what this section of the book is all about for, as the entertainer Sophie Tucker observed, 'I've been rich, and I've been poor: rich is better.' Not, I hasten to add, that I am suggesting you get rich for the sake of it. My interest is in making sure you have sufficient money to be free – free from the worry of not having enough and free to choose how you spend your time.

There are some widely held misconceptions about how to get rich. Some people think the only way they will manage it is by owning their own business; others feel the Lotto offers them their best chance; a third group seem to imagine it will happen all by itself.

In my experience, the only way to get rich is to take it slowly and steadily.

Set aside part of your income every month and invest it wisely and you will be amazed at how – over the years – it grows.

Many people feel that there is not much difference between savings and investment, but to my mind there is a clear distinction:

- *Saving is all about short-term goals. It's the money you tuck away on a regular basis to pay for your holidays, or in case of emergency. Because it's money that needs to be available to you it can't be tied up where you can't get your hands on it.*

- *Investment, on the other hand, is all about medium- to long-term goals. You invest to ensure yourself a more prosperous and secure future. You may invest a lump sum, or on a regular basis, but the real thing is (barring an unforeseen crisis) you should be able to leave your money to work for you undisturbed for a reasonable period of time.*

Accordingly, this section is divided into two chapters. In the first you'll discover the best possible way to save your money with a view to building your own emergency fund. In the second, you'll learn how to invest your money in such a way as to build your wealth. Between the two you'll have all the tools you need to make your money grow, and grow and grow...

15
SAVING FOR A RAINY DAY

THE QUICKEST, MOST EFFICIENT WAY TO BUILD UP AN EMERGENCY FUND

One of your key financial objectives should be to have some easily accessible cash savings to pay for larger expenses or simply in case of a 'rainy day'. In this chapter you will discover:

- why it is so important to have cash savings
- how much savings you should build up
- the best way to make your savings grow.

GOOD, OLD-FASHIONED SAVINGS

We are lucky enough to live in a country where the state will provide a safety net for widow(er)s, those who are seriously ill or disabled, pensioners and anyone in dire financial straits. However, the amount on offer is relatively meagre and won't cover most of the day-to-day financial crises ordinary people face. For instance, the state isn't going to help you with an unexpected bill for repairs to your home or car. Nor will they pay all your regular bills if you find yourself without an income for any reason. The fact is you should have a bit of cash tucked away – good, old-fashioned savings – just in case you ever need it. You should probably also have some extra cash to hand so that you can take advantage of an unexpected investment opportunity, for capital expenditure or just in case you see something you want to buy.

Saving up money to create a safety net requires a degree of commitment. It is in our nature, after all, to spend rather than to save. But if you can motivate yourself to tuck a little bit away each month I promise you'll never regret it!

SAVING MADE SIMPLE

It is one thing to think 'I must build up my savings' but often quite another thing to actually do so. Saving can only be achieved by conscious effort.

Ideally, you should open your savings account somewhere convenient and arrange to make regular payments into it. For instance, you might set up a standing order to transfer a regular amount each month from your bank current account to a deposit account. Some employers offer 'payroll deduction' schemes where the money goes straight from your salary to a savings account. Also, if you are entitled to receive a child allowance from the state you could consider saving all of this on an automatic basis. The real thing to remember is that a savings plan should be regular, and sacrosanct.

HOW MUCH IS ENOUGH?

Just how much savings you should aim to accumulate will be determined by your personal circumstances.

- A single person in his or her 20s without any responsibilities and low overheads probably only needs to have enough cash to cover – say – three months' worth of expenditure.
- A couple with children, a mortgage and a car to run should probably aim to build up as much as six months' expenditure.

If you aren't already lucky enough to have a lump sum available to form your safety net, then the best way to build it up is to establish a pattern of regular saving each week or each month. Remember, something is better than nothing – even if it is a relatively small amount, it will soon add up.

YOUR SAVINGS STRATEGY

If you have – say – six months' worth of expenditure saved up and you don't need instant access to all of it, my advice is to keep about a third where it is readily available and the rest where you can access it by giving notice. This strategy will allow you to earn extra interest.

Incidentally, if you are in a permanent relationship, then ideally you should both have access to the emergency fund. In the event of some problem affecting one of you, the other may need to use this money.

EMERGENCY FUND: THREE BASIC REQUIREMENTS

An emergency fund should meet three basic requirements:

1   It should provide you with total security. Your savings must not be at risk.

2   It must earn as much interest as possible under the circumstances.

3   It must provide you with the level of access you need.

For these reasons the number of options available to you are limited pretty much to those listed below.

Deposit accounts

If you leave money on **deposit** with a bank, building society or credit union they will pay you interest. How much interest you earn can vary according to:

- how much money you have on deposit
- the length of notice you have to give before you can make a withdrawal (notice accounts/fixed rate accounts)
- the commitment to saving regularly (check out Regular Saver Accounts).

Rates can vary substantially and change all the time. Shop around and don't be afraid to move your money to where it can be earning more for you. Remember, currently the Deposit Protection Scheme will guarantee €100,000 of your savings. In addition, that portion of deposits in excess of €100,000 held with the six Irish-owned banks and not covered by the Deposit Protection Scheme is covered to an unlimited amount by the Eligible Liabilities Guarantee Scheme (ELGS). This scheme is due to expire on 31 December 2012 and its continuance will be reviewed by the EU.

State Savings from NTMA

Available from An Post, these offer a good range of savings products, all of which give competitive returns and some of which are tax-free. If you want to build up an emergency fund the two most appropriate accounts to consider are the **Instalment Savings** scheme or the **Instant Access** deposit account. An Post's Instalment Savings scheme requires you to make regular monthly payments for at least one year of between €25 and €500. In exchange, you will enjoy tax-free growth. An Post's Instant Access deposit account is very similar to a bank or building society deposit account. The interest rate isn't high, but it is competitive and you do have instant access. Once you've built up your emergency fund you may like to consider transferring your money into either an An Post **savings bond** or An Post **savings certificates**. Both are designed for medium- to long-term growth (at least three years), but you can get your money quickly if you need to. In addition, it's worth keeping in mind that the interest earned on savings bonds and certificates is tax-free. The National Solidarity Bond (either a 4- or 10-year investment) enjoys an element of tax-free returns, with the 10-year Bond returning a net 47% on maturity (€10,000 = €14.700 after 10 years).

SAVINGS AND TAX

On deposit accounts, deposit interest retention tax (**DIRT**) is levied at source on your interest at a standard rate of 30%. However, if you are not liable for income tax and you or your spouse are over 65 years of age or you are permanently incapacitated, then you are entitled to claim back any DIRT deducted from your interest. You can make a back claim for DIRT tax for up to four years. Send a DE1 form to your deposit taker to reclaim the tax. The institutions will then pay you a gross return. Otherwise, use the 'old system' for back claims.

MONEY DOCTOR WEALTH CHECK

How to reclaim DIRT

Nothing could be easier than reclaiming DIRT. All you do is complete a short form available from any larger post office, bank, building society or tax office. You'll need to attach evidence of the DIRT that you have paid. This is done by asking the financial institution (or institutions) concerned to provide you with a special certificate. The DE1 leaflet is available at www.revenue.ie/leaflet/dde1.pdf for those who wish to claim exemption from paying DIRT.

THE MONEY DOCTOR SAYS...

- Saving on a regular basis may not always be easy but it will bring you real peace of mind.

- You should have an emergency fund in place sufficient to cover all your bills for between three and six months.

- As with everything: shop around. You could earn a considerably greater return by moving your money to where the best rates are.

- Watch out for Regular Saver Accounts – you save from €100 to €1000 per month up to 12 months at very attractive rates. E-mail me for details of these deposit takers and their interest rates and terms.

16
INVESTMENT STRATEGIES YOU CAN COUNT ON

HOW TO MAKE YOUR MONEY GROW AND GROW AND GROW

Every investor faces the same conflict: how to balance risk and reward. Should you accept a lower return in exchange for peace of mind? Or should you attempt to make your money grow more quickly and face the possibility of losses? In fact, the best solution to the dilemma is: neither. As this chapter will demonstrate, the optimum way to build up your wealth is to:

- Set clear objectives. Know where you are going and what you want to achieve.
- Diversify. Invest your money in more than one area to combine growth and security.
- Be consistent. Don't chop and change but stick to your strategy.
- Stay on top of it. Keep an eye on performance all the time.
- Avoid unnecessary expenses and charges.

In addition to outlining a proven method of making your money grow, the chapter summarises all the major investment vehicles you should consider, providing you with 'insider' tips in relation to:

- pooled investments
- stocks and shares
- property
- tax-efficient investment.

BASIC INVESTMENT PLANNING

As discussed in earlier chapters your primary investment priorities should be to:

- build up an emergency fund

- start a pension plan
- buy your own home.

What you should do next will depend on your circumstances. Whether you have a lump sum to invest or simply plan to save on a regular basis, your objectives will basically revolve around the following questions:

- How much money is involved?
- How long can you tie your money up for?
- What type of return are you looking for?
- What risks are you willing to accept?
- To what extent is tax an issue?

Let's look at each of these in turn.

How much money is involved?

If you are saving regularly, then you have a choice between investing in a specially designed longer-term plan or building up 'blocks' of capital and investing each one somewhere different.

If you have a lump sum – or as you build up 'blocks' of capital – then the choice of investments available to you opens up. For instance, with some capital available, property investment becomes an option, as does buying publicly quoted shares.

You must have a clear idea in your mind about how much you plan to invest and in what form. If you are saving on a regular basis, consider how long this will be for. Bear in mind that regular savings products have advantages and disadvantages. On the one hand, they tie you in and there can be strict penalties for early encashment or withdrawal. On the other, they force you to be disciplined and take away the tricky decision of how to invest your money. You should also think about the cost of such plans.

How long can you tie your money up for?

Is there a date you need your money back? In other words, are you investing for something specific or just to build your overall wealth?

Investments have varying degrees of accessibility or **liquidity**. An investment that allows you to get at your money immediately is considered 'highly liquid'. Cash in a deposit account or publicly quoted shares, for instance, are both liquid. Property and pension plans are not.

How long you stay with any particular investment will partly be determined by the investment vehicle itself (a ten-year savings plan is – unless you break the terms – a ten-year savings plan) and partly by events (there may be a good reason to sell your investment).

What type of return are you looking for?

Returns vary enormously. The graph below shows how, up to 2004, €1,000 would have grown over almost 20 years had you invested it in different ways.

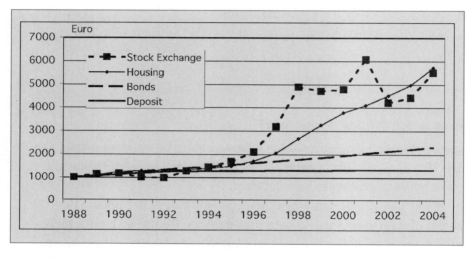

Since 2004, this graph has practically reversed, with bonds as the main winner. This highlights the diversification philosophy.

What risks are you willing to accept?

In general, *the higher the return, the greater the risk*. The highest possible returns are to be made from investments such as **commodities** and **spread betting** – but in both cases you can actually lose substantially more than your original investment. The lowest returns are to be made from investments such as bank deposit accounts and An Post savings plans – where your money can be considered 100% secure.

In formulating your overall investment strategy, you need to consider your approach to risk. Are you willing to accept some risk in order to boost your return? How much? Remember, if you want your money to grow, there has to be an element of risk. Email consultation@moneydoctor.ie for a risk questionnaire.

To what extent is tax an issue?

If you are a higher-rate taxpayer – or expect to be – then you need to consider to what extent tax saving is an issue for you. Bear in mind that there are a number of highly tax-effective investment options available – though all carry above-average risk. Remember, too, that capital gains are taxed at a much lower level than income – which may make this a more attractive option for you (see Chapter 26).

A proven investment strategy

The saying 'don't put all your eggs in one basket' is extremely relevant when it comes to building wealth. In fact, it forms the basis of the only investment strategy I believe can be relied upon: **diversification**. If your investment strategy is too safe, then you won't enjoy decent growth. If your investment strategy is too daring, then you risk losing everything you have been working towards. The solution? To diversify your investments so that your money is spread across a range of areas. Which leaves you two simple decisions:

1   In which areas should you invest your money?
2   How much should you invest in each area?

As already mentioned, you should start by diversifying into the three most important areas of investment – your emergency fund, your pension and buying your own home. Having done this, I would suggest putting your money into the following five areas:

1   Pooled investments.
2   A 'basket' of directly held stocks and shares.
3   Investment property.
4   Higher risk and tax-efficient investments.
5   Alternative investments such as art, antiques, gold and other precious metals.

Within each area there is much scope for choice, allowing you to vary the amount you invest, the length of your investment, the degree of risk and so forth. You must decide for yourself what mix of investments best suits your needs.

The information on the next pages will give you a feel for the various opportunities available. Your next step will depend largely on how active a role you want to play. One option is to investigate each area thoroughly yourself. Another option is to allow an authorised adviser to handle it all for you. My own suggestion would be to go for a combination of the two. Educate yourself, keep yourself informed, but let an expert guide and support you.

When long-term means long-term

One of the biggest mistakes investors make is that they forget their own financial objectives. If you are investing for long-term, capital growth – a good, solid gain over, say, 20 years – then if you change your strategy half way through you must resign yourself to a poor return and even losses. This is true regardless of the investment vehicle you are using.

If a change of strategy is unavoidable, then try and give yourself as long as possible to enact it.

There are various areas where investors seem particularly prone to chopping and changing. Long-term savings plans – such as endowments – is one. The stock market is another. In every case (leaving aside some sort of personal financial crisis) the usual reason is despondency over perceived lack of growth or falling values. If you have chosen your investments well you shouldn't be worrying about the effect of a few lean years or an unexpected dip in values. If you are concerned that you have made a bad investment decision in the first place do take professional advice before acting. The biggest losses come when an investor panics.

POOLED INVESTMENTS

A **pooled investment** – sometimes known as an investment fund – is a way for individual investors to diversify without necessarily needing much money. Your money – along with the money of all the other participants – is pooled and then invested. Each pooled investment fund has different, specified objectives. For instance, one might invest in the largest Irish companies, another in UK companies, a third in US gilts and a fourth in Korean property. In each case the fund managers will indicate the type of risk involved. They will also provide you – on a regular basis – with written reports or statements explaining how your money is performing.

Since it would be impossible for all but the richest of private investors to mimic what these pooled investments do, they are an excellent way to spread your risk. A typical fund will be invested in a minimum of 50 companies and will be managed by a professionally qualified expert.

The fund managers make their money from a combination of commission and fees:

- There is often an entry fee of up to 5% of the amount you are investing.
- There will definitely be an annual management fee – usually 1% of the amount invested, though the more successful ones charge 2%+.
- If you want to sell your share in a pooled investment, you may also be charged a fee.

It is sometimes suggested in the media that fund managers are rewarded too highly. My view is that if a fund is meeting its objectives, then it is only fair that the fund managers recoup their costs and earn a fee for their expertise. I wish journalists would put more effort into reporting performance figures and less into complaining about whether a manager is charging 0.85% a year or 0.93%!

A couple of other points before we look at all the options in a little bit more detail:

1 The funds described below are all medium- to long-term investment vehicles. In other words, you should be thinking about leaving your money in them for an absolute minimum of five years – and more like ten years or even longer.

2 Although past performance – as it always says in the small print – can be no guide to future performance it is still useful to know. One thing to note is who is making the actual investment decisions and how long they have been doing it for. If the individual manager of a fund has changed recently then the past performance may not be so relevant.

I include several different types of investment in this category:

- tracker bonds
- unit trusts and other managed funds
- with-profits funds
- stock market 'baskets' (or guaranteed stock market active funds).

This is because all of them are what I would describe as 'tailor-made investment vehicles'. That is to say they have been specifically designed to meet the needs of ordinary, private investors. This is in direct contrast to, say, un-tailored opportunities – such as buying a publicly quoted share or an investment property – which aren't aimed at any specific group of investors.

Tracker bonds

This is a fund that guarantees to return your initial investment *plus* a return based on a specific stock market index or indices. For example, it might give you all your money back after five years *plus* 80% of any rise in the FTSE 100.

Unit trusts

Your money is used to purchase 'units' in an investment fund. The price of the units will vary according to the underlying value of the investments. For instance, if the unit trust specialises in European technology shares then it is the value of the shares it holds which will determine the price of the units. You can sell your units at any time but you should be wary of buying and selling too quickly as charges and fees can eat up your profit.

Unit-linked funds

As above, but with the added element of a tiny bit of life insurance so that they can be set up and run by life insurance companies.

Managed funds

Again these are – in essence – unit trusts. The term is used to denote a fund which makes a wide spread of investments – thus theoretically reducing the risk – though you should not assume that this is the case.

Specialised funds

A fund that concentrates on a very specific market opportunity – such as oil shares or companies listed in an emerging market. This is obviously riskier but if the underlying investment performs well, then you will make above-average returns.

Indexed funds

This is a fund that aims to match the overall market performance. For instance, you might have a fund that plans to achieve the same return as the UK's leading 100 shares (FTSE 100) or Europe's top index, Eurostoxx 50.

With-profit funds

These funds are run by insurance companies and they guarantee a minimum return *plus* extra bonuses according to how the fund has performed over the longer term. These bonuses might be added annually (**annual bonus**) or when the fund is closed after the agreed period of time (**terminal bonus**). The terms, conditions, objectives and charges for these funds vary enormously.

Stock market 'baskets'

Investors or their advisers choose a number of stocks, which can range from blue chip shares (such as the big corporates and retail groups) to downright risky stocks. Depending on how risk-averse you are, a percentage of your 'basket' will be conservative solid choices, while the smaller percentage will be a little bit of a gamble. **Diversification** is again the buzz word – the greater the spread or choice of stocks, the softer the fall if there is to be a fall.

SPECIALISED STOCK MARKET STRATEGIES

Futures, options, hedge funds, exchange-traded funds, derivatives, contracts for differences (CFDs) and the like all form part of the specialised investment sectors of the stock market. Good solid advice is essential if you wish to participate in this area.

ALTERNATIVE INVESTMENTS

There is a large number of alternative investment options, all of which come with varying amounts of risk. Some, such as gold or other precious metals, are easy to buy and sell. Others, such as art, may have a limited market, making them difficult to find a buyer for when you want to dispose of them. Examples of alternative investments include:

- paintings and other art
- antique furniture and other objects
- debentures at Wimbledon
- rock memorabilia
- gold and other precious metals
- diamonds and other precious gems
- wine

- jewellery
- collectibles such as rare stamps, coins, classic cars or watches.

In general, alternative investment is 'direct' – this is to say, you purchase the actual items. Specialist knowledge is vital if this is to be a genuine investment and you should not consider alternative investments until you have a reasonably high net worth and a portfolio of more conventional investments since the risks can be high.

MONEY DOCTOR WEALTH WARNING

Think carefully before you buy an annuity

If you have a lump sum to invest and you are aged at least 65, then one option is to purchase an **annuity**. The key advantage of an annuity is that it guarantees you an income for the rest of your life. The key disadvantage is that, once purchased, you cannot get your lump sum back. Furthermore, when you die the income stops and nothing will normally be returned to your estate.

Annuities are purchased from life assurance companies, and the return is linked to your age. The younger you are, the lower the return you can expect to receive. It's possible to take out a 'joint-survivor annuity' if you're married. With these, when either you or your spouse dies the income continues at a reduced rate until the death of the other. Joint-survivor annuities produce a lower return – or income – than single-life annuities.

At the moment annuity rates, like interest rates, are relatively low. If you were a male, aged 65, and you wanted to generate a guaranteed income of €1,000 a month, you would need to invest €190,000. However, if you were aged 75, you would only need to invest €130,000.

Annuity rates differ from insurance company to insurance company, and from day to day. It is possible to arrange for your annuity rate to be linked to inflation, and some companies will also guarantee you a minimum return if you die within five years of purchasing the annuity. Finally, you should be aware that the income from an annuity is subject to income tax.

If you've got a limited amount of capital and you're worried about supporting yourself through your retirement years, an annuity could well be the perfect solution. However, I would advise getting professional help to make sure that you purchase the best-value annuity for your needs.

A low-risk, medium-term investment option

For a low-risk, medium-term investment option, consider **guaranteed bonds**. These offer above-average returns in exchange for you locking your money in for an agreed period. Some offer limited penalty-free withdrawals or provide a regular income for the term of the bond.

INVESTING IN STOCKS AND SHARES

Direct investment in the stock market is not for everyone. The risk associated with buying individual shares is obviously much greater than when buying into a diversified portfolio of shares – which is essentially what you are doing with a pooled or investment fund. If the share price goes up – yes – you can make a small fortune. But if the price falls or the market crashes then your shares can become worth a fraction of what you paid for them.

For an investor with limited funds, buying shares is probably not a sensible option. However, once you have started to build your capital wealth you should definitely consider adding individual share holdings to your portfolio of investments:

- Over the longer term, the stock market has shown a greater return to investors than any of the alternatives including property.
- Irish investors are not limited to the Irish stock market – you may buy shares anywhere in the world.
- The charges for buying and selling shares have dropped dramatically, making it feasible to buy and sell in much smaller quantities.
- There are excellent sources of advice on which shares to buy and sell.
- Shares have widely varying degrees of risk.
- One of the big advantages to share ownership is that you literally own part of the company itself and its assets.

- Share ownership should bring you a regular income in the form of dividends plus capital appreciation (if the company is doing well).

Private investors have a choice of doing their own research and making their own decisions or seeking professional help from a stockbroker. Either way, if you are tempted to start buying and selling, you should arm yourself with as much information as possible. Remember, it is ultimately your decision what happens to your portfolio. You should always keep a close watch on what is happening to any company whose shares you have bought, the sector it operates in and the market as a whole. I would particularly recommend the internet for information purposes.

How to read the financial pages

If you do decide to buy stocks and shares, you can keep track of their performance by reading the stock market pages in your daily newspaper. Next to the name of your company you'll find the following information:

High. This is the highest price that your particular company share has reached in the past 12 months.

Low. This is the lowest price that your share has reached in the past 12 months.

Share price. This is the average price paid for your share at close of business on the previous day.

Rise or fall. This is usually represented by a (+) or (-) symbol, and it lets you know how much your share increased or fell by in the previous day's trading.

Dividend yield. The dividend yield is the relationship of a share's annual dividend to its price. The figure will be before tax. For instance, if the dividend yield was 5.8%, and if you'd purchased €100 worth of shares at the current price, you would receive an annual income of €5.80 before tax.

P/E. This stands for **price-earnings ratio**, and it is one of the methods experts use to value a share. The price-earnings ratio is calculated by dividing the company's share price by the after-tax earnings due to each share over the company's most recent financial year. A high price-earnings ratio means that the market is confident in the company's future. But, by the same token, it could mean that the shares are over-priced. A low price-earnings ratio implies a lack of market confidence in the shares but the potential for an investor to pick up a bargain.

Dividend payments

When you own shares in a company you are entitled to a share of the profits – pre-supposing there are profits to be shared. This share is referred to as a dividend, and it is paid twice a year. The first payment is called an 'interim dividend' and the second payment is called a 'final dividend'. Several weeks before the dividend is due to be paid the company directors will announce how much it is to be. A few weeks after this they will 'close the register of shares'. Although you can still buy and sell the shares, if you do so while the register is closed you won't be entitled to the forthcoming dividend. During this period the company shares will be marked XD – which is short for ex-dividend – in the newspapers.

Shares and tax

Irish shares are liable to two different types of tax. First, you'll have to pay income tax on any profits (in other words, 'dividends') you receive. In fact, when you receive a dividend from an Irish company they will have already withheld tax at the standard rate of 20%. If the amount of tax withheld exceeds your liability for that particular year you can claim a refund. However, if you are in fact a higher-rate taxpayer, you'll have to pay the difference between the standard rate and the higher rate when completing your annual tax returns. Second, when you sell your shares, if you've made a gain, you'll be liable for capital gains tax at 30%.

Choosing a stockbroker

The only way to buy and sell shares is through a registered stockbroker. When you do this, you will either pay a flat fee or commission, depending on whether the stockbroker is also advising you and/or the size of the transaction.

If you don't need advice when buying or selling, then you will require an execution only service. In this instance your main concern should be to keep the costs down to a bare minimum. Online services tend to be the cheapest, but it is well worth checking with your bank and the leading stockbrokers just to make sure.

Stockbrokers will be happy to provide you with an advisory service. You'll pay a higher level of commission for this (up to an average of 1.25%) but – of course – you'll benefit from your stockbroker's knowledge of the market.

There is no official minimum value regarding the volume of shares you can purchase. However, there's the minimum level of charges, usually around

€25, so it probably doesn't make much sense to buy less than €1,000 worth of shares at a time.

If you want a list of Irish stockbrokers, then contact:

The Irish Stock Exchange
28 Anglesea Street
Dublin 2
Tel. (01) 617 4200

MONEY DOCTOR WEALTH CHECK

Why not start an investment club?

If you'd like to dabble in the stock market but only have a relatively small amount of money to invest, why not start an **investment club**? An investment club is when a group of friends or work colleagues pool their resources and make buy-and-sell decisions together. My own experience of investment clubs is that they regularly out-perform the stock market because those involved take a real and detailed interest in every investment decision. However, you need time and patience.

Bonds

A **bond** is a long-term, fixed interest investment. Bonds are issued by public companies and also by governments as a way of raising money and are, in effect, loans by you to a company or the government. Government bonds are usually referred to as **gilt-edged** securities or, for short, 'gilts' (see below). Bonds have a face value and term – expressed as a **maturity date**.

For instance, if you had purchased a 15-year €100 bond in a Dutch health insurer in 2002 for a face value of €99.10 – the discount is 90c – at a yield of 6.375% (the **coupon**) you would receive an annual income of €6.38 until the bond reaches its maturity date in 2017 if it is not 'called in' beforehand. On maturity, you are guaranteed to receive €100.

What if you want to cash in your bond sooner? There is a thriving market for second-hand bonds. For instance, the example I mentioned above is currently worth €122.37 with a yield of 3.925%. The second-hand value of a bond will be linked to the underlying security, the rate of interest, and the length of time until it matures.

Gilts

Gilts are the name given to government stock. Governments over the years use 'stock' (rather like an IOU) to raise money to fund their spending. They offer investors a fixed rate of interest for a set period of time in exchange for the use of their savings. The interest is paid without DIRT being deducted – making them very tax-efficient for some non-taxpayers. As interest rates in general fall, government stock tends to rise in value. Gilts are a totally secure and inexpensive way to invest. The returns are usually above average and the cost of buying stock is low – normally a one-off charge of 1%.

PROPERTY

It is easy to understand why so many private investors are attracted to residential and even commercial property:

- Property values have risen and fallen dramatically over the last 30 years.
- It is possible to fund up to 75% of the purchase price with relatively inexpensive loans.
- Rental income from property can cover all the expenses – interest, maintenance, tax and so forth.
- Your investment is in bricks and mortar – something solid – that you can actually see.
- If you make a gain when you sell the property, you will pay substantially less tax – because it is not 'income' but a capital gain and thus taxed at a lower level – currently 30%.

Looking at how property prices have increased over the last 20 years, if you had borrowed €180,000 to buy a €200,000 property some 20 years ago, you would have seen your €20,000 deposit turn into €341,200 profit! Not so much in the last 5 years!

Clearly, property prices rise and fall, so you would be unwise to assume that this is a one-way bet. If the market does fall, you may find it hard to sell the property and take out your money as we have witnessed over the last 5 years. Also, the supply of property to rent has risen so much that in some areas it is now harder to find and keep tenants.

On the other hand, as the old saying goes, 'they aren't making any more of it', and as planning restrictions become tighter there is every reason to believe that property will continue to be a highly attractive investment in the future. The golden rule, in my opinion, is to pick a location and type of property that is always easy to rent, near public transport and requiring little maintenance.

MONEY DOCTOR WEALTH CHECK

Tax treatment of rental income

Basically, your rental income will be treated the same way as if it was income you had earned by self-employment. You will be allowed all your expenses including:

- wear and tear on furniture, currently an eighth of the cost for each of the following eight years

- any charges made by a management company or letting agent

- maintenance, repairs, insurance, ground rent, rates, PRTB and so forth

- the cost of any other goods or services you supply to your tenants (such as cleaning).

With regard to relief on interest payable on loans borrowed to purchase, improve or repair a rented property this is allowable (only 75% of the interest) except – roughly – from the period 23 April 1998 to 1 January 2002. If you bought rental property during this period, you should seek professional advice or contact the Revenue Commissioners to clarify your position. **Do note that not all your property expenses will be allowable for tax relief in the year in which they are incurred. For instance, the cost of 'wear and tear' will be spread over several years.** For more information about tax treatment of property see Chapter 24.

TAX-EFFICIENT INVESTMENT OPTIONS

Financial experts often comment that 'you should never let the tax-saving tail wag the investment dog'. In other words, you shouldn't invest in anything simply to enjoy the tax savings but should always consider the underlying value of the opportunity.

When it comes to **property investment** there were a number of tax incentives designed to make certain types of property more attractive. Most of these have been phased out or will be by 2017.

- In Budget 2012, a new **Employment and Investment Incentive Scheme (EII)** was introduced to replace the BES Scheme. The current BES Scheme will remain in place until 31 December 2013.

THE MONEY DOCTOR SAYS...

- Don't put all your eggs in one basket. Divide your savings and investments into different parts so that if one area doesn't perform as hoped your overall financial objectives can still be met.
- Remember, the stock market has outperformed all other investments over the long term. You can take advantage of this by investing in a pooled fund such as a unit trust or by investing directly in shares.
- You must keep reviewing your investment decisions even if you get a professional to help and advise you.
- Investment is for the long term – anything from five years upwards. Don't allow short-term rises and falls to distract you from your long-term strategy.

MONEY DOCTOR WEALTH WARNING

As with everything, if you get professional help, make sure that they are unbiased and don't only represent one or two firms. Some so-called experts will sell you their solution without listening to your objectives. Email consultation@moneydoctor.ie for more information on investments.

PART 7

PLANNING FOR A RICHER RETIREMENT

Until twenty or thirty years ago the word 'retirement' was associated with a certain age. Women, if they worked, retired at 60 and men at 65. Life expectancy was shorter and money was scarcer.

Today, retirement has taken on a whole different meaning. With a bit of careful planning it is now common for people to give up work and 'retire' from their late 40s onwards. There is also a strong trend towards second and even third careers.

So when we talk of retiring – yes – we mean giving up work, but we also mean having enough money to do what we want.

Thankfully, successive governments have encouraged the trends I am describing and have rewarded those who save for their retirement with very, very, very tasty tax breaks. Also, there are some relatively new pension structures that offer incredible flexibility.

Anyway, in this section you will learn how it is possible to ensure that when you retire (whenever it may be), you have sufficient wealth to lead a comfortable life. Specifically, you will discover how to:

- *decide what sort of pension you will need*
- *assess your current pension prospects*
- *understand all the various options open to you*
- *arrange a pension that will ensure a comfortable retirement for you*
- *retire early and*
- *find someone you can trust to steer you through the pensions minefield.*

I must emphasise that no one should be complacent about retirement planning. Even if you have a pension, you must review it on a regular basis. You could be a long time retired, anything from 20 to 40 years, so you need to get it right.

17
RETIREMENT BASICS

HOW TO TAKE ADVANTAGE OF THE PENSION OPTIONS OPEN TO YOU

In this chapter we will look at why pension planning is so important and also learn about what I call 'retirement basics' – such as understanding what your existing entitlement (if any) is – together with general planning advice.

WHY YOU SHOULD MAKE PENSION PLANNING YOUR NUMBER ONE PRIORITY

The only people who don't have to worry about retirement planning are those lucky enough to belong to a really first-class pension scheme (one with generous, cast-iron benefits) or who are so rich that money will never be a problem.

For the rest of us, pension planning should be a top priority – more of a priority, in fact, than almost any other financial decision we take. Frankly, it doesn't matter if you haven't bought your own home or invested a single penny of your money provided you have a good pension plan. I say this because, thanks to longer life expectancy, many people will spend anything from 20 to 40 years in retirement.

Typically, as we get older and progress in our careers we earn more money. However, on retirement we are no longer able to earn an income and must rely on either our savings or state benefits. Our earnings are therefore usually at their highest just before we retire. And unless we have made proper provision they will be at their lowest just after we retire. This can result in a massive drop in lifestyle at the point of retirement.

This is where the concept of **income equalisation** comes in – that is, reducing your disposable income when you are earning good money to help increase your income when you are not able to earn. We reduce our disposable income now by putting money into a pension scheme that can be used to increase our retirement income. It is still likely that when we retire our income will fall, but with this type of planning the transition will be far less of a shock to the system.

MONEY DOCTOR WEALTH WARNING

Is your company or government pension going to let you down?

Are you in a company or government pension scheme – outside the state pension which you would be entitled to at age 66? You should check on a regular basis, certainly every other year, that it is actually going to meet your needs on retirement. A growing number of pension schemes are producing disappointing returns and you should not be complacent. Very few company schemes provide enough money to ensure a comfortable old-age income. Get expert help too, because whereas companies are obliged to give you details of your benefits (and losses), you might not necessarily understand them. You can't rely on whoever is operating the scheme to provide you with the information you need.

IT IS NEVER TOO EARLY OR LATE TO BEGIN

Given that it is not impossible that your retirement may turn out to be a longer period than that of your working life, it isn't surprising that pension experts stress the importance of starting to plan early.

Nevertheless, if the number of men and women in their 40s, 50s and even their 60s consulting the Money Doctor on pension planning is anything to go by, a huge percentage of the population don't start thinking about their retirement until it isn't that far away.

Obviously, the later you leave it, the more of your income you will have to devote to building up a decent pension fund and the less well off you can expect to be once you stop work. But just because it is never too late to begin, it doesn't mean you should go to the wire. Every single day counts.

START BY TAKING STOCK

The first step towards a comfortable retirement is to take stock of where you are now in pension terms:

- Are you part of one or more companies or occupational pension schemes already?

- Are you entitled to a state pension by virtue of your employment?
- Are you entitled to a non-contributory old age pension?
- Do you need more than a third of the average industrial wage to live on? Because that is roughly what the state pension will give you!
- Have you started a pension plan in the past?

If you answer 'yes' to any of these questions then you need to find out what your existing pension is going to be worth to you.

You also need to consider what other assets you have. Will your home be paid for by the time you retire? Have you any other savings or investments? By the same token, are there any other debts that you will need to discharge before retirement?

WHERE DO YOU GO FOR THE ANSWERS TO ALL THESE QUESTIONS?

The easiest thing to do is to get a qualified professional to do the work for you, in other words, either an accountant (if they specialise in this area) or an independent, regulated financial adviser. The alternative is to approach all the relevant parties yourself. That is to say:

- your current employer and any past employers
- the managers of any pension scheme you may have started in the past
- the Department of Social Protection (check your telephone directory for the relevant department or Chapter 5)
- the Pensions Board (Verschoyle House, Mount Street, Dublin 2).

If you are unhappy with any aspect of the way a non-government pension scheme has been administered, then you should contact the:

Pensions Ombudsman
36 Upper Mount Street
Dublin 2.

THE MONEY DOCTOR SAYS...

If you are self-employed or you are not in an employer-sponsored pension scheme then, unless you take action, you'll have to rely on the state. You can guess how well off that will leave you.

HOW MUCH WILL YOU NEED WHEN YOU RETIRE?

The whole concept of retirement has been turned on its head in recent years. As a population we are:

- giving up work sooner – often in our late 40s or 50s
- living longer and healthier lives
- leading more active lives in retirement.

We also expect a much higher standard of living. As a result we need more money in retirement than our predecessors. Here are some things you will need to consider:

- Will you need a lump sum on retirement to pay off debts or to invest for a regular income?
- Will you still have unavoidable expenses (such as children's education) to pay for? Perhaps your mortgage will continue until you are 70 or 75.
- How much of an income will you need? Could you manage on half of what you earn now? Public sector employees receive *half* of their normal annual income on retirement after 40 years service. How many realise this? Could you manage on a quarter?

What changes would you have to make in your lifestyle if the only money you had coming in after retirement was the state pension?

Do you have anyone else to provide for? Your spouse, for instance? What will happen if you die before they do?

Our civil servants receive an index-linked income of up to half of their final pay, a tax-free sum of up to one-and-a-half year's salary, and a half-pension for their spouses after they die. Only a very tiny percentage of private-sector schemes offer this type of benefit.

What's more, if you work in the private sector and wanted to receive the same sort of benefit from the age of 65, you would have to put about 15% of your income into a pension fund from the age of 20 and even 40% when aged over 60.

THE GOOD NEWS

There are three excellent reasons why you shouldn't despair, regardless of whether you have any sort of pension in place already:

1 The government realises that it is vital to encourage you to save for your retirement so they will give you *huge* tax incentives to do so. For every €1 invested in a pension, you will receive 20c or 41c back depending on your tax margin and excluding USC. Plus, all growth in the fund is tax-free, and 25% of the fund can be taken as a tax-free lump sum (or €200,000, whichever is the lesser).

2 Good planning at any age can optimise your retirement income.

3 By taking action now, you can alter your position dramatically. It is only people who continue to ignore the risks they are running who face the possibility (one might say certainty) of an impoverished retirement.

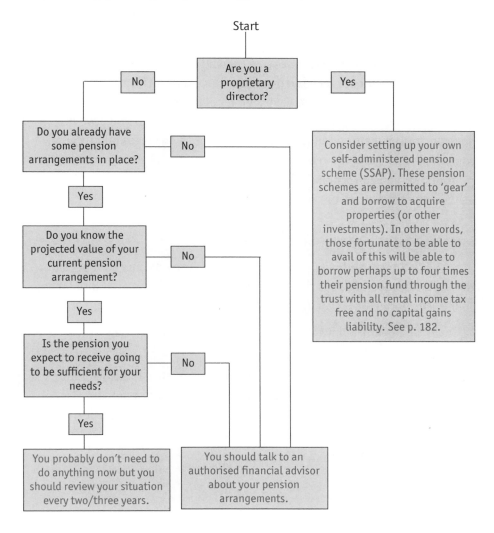

WHAT TO DO IF YOU WORK IN THE PRIVATE SECTOR

If you work for someone else you will be in one of two situations:

- either you will be in a company or occupational scheme or
- you won't be in any scheme at all.

If you are in a company or occupational pension scheme, then you will need to ascertain how good the scheme is, the sort of pension you can expect, what other benefits you may be entitled to and whether it is possible to increase your pension by making **additional voluntary contributions** (AVCs). If, on taking expert advice, the existing pension scheme doesn't appear to be that good, then concentrate on those AVCs.

Don't forget any schemes you may have been in during your previous employment.

If you aren't in your employer's scheme (and all employers are now obliged to operate a scheme under recent legislation – **personal retirement savings accounts** or PRSAs – or at least have a direct debit provision from your salary to such an investment) then you should consider joining. If you have no pension arrangements at all (and you don't want to do something through your employer) then you need to start a scheme of your own.

Your own pension scheme might be a personal pension plan or a PRSA. I'll be looking at these options in greater detail in the next chapter.

WHAT TO DO IF YOU WORK FOR YOURSELF

If you work for yourself, you are going to have to provide your own pension. The big advantage of this is that you can design a pension plan that matches your needs perfectly:

- It will be flexible, allowing you to invest on a regular basis or with lump sums.
- You'll have the choice of investing your money in an established fund or starting your own if you are a company owner, proprietary director (i.e. have at least a 5% shareholding in your company) or a senior company employee (e.g. a **small self-administered** pension scheme – SSAP) or self-directed trusts.

- If you own your own company you could even consider setting up a company scheme.

THE MONEY DOCTOR SAYS…

- You are probably, to quote a line from the TV programme *Black Adder*, 'perfectly happy to wear cotton without understanding how the weaving process works'. By the same token, you shouldn't feel that you need to understand pensions legislation in its entirety to make your retirement plans!

- Action is imperative. If you have a really good pension plan, allowing you to retire early, you don't need any other investments (not even a house).

- The sooner you act, the better it will be, but it is never too late to start. Extra tax benefits may apply the older you are. It's certainly never too late to enquire – consultation@moneydoctor.ie.

18
PENSIONS MADE EASY

STEP-BY-STEP INSTRUCTIONS ON HOW TO MAKE YOUR RETIREMENT DREAMS COME TRUE

This chapter contains detailed instructions on retirement planning – all the information, advice and tips you need to make your own decisions about what you need and want.

A QUICK GUIDE TO PENSION SCHEMES

One of my teenage daughter's favourite expressions is 'too much information'. This may be the reaction many of you have when trying to understand the pension system. Nor is it any wonder when you consider how complicated the various options are. Opening a book on the subject at random (a book aimed at ordinary consumers, by the way), my eyes fell immediately on the following sentence:

> *Where a 5% Director chooses the New Retirement Options, they must first ensure that the total fund accumulated would not result in a situation where the maximum benefits would be excluded had they gone down the traditional annuity purchase route.*

My own view is that you should inform yourself, in the same way that you would inform yourself before making any major purchase, but that unless you find the topic fascinating don't waste your time grappling with the minutiae. Instead, let an independent and authorised expert advise you. Here, then, is my quick guide to pension schemes.

LET'S BEGIN AT THE VERY BEGINNING...

Basically, a pension scheme, or a retirement plan, or whatever you want to call it, is a way of saving money specifically for **your retirement**. What differentiates it from an ordinary savings plan is that you will receive substantial help from the Revenue and, in exchange, access to your savings will be restricted. How restricted? Well, it will vary but typically you won't be able to touch any of the money you have saved until you reach a minimum age (this will vary according to the scheme and even the sort of job you have) and even then you won't be able to get your hands on all of it as a tax-free lump sum.

There are three basic employment categories and the pension options can be defined as follows:

- employee
- self-employed
- directors.

Employee

Occupational pension schemes. Money invested in these schemes is locked away until you actually retire. At this point there will be restrictions on how you take the benefits. For instance, you'll only be allowed a limited amount as a lump sum – tax-free – and the rest will have to be taken as an income.

Defined benefits. This is the Rolls Royce of schemes and extremely valuable. It can be either a contributory or non-contributory scheme – invariably, the employer will make contributions to the scheme. With this type of pension the employer guarantees you a certain percentage of your final salary, as a pension for life, for every year you have been working for them. Depending on the particular scheme, this can be up to 66% of the annual average of your last three years' income. You can also elect to take part of your benefits as a tax-free lump sum of up to one-and-a-half times your salary. The beauty of defined benefit schemes is that, irrespective of fund performance, you are guaranteed to receive the promised pension. It is the trustees of the scheme who have to worry about how they are going to fund what could be a very expensive company cost. More and more employers are opting out of the defined benefit pension because of cost, a trend exacerbated by the poor pension fund performances of the late 1990s and first part of this century. Defined benefit schemes undoubtedly provide the best pension benefits. However, you should note that benefits are based on how long you have been working for that company. If you have a relatively short number of years' service, you can still top up your pension benefits by making some contributions through additional voluntary contributions (AVCs). Also remember that over 70% of defined benefit schemes in Ireland are insolvent, so ensure that *your* company will be able to meet its future commitments.

Defined contributions. Your pension is based on the growth of your monthly contributions (again the employer will usually also make contributions to your pension) up to maturity on retirement age. Unfortunately, there is no guarantee of how much you will receive on retirement as values may fall as well as rise. Your fund is purely down to how fund managers perform and how much you have invested. It is vital therefore that you be fully briefed and communicated with on a regular basis so that you can take corrective action if necessary. That corrective action may be an AVC.

Additional voluntary contributions (AVCs). Depending on your own existing pension contributions and your age, you could put up to 40% of your annual income into an AVC. You can offset the entire 40% against your income tax liability, making this procedure a very tax-efficient one. Furthermore, most employers will deduct your AVCs directly from your wages. There is also greater flexibility about how and when you take the benefits and you won't have to pay for setting up a scheme of your own. If your employer's pension scheme has a good investment performance or guaranteed benefits, then putting more money into it via an AVC can make excellent financial sense.

Check with an authorised adviser for specific details, as there are so many regulations and you want to ensure you're making the right decision.

No occupational pension scheme is available to you. If your employer does not offer an occupational pension scheme, you have the same options as someone who is self-employed (see below). The one exception is that your employer is required, by law, to provide you with a payroll deduction facility to a nominated PRSA provider or face a €15,000 fine.

Self-employed

Personal Retirement Savings Accounts (PRSA)/personal pensions – with the 2002 introduction of PRSAs, pensions became more accessible and less expensive to start. PRSAs have maximum charges of 5% of each premium paid plus 1% a year of the accumulated fund. The affordable pension is here to stay. Benefits include:

- it's low cost
- generous tax relief at your marginal rate. Depending on your age this can be on contributions of up to 40% of your income

- it's easy to understand – you decide how much you want to invest and where you want the money invested

- it's portable in that you can bring the pension with you from employment to employment together with flexibility in being able to adjust your annual contributions depending on your circumstances, and flexible about how you use the fund on retirement

- when you retire, you can have up to 25% of the fund as a tax-free lump sum (useful for paying off a mortgage) up to a maximum of €200,000 and

- it's suitable for people who work for themselves, have no company scheme or change their employment frequently.

In theory, a PRSA is a simplified version of a personal pension plan. In practice, the rules governing PRSAs are just as complicated. You should seek independent advice.

Directors

If you are a director, you can avail of a **director's executive pension** (if you have 5% or more shareholding in your company). In fact, the advantages offered by company schemes are so good that if you are self-employed (a sole trader), it may be worth your while to form a limited company in order to take advantage of them yourself. If you do own your own company, then setting up a company pension scheme will probably be the best route for you. The main reason for this is that the limits for which the Revenue will give tax relief on pension contributions are significantly higher for a company investing in a company pension scheme than for an individual investing in a corresponding PRSA or personal pension.

Company schemes can be arranged to benefit as many employees as you want, just you, or selected members of your staff, as you prefer. Note that this route is particularly good for anyone who has left it late in life to plan for his or her retirement.

- As there is no benefit in kind on contributions to a company pension scheme, your company will be able to put substantial tax-free money into your pension.

- There is greater flexibility with regard to your retirement date.

- You have more control over where your contributions are invested.

- You can take a portion of your fund tax-free – so tax breaks on the way in and the way out!

MORE ON PRSAs/PERSONAL PENSIONS

Small self-administered pension schemes (SSAP) or self-directed trusts

Under most pension arrangements it is left up to fund managers to determine what the pension funds actually invest in. However, if you want more direct control on the actual assets that make up your pension fund you can always set up an SSAP. Here you appoint a **pensioner trustee** to run your pension but you dictate what it invests in. For example, if you want to invest in shares you can pick the individual shares as opposed to just a managed fund.

Recent legislative changes have also brought in for the first time a provision which allows pension funds to borrow for **property acquisition**. This effectively means that you could borrow within your pension fund to buy an investment property (at arm's length – not your own company's offices, your holiday hot spot or your granny's flat) and both the rental income contributions and your own monthly contributions will be paid into your pension fund tax-free, while all along your fund (i.e. your property) should be appreciating as you are making those contributions. There is also the added benefit that no capital gains liability is incurred and your estate keeps the asset (i.e. your property) after you die.

I think that for the company executive, the SSAPs/self-directed trusts will grow considerably over the coming years as a result of the introduction of that one provision, allowing pension funds to borrow or gear perhaps up to four times the fund value to buy investment property. SSAPs are not just confined to property. Shares, investments and even complex financial instruments (e.g. hedge funds) can be incorporated into SSAPs. Email me for a free brochure on self-directed trusts at jlowe@moneydoctor.ie.

BIG TAX RELIEF – THE REVENUE COMMISSIONERS ARE ON YOUR SIDE

I have made repeated mention of the huge tax incentives offered to those who invest in a pension. These include:

- Tax relief at your marginal rate of tax. So if you are paying tax at 41% when you put €100 into your pension fund it will only cost you €59. Put another way, pension funds almost double the value of your savings before the money has been invested in anything. Even at 20% taxable, the fund would have to drop by 20% before losing out.

- Investments grow tax-free. If you put money into your own company scheme it is a legitimate business expense for tax purposes and profits within the pension fund are tax-free (e.g. dividends and interest).

- Put another way, if a gross premium of €5,000 were paid for 20 years, the value of the premiums would be €100,000 at the end of the period. Thanks to the tax element, the net cost **from after-tax income** (if the tax remains at 41%) is €59,000. To achieve the same return on investing, the net income would need an annual compound return of 6%! This is the value of the government's contribution and it is given **for free**.

- While it is in a pension fund, no income tax or capital gains tax is payable on your investment.

- All pension schemes allow you to take out a certain portion of your fund tax-free when you come to retire.

- PRSI is not payable once you are 66.

There are limits on the amount you can invest into a pension fund and still get the tax relief. Check with your authorised adviser for details or consultation@moneydoctor.ie.

WHAT HAPPENS TO YOUR PENSION CONTRIBUTIONS?

If you are part of an occupational pension scheme, then your money will be invested by the scheme's managers. If it is a big scheme, they may invest it directly themselves. Most companies, however, use the services of professional fund managers who invest in everything from stocks and shares to property and commodities. Performance will be determined by how well the scheme is managed and if you are in a 'defined contribution' scheme, you need to pay close attention to this. For employer-sponsored schemes (e.g. occupational pension schemes) trustees play an important role as they look after the investment decisions on advice from fund managers.

If you set up your own personal pension plan or your own company sets up a company scheme, then you have much more control over how your contributions are invested while you have to make the investment choices. Most opt for equity funds – where your money is pooled and invested in stocks and shares. Such funds will have varying returns and different levels of risk. As you near retirement you will be less likely to place your fund in a higher-risk investment than you would if you were in your early 30s.

MONEY DOCTOR WEALTH WARNING

Don't buy a pension from someone who can't offer you choice

All the financial institutions involved in the retirement market, and I'm speaking chiefly about life insurance companies and banks, employ salespeople whose job it is to promote their own company's pension products.

One such example is that of a young solicitor who was persuaded to take out a bank assurance pension plan at a premium of more than €500 per month, based on her expectation of a certain income on retirement in keeping with her current levels of salary. After a couple of months she cancelled the policy because she wasn't asked one of the most important questions: 'Can you afford to pay this amount each month into a pension scheme?'

While it is important to aim for a similar level of income to retire on, it is equally important to be able to afford it and have a life in the meantime. Ideally, you should not choose a pension from someone who only represents one company. You should always deal with someone independent who is authorised to tell you about every single option available to you. Pension fund performance and management fees vary enormously. Buying without comparing the whole market could cost you a great deal of money.

WHAT IS IT GOING TO COST?

Almost without exception, the pension industry gets paid on **commission**. This commission comes out of your monthly payments. The amount will vary according to the type of pension scheme you join or set up. Many schemes (but not all) will involve an initial, one-off fee followed by an **annual management charge**. To give you an example, for a standard PRSA the maximum annual management charge is 1% of the accumulated fund, whilst the initial set-up fee is capped at 5% of the premiums. When you take out a pension, your authorised adviser will explain, in full, what charges you are paying. Remember, however, the charges are one thing, but what is it going to cost to provide an income?

Having a pension is one thing, but having a pension which is going to provide you with the income you think you will need is another. One example of this was a shop-owner who sought advice on investing a lump sum. One suggestion was to look at investing this in a pension. However, he indicated that he was alright here as he had already put a pension in place. It transpired that this 45-year-old shop-owner was currently earning €50,000 a year and had just taken out a pension plan for €400 a month. He was shocked to learn that if he kept contributions at this level, and took the state contributory pension into account, he could expect to have a total after-tax retirement income of around €750 a month (in today's terms) at age 65 – a fraction of what he currently earned.

You get what you pay for. One way of looking at it is to look at what level of income you think you need and finding out how much it would cost to provide this. You may not be able to afford the cost now but at least you will know what to expect.

Below is a table showing the approximate costs of funding a total after-tax income of €1,250 a month and €2,500 a month in today's terms should you retire at 65. They assume that you will be entitled to the state contributory pension. These figures are meant as a guide only, and make a number of assumptions. You should discuss your own particular circumstances with a financial adviser or get in touch consultation@moneydoctor.ie.

	Aged 25	Aged 30	Aged 35	Aged 40	Aged 45	Aged 50	Aged 55
€1,250pm	€191pm	€255pm	€347pm	€482pm	€673pm	€1,001pm	€1,681pm
€2,500pm	€341pm	€457pm	€623pm	€864pm	€1,207pm	€1,790pm	€3,019pm

The above figures are before tax relief and assume that contributions are increased by 5% a year, inflation is 5% a year and the state pension increases by 5% a year. It also assumes that the funds the pension is invested in increase by 6% a year and that the tax rates on retirement are similar to today.

WHAT BENEFITS SHOULD YOU BE LOOKING FOR?

How do you judge a pension scheme? Here are some tips:

- If it is a defined benefit scheme, then you should judge it primarily on what percentage of your salary you'll receive once you retire. Remember, these are the only schemes where the benefit is guaranteed based on service and salary. (Public sector employees receive ⅟₈₀ for every year of service, so 40 years will return half their annual salary. Should they bolster this?)

- Depending on the type of pension plan you have you will be given a certain portion, by way of a tax-free lump sum, of the fund's value. Establish how much.

- Death-in-service benefit. Essentially, this is life cover giving your beneficiaries a lump sum and/or income should you die before retirement age.

- Death-in-retirement benefit. This gives your beneficiaries a lump sum and/or an income if you die after you have retired. Generally covers the first 5 years.

- The minimum retirement age (for occupational pension schemes it is 60, but if you own your company you can take a well-earned rest at age 50).

- How much will your pension income increase each year after you have started claiming it? Will it increase in line with the cost of living? More than the cost of living?

- Any special benefits offered to your spouse or other dependants.

WHAT HAPPENS WHEN YOU RETIRE?

This will depend on your employment status and scheme.

For **defined benefit schemes**, you will receive a tax-free lump sum and a guaranteed annual income, usually index-linked and based on your service.

For **defined contribution** schemes, the accumulated fund on retirement is used to buy an annuity income based on how much is in the fund after taking out an allowable portion by way of a tax-free lump sum.

An annuity is a guaranteed fixed income for life (mostly guaranteed for the first 5 years on retirement, after which the insurance company keeps the fund). The Finance Act 1999 introduced a new alternative: Approved Retirement Funds (ARFs), which allow pension-holders to retain greater control, choice of investments and flexibility – plus, importantly, the ability to pass on any residual balance in the fund to their estate on their death.

The Finance Act 2006 introduced a new requirement to draw income from ARFs called 'imputed distribution':

- 1% in 2007
- 2% in 2008
- 3% in 2009
- 5% in 2010
- 6% in 2012

The Finance Act 2011 saw the extension of the ARF option to members of Defined Contribution Plans (AVCs and PRSAs), so they were not confined to buying an annuity on retirement.

THE MONEY DOCTOR SAYS ...

- The tax benefits of having a pension are enormous. For a taxpayer on the higher rate of tax, putting €100 into a pension will currently only cost €59. This is a bargain by anyone's standards.

- If your pension incorporates life cover you may receive extra tax relief.

- The pension end-game is important. Make sure that whatever contributions you make to a pension plan are sufficient to meet your monthly needs when you retire.

- Please, please take independent professional advice. I am repeating myself, I know. But only someone who is authorised to advise you on every pension available is going to guarantee you the most appropriate pension for your needs.
  Email consultation@moneydoctor.ie.

PART 8

WHY PAY MORE TAX THAN YOU HAVE TO?

Would you like to slash your 2013 tax bill quickly, easily and without having to plough through a lot of incomprehensible jargon? Then this section is for you. Because in plain English – using plenty of examples and case histories – I am going to explain how, as a taxpayer, you can:

- *make certain that you don't pay a single cent more tax this year than you have to*
- *reclaim any tax you may have overpaid in previous years*
- *plan your finances so that future tax bills are kept to a bare minimum.*

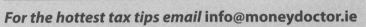

MONEY DOCTOR WEALTH CHECK

***For the hottest tax tips email* info@moneydoctor.ie**

Because tax rules sometimes change during the year and because the Money Doctor's team of tax advisers are always searching for new ways to save you tax. So for the hottest tax tips email info@moneydoctor.ie *today.*

To make it as easy as possible to find the tax-saving information you require I've divided this section up into lots of short chapters. From the list below you can check which chapters are relevant to your circumstances:

Chapter 19: *Tax basics. An overview of how the Irish tax system works – and your part in it!*

Chapter 20: *Income tax basics. The first steps towards reducing your income tax bill.*

Chapter 21: *All about income tax credits. How tax 'credits' and 'allowances' can help you save money.*

Chapter 22: *PAYE. How to make the Pay As You Earn (PAYE) tax system work in your favour.*

Chapter 23: *Income tax for the self-employed. How to reduce your income tax bill if you work for yourself.*

Chapter 24: *Tax and property. Property investor? How to ensure you keep your tax bill to a minimum.*

Chapter 25: *Tax and the company car. How motorists can drive down their tax bill.*

Chapter 26: *Capital gains tax. Lots of useful tips on how to reduce, delay and avoid capital gains tax. If you think you may be selling any of your assets (including a property) during 2013 or in the foreseeable future then you need to read this chapter.*

Chapter 27: *Capital acquisition tax. The purpose of capital acquisition tax is to tax gifts and inheritances – and the purpose of this chapter is to make sure that your gifts and inheritances aren't taxed!*

Chapter 28: *Love, marriage and lower taxes. Extra tax benefits for those who are married.*

Chapter 29: *Tax for the ex-pat. Tax planning tips for those living and working abroad.*

Chapter 30: *Special tax advice for farmers. Special tax tips for farmers and farming businesses.*

MONEY DOCTOR WEALTH CHECK

Could you take advantage of the seed capital scheme?

If you're thinking of starting your own business – and you've never been in business before – then you may be able to take advantage of something called the seed capital scheme. To be eligible you have to have been employed on a PAYE basis and you have to have capital of your own (or be able to borrow capital elsewhere) to invest in the new venture. Under these circumstances the government will give you an income tax rebate of up to €100,000 (relating to the PAYE paid in the six years preceding cessation of your employment) to help you get your new business off the ground. Because the seed capital scheme is essentially returning or rebating tax you've paid in the past, it doesn't stop you from taking advantage of other government incentives such as grants and employment incentives. Furthermore, you can claim this rebate pretty much regardless of the sort of business you are establishing.

19
TAX BASICS

GETTING TO GRIPS WITH THE TAX SYSTEM

There are really only two things you need to know about Irish tax to start
beating the system. Firstly, most people are hit hardest by just three taxes and
it is these that you want to concentrate on reducing or – better still – avoiding
completely. They are:

- income tax
- capital gains tax (CGT)
- capital acquisition tax (CAT).

(Of course, there are many other taxes, such as stamp duty and deposit interest
retention tax [DIRT], and, believe me, I am not going to ignore them. But it is
the first three that will probably offer you the biggest scope for juicy savings.)

Secondly, the beauty of the Irish tax system is that it consists almost entirely
of exceptions. There are, literally, hundreds of different reasons why you
might not have to pay a particular tax. So, cutting your tax bill is simply a
matter of either:

- studying these reasons to see which ones apply (or could be made to
  apply) to your own circumstances so as to save you tax
- looking at your circumstances and seeing how they might be altered
  to give you a tax advantage.

Let me give you a quick example. In theory, if you are single, the first €32,800
of your 2012 income should be taxed at 20%, and anything over this sum
should be taxed at 41%. In practice, there is a minimum income (**income
exemption limit**) you have to receive before you pay any tax at all (this could
be as high as €36,000 depending on your age and circumstances) and once
your income exceeds this level there are all sorts of allowances, credits and
other ways to reduce the amount you actually have to part with.

How old you are, where you live, your marital status, the source of your income, any borrowings you may have, your health, the health of your family… all these factors and many, many others can be used to slash your tax bill.

It is not inconceivable that you could have an income of as high as €75,000 and not actually have to pay a single cent in tax – except for USC!

KEEPING IT LEGAL

The difference between legal tax saving – which is called **tax avoidance** – and illegal tax saving – which is called **tax evasion** – was once described as being 'the thickness of a prison wall'. It is perfectly legal to use our tax laws in any way you can to reduce the amount of tax you pay. Naturally, all the tax-saving suggestions in this book are 100% legal.

GET TO KNOW YOUR TAX LIABILITIES

AND THE REVENUE COMMISSIONERS IN THE PROCESS

Here is a list and brief description of taxes affecting individuals:

Income tax

This, as its name implies, is a tax on annual income. How much you have to pay is linked to:

- how much you earn
- your personal circumstances
- what tax credits and allowances you are entitled to.

If you are an employee you pay your income tax monthly but if you are self-employed you pay it annually. Either way, there are dozens of income tax-saving tactics available.

Capital gains tax

If you buy something at one price and either sell it later for a higher price or give it away when it is worth more than you paid for it, then you will have made a capital gain. This gain may be taxed – depending on all sorts of factors including:

- how big the gain is
- what sort of gain it is
- the rate of inflation
- allowable expenses.

It is paid annually. As with income tax there are plenty of ways in which to reduce your liability to capital gains tax. See Chapter 26.

Capital acquisition tax

This is a tax on gifts and on inheritances. The person receiving the gift or inheritance pays it. Whether tax has to be paid will depend on a variety of factors including:

- the amount of money or the value of the property involved
- the relationship between the parties involved
- the nature of the gift or inheritance.

Once again, it is paid annually and there are any number of ways in which it is possible to avoid and/or reduce this tax. See Chapter 27.

Stamp duty

If you are buying a property you will be liable for **stamp duty** – which is a one-off tax. You'll also have to pay stamp duty – at a considerably lower level – on your mortgage deed. For individuals, it is very hard to legally reduce or avoid this form of taxation. See p. 137 for matrix.

Pay Related Social Insurance (PRSI)

If you are employed or self-employed you will have to pay PRSI at 4% on all your gross income, with the first €127 per week exempt. There is little scope for legally avoiding PRSI.

   However, PRSI is no longer payable once you reach the age of 66.

Value Added Tax (VAT)

This is a tax on your spending. It is charged at different rates from 0% to 23% – depending on what you are buying. Businesses and the self-employed have some opportunities for avoiding or reducing their VAT liability – individuals are limited in their options.

Do you have to fill in a tax return?

One question I frequently get asked – especially by those in retirement, regular employment, or receiving welfare payments – is whether or not they are legally obliged to complete an annual tax return. Let us start by considering who must fill out that dreaded form whether they want to or not. Into this category falls:

- anybody who works for themselves – full- or part-time
- anyone with a second income, even if it's from casual work like cleaning or baby-sitting
- all company directors
- anyone in receipt of income that hasn't already been taxed – for instance, a private pension or dividends from an overseas investment
- anyone who has made a capital gain
- anyone with rental income from a property
- anyone who has received or made a gift
- anyone who has received money of any sort that may be liable to tax here in Ireland.

The fact that you may be paying PAYE does not exclude you from having to complete a tax return. Indeed, even if you're on PAYE it may be to your advantage to complete a tax return as it could reduce your tax bill for the year.

So who *definitely* doesn't have to complete a tax return? If you fall into any of the following categories, you are off the hook:

- You have a relatively low income. See p. 199 for details.
- You have absolutely no income.
- You pay your tax through the PAYE system, and haven't received any other money that might be liable to tax.

MONEY DOCTOR WEALTH CHECK

Take advantage of the taxperson

Many people forget that the Revenue Commissioners are there to serve you. They publish a wide range of brochures designed to assist taxpayers, and you'll also find an enormous amount of information online at their website (www.revenue.ie). Your local tax office will be delighted to answer questions for you, and you can also telephone them on their information helpline, details of which you'll find in the 'Useful Addresses' section (Appendix 8). The Revenue Commissioners also have a highly efficient on-line service called, oddly enough, the Revenue On-line Service or ROS. This internet facility allows you to file your tax returns, make payments, and access your personal revenue data any time, night or day. Registering is a simple process, and the software is easy to use and compatible with every type of computer. When completing a tax return you will also find that it saves you a vast amount of time since you won't have to wade through all the relevant sections looking for the questions you need to answer. However, it is not yet available to everyone.

20
INCOME TAX BASICS

THE FIRST STEPS TOWARDS REDUCING YOUR INCOME TAX BILL

'Income tax', claimed Will Rogers, 'has made more liars out of the American people than golf.' Being a patriotic soul I like to think that we Irish people are above such deceit. Not that we mightn't be tempted when it comes to income tax – if only because the thing is so wretchedly confusing.

The Revenue Commissioners (who appear to be allergic to plain English) hardly help by defining income tax as being the tax:

> payable on your taxable income, i.e. your total assessable income tax for a tax year, less deductions for any non-standard rate allowances (not tax credits) to which you may be entitled.

Then, as if this wasn't sufficiently obscure, they divide 'income' into several different categories which they call – unhelpfully – **schedules**. The schedules are then divided into 'cases'. And so it goes on.

Unfortunately, if you are going to make a serious attempt to reduce your income tax bill, you really need to understand how the Revenue Commissioners are actually taxing you. Therefore, the first part of this chapter is devoted to a basic, jargon-free guide to income tax. However, once the terms of engagement, as it were, have been explained we will get straight down to all the different ways in which you might cut – or even avoid altogether – your income tax liability.

WHAT SORT OF INCOME DO YOU HAVE?

In order to differentiate between the different types of income people receive, the Revenue Commissioners classify income under a number of different headings or 'schedules'. Since accountants and other financial professionals refer to these schedules all the time, it's quite useful to know what they are:

> **Schedule C** relates to organisations like banks that have deducted income tax from certain payments. You almost certainly won't have to worry about this.

Schedule D is divided into five separate classes referred to as 'cases'.

- Case I relates to profit from a trade.

- Case II relates to profits from a profession.

- Case III refers to interest not taxed at source, and all foreign income.

- Case IV refers to taxed interest income not falling under any case schedule.

- Case V refers to rental income from properties in Ireland.

Schedule E basically covers all the money earned from regular employment, and is technically defined as 'income from offices or employments, together with pensions, benefits in kind, and certain lump sum payments arising from an office or employment'.

Schedule F covers dividends and other distributions from Irish-resident companies.

Whenever you deal with the Revenue Commissioners in relation to income tax you'll find that they make reference to the above schedules and cases. It is always worth checking that they have your income correctly classified as – if they don't – it could help to reduce your tax bill.

A QUICK EXPLANATION OF INCOME TAX RATES

For many years, income tax has been levied at a different rate according to the amount of income involved. There are currently two different rates in Ireland – 20% and 41%. Which rate of tax you'll pay will depend on your circumstances and income. For instance, for 2012 if you are a single person the **first €32,800** of your income will be taxed at **20%** and the balance would be taxed at 41%. It is worth remembering that these tax rates can change from year to year.

The table overleaf shows the different tax bands and rates for 2012. As you will see, taxpayers are divided into four different groups. These are:

- single people and widow(er)s
- one-parent families
- married couples where only one spouse is working
- married couples – where both spouses are working.

Rates of income tax

Single/widowed without dependent children	€32,800 @ 20% Balance @ 41%
Single/widowed qualifying for one-parent family tax credit	€36,800 @ 20% Balance @ 41%
Married couple (one spouse with income)	€41,800 @ 20% Balance @ 41%
Married couple (both spouses with income)	€41,800 @ 20% (with increase of €23,800 max.) Balance @ 41%

Universal Social Charge (USC)

An income levy was introduced in the budget of October 2008 and increased in the supplementary budget of April 2009. In the Budget of December 2010, it was abolished and replaced as one part of the Universal Social Charge (see page 337). If your income is less than €10,026, you pay no USC. Once your income is over this limit, you pay the USC on *all* of your income.

Rates
People under age 70 (2012)

Rate of USC	Income band
2%	Up to €10,036
4%	€10,036–€16,016
7%	€16,016

Medical card holders and people over age 70 (2012)

Rate of USC	Income band
2%	Up to €10,036
4%	Over €10,036

A full medical card (including a Health Amendment Act Card) allows you to qualify for the 4% rate. This does not apply to people who hold a GP Visit Card, a Drugs Payment Scheme Card, a European Health Insurance Card or a Long-term Illness Scheme Card. If a person reaches age 70 at any stage during the year they will benefit from the maximum 4% rate for that whole year.

Some good news for anyone on a low income

If your income falls below a certain level, you are completely exempt from income tax. The chart below sets out the maximum amount of income you can receive – according to your circumstances – this year without paying a single cent in tax. It's worth noting that if you earn income over the amounts set out below, you will be eligible for something called 'marginal relief', which is explained below.

Low income exemption limits

Single/widowed	Exemption limits for 2011
65 or over	€18,000
Married	
65 or over	€36,000
Additions to exemptions limit for dependent children (€)	
1st and 2nd child (per child)	€575
Each subsequent child	€830
Marginal relief tax rate	40% of the amount by which the total income exceeds the exemption limit.

Taking advantage of marginal relief

Supposing you are on a relatively low income, but you earn slightly more than the amount necessary to avoid tax completely? Recognising that it would be unfair to tax you too heavily, something called marginal relief exists. Any individual/married couple whose total income from all sources is slightly over the exemption limit may qualify for marginal relief but it will only be granted if it is more beneficial to the claimant than their tax credits. It restricts the tax payable to 40% of the difference between your income and the appropriate exemption limit. The exemption limits vary depending on age, marital status and the number of qualifying dependent children. As this is quite complicated, let me explain it with an example:

Marginal relief advantageous

Over 65 married with two children

	€		€
Total income	36,000	Total income	36,000
Tax @ 20%	7,200	Less: Exemption	36,000
Less: Tax credits	5,440	Excess	nil
Tax due	1,760	Tax @ 40%	nil

PERSONAL CREDITS AND TAX ALLOWANCES

Although you are liable to pay income tax at the rates outlined, you are entitled to claim all sorts of **personal tax credits** and **allowances** which will help you to reduce this bill by a fairly substantial amount. You'll find a complete guide to all the income tax credits and allowances in the next chapter.

PRSI – another form of income tax

The initials PRSI stand for **pay related social insurance**. Because it is calculated as a percentage of your income it is effectively a form of income tax.

The purpose of PRSI is to raise money to provide all sorts of social welfare benefits – these range from invalidity pensions to redundancy pay, and from a bereavement grant to a maternity benefit. Your ability to claim social welfare benefits is linked to your having paid your PRSI. It is, therefore, worth remembering the following points:

- How much PRSI you have to pay will depend on your job. There are three key categories: private sector employees, public sector employees, and the self-employed.

- Your entitlement to benefits is normally based on your contributions made two years before the benefit year in which you claim! In other words, what you paid in 2011 will determine what you can claim in 2013.

- The level of PRSI you have to pay is calculated as a percentage of your gross income, less any payments to an approved pension scheme or certain other health schemes.

- If you earn less than €127 a week, you don't have to pay any PRSI at all.

- You can volunteer to pay PRSI, or pay it at a higher level, if this is to your advantage.

It's worth noting that the employee and employer normally share PRSI contribution costs. Most employees, of course, pay their PRSI through the PAYE tax system.

A summary of the benefits to which you are entitled under PRSI is to be found in Chapter 5. It is, perhaps, worth mentioning here that to claim a **social insurance benefit** it is necessary to have a minimum number of PRSI contributions. Confusingly, the word 'contribution' means not just the PRSI you've paid, but also your PRSI credits. PRSI credits are awarded to someone who would normally have been making a contribution but for various reasons did not do so. For instance, you would receive PRSI credits during any weeks when you received a disability benefit or unemployment benefit. You also receive credits when you first start working.

If there were an Olympic category for the 'most complicated tax in the world', then PRSI would probably win a gold. If you need help with your PRSI then I would suggest either talking to an accountant or else contacting the Department of Social Protection or – alternatively – the Revenue Commissioners.

21
ALL ABOUT INCOME TAX CREDITS

HOW TAX 'CREDITS' AND 'ALLOWANCES' CAN HELP YOU SAVE MONEY

Depending on your circumstances, you can reduce your income tax bill by claiming certain **tax credits** and **allowances**. A great deal of confusion exists over the difference between 'credits' and 'allowances'. The key points to remember are:

- A tax credit is money off your actual tax bill. So, if you have a tax bill of €1,000 and tax credits of €800, you only pay €200 in tax.

- A tax allowance reduces the amount of income on which tax is payable. How much it will be worth to you will depend on the rate of tax you pay. For instance, if you pay income tax at 20% then a €1,000 tax allowance will save you €200 of tax.

The old system of tax allowances has largely been replaced by tax credits.

Every year you are sent an annual **tax certificate** referred to, somewhat long-windedly, as the 'notification of determination of Tax Credits and standard rate cut-off point', which sets out full details of all your tax credits together with the income level at which you will start to pay the higher rate tax.

HOW TAX CREDITS WORK IN PRACTICE

Before going into detail about all the different personal tax credits that exist, let's just look at how they work in practice. In 2012, John O'Brien, a single taxpayer on PAYE, pays tax at 20% on the first €32,800 of income and 41% on anything above this sum. His tax credits amount to some €3,300. I've shown on the next page how his tax credits reduce his tax liability on an assumed income of €40,000.

Income	€40,000	
Tax €32,800 @ 20 %		€6,560
* Tax €7,200 @ 41%		€2,952
Total tax before tax credits		€9,512
Deduct tax credits		
Single tax credit	€1,650	
PAYE tax credit	€1,650	€3,300
Tax payable		€6,212
*€40,000 less €32,800		

CHECK YOUR TAX CREDITS EVERY YEAR

Do remember to check that you're claiming all your tax credits every year. It's also worth bearing in mind that you can go back to the Revenue Commissioners and claim tax credits that you failed to take advantage of for the previous four tax years.

A COMPLETE GUIDE TO PERSONAL TAX CREDITS AND ALLOWANCES FOR 2013

Over the next few pages you'll find brief details of all the different tax credits and allowances for which you may be eligible.

Single person's credit

You can claim this if you're single; if you're married but decide to opt for single/separate assessment or if you're separated and you and your former partner have not opted for joint assessment. It is worth €1,650 for 2012.

Married person's credit

This is double the single credit, and it's granted to married couples who have opted to be assessed together. It can also be claimed by separated couples where one partner is maintaining the other and is not entitled to claim tax relief on the maintenance being paid. For more details on tax relief for separated and divorced couples see Chapters 32 and 33. The married person's credit is worth €3,300.

One-parent family credit

If you have a dependent child and you are unmarried, widowed, separated, divorced or deserted (that is, your spouse has left but you are neither separated nor divorced), then you can claim the One-parent Family Tax Credit of €1,650. This is in addition to your normal personal tax credit.

Widowed parent credit

A special credit is granted to widowed parents for the first five years following the year of bereavement. For the year 2012 the credit is: €3,600 in the first year; €3,150 in the second year; €2,700 in the third year; €2,250 in the fourth year; and €1,800 in the fifth year.

Special age credits

If you are over 65 – or if your spouse is over 65 – then you receive an extra credit. If you're single or widowed this is worth €245. For a married couple it is worth €490.

The home carer's credit

If you care for someone who's elderly (defined as being over 65) or incapacitated, you may be eligible to claim an additional credit of up to €810. The home carer credit is only available to married couples where one spouse cares for one or more dependent people. You can't claim if you are looking after your own spouse. The maximum income of the home carer to claim maximum relief is €5,080. A reduced tax credit applies where the income is between €5,080 and €6,700.

A new childminding relief was introduced in 2006. Where an individual minds up to three children (other than their own children) in the minder's own home, no tax will be payable on the childminding earnings received provided the amount is less than €15,000 per annum. If the childminding income exceeds this amount, the total amount will be taxable, as normal, under self-assessment. An individual will be obliged to return their childminding income in their annual tax return.

Incapacitated child credit

If you are looking after an incapacitated child, then you're entitled to claim a tax credit of €3,300. Note that the child must be under the age of 18 or, if over the age of 18, must have been incapacitated before reaching 21 years of age or whilst still receiving full-time education.

Dependent relative credit

If you can prove that you maintain, at your own expense, a relative who cannot live independently (or a widowed mother whether incapacitated or not), you can claim a tax credit of €70 per year provided the relative's income does not exceed €13,873 per year.

Incapacitated person's allowance

An allowance of €50,000 is available to any taxpayer who is incapacitated and has to employ someone to look after them. The same allowance is available to any taxpayer who is employing someone to look after an incapacitated spouse. In fact, the allowance is available where a family employs a carer to look after a totally incapacitated person. Clearly, to take advantage of this allowance you need to have an income, and because it's an allowance (as opposed to a tax credit) the value of the benefit will be determined by your marginal – or top – rate of tax.

Blind person's credit

If you are blind, you can claim a tax credit of €1,650. If both you and your spouse are blind then you may both claim, bringing the total credit up to €3,300. An additional allowance of €825 is available to any blind person who uses a guide dog. This allowance is at marginal rate (up to 41%).

PAYE credit

If you pay tax by the PAYE system you're entitled to a PAYE credit of €1,650. If you're married, and both you and your spouse are on PAYE, then there is a doubled credit. However, you should bear in mind that you cannot claim the PAYE credit if you are the director of a company and control, either directly or indirectly, 15% or more of the shares. You can't claim it, either, if you employ your spouse (either as an individual or as a partner in a firm).

Medical insurance

If you take out medical insurance, the premium you pay will already have been discounted by the standard rate of tax (currently 20%). The insurance company will receive this tax relief directly from the government so there is no need for you to make a separate claim. It is worth noting that you can enjoy this tax relief even if you don't pay tax!

Permanent health insurance

If you are worried about a drop in your income as a result of an accident or illness, and you take out permanent health insurance to protect you against this eventuality, your contributions will be tax deductible. Do note, however, that the amount of relief you can claim must not be more than 10% of your total income for the year of assessment. Do remember that any benefit you claim under a permanent health insurance policy will be liable to income tax.

Medical expenses relief

If you have to spend money on medical care, or non-routine dental treatment, then you can claim tax relief at the standard tax rate. You should note that:

- You can claim for yourself, your spouse or any other person for who you claim tax allowances.
- The allowance can be shared among a number of people so that if, for example, several children are paying for their parent to receive treatment, each can claim.
- You may even be able to claim the cost of travelling to and from the hospital or other treatment centre.
- When it comes to medical expenses most things are eligible for tax relief, from an ordinary visit to a doctor to hearing aids, and from physiotherapy to the cost of gluten-free food for cœliacs.
- Note that all expenses in relation to maternity care are fully allowable.

There are a few exceptions you should be aware of including routine dental treatment, having your eyes tested, and the purchase of spectacles or contact lenses.

- For nursing home expenses, relief is available at your marginal rate of tax.

Relief for long-term unemployed people

If you have been unemployed for at least 12 months, and you then return to work, you will receive an additional personal allowance as well as a child tax allowance if, of course, you have one or more children. The allowance lasts for three years, and the amounts are set out below:

	Personal tax allowance	Child tax allowance (for each qualifying child)
Year 1	€3,810	€1,270
Year 2	€2,540	€850
Year 3	€1,270	€425

Third-level college fees

You may be able to claim tax relief on tuition fees paid for approved:

- Undergraduate courses

- Postgraduate courses

- Information Technology (IT) and

- Foreign language courses.

You can claim tax relief as long as you have actually paid the fees, either on your own behalf or on behalf of another person in private or publicly funded third-level colleges.

For the 2012 tax year and thereafter you can claim the Student Contribution as part of the tuition fees tax relief. The maximum annual relief for tuition fees including the Student Contribution is €7,000 per person per course.

If you are claiming for a full-time student, there is no tax relief on first €2,000 of all tuition fees for the 2011/2012 academic year. If the claim refers to a part-time student, there is no tax relief on the first €1,000 of tuition fees for the 2011/2012 academic year. For the 2012/2013 academic year, there is no tax relief on first €2,250 of tuition fees for a full-time student and €1,125 for a part-time student.

If you are claiming for more than one student, you will get full tax relief on the Student Contribution for the second or subsequent students. Tax relief is given at the standard rate and there is no limit on the number of individuals for whom you can claim.

Charitable donations

If you are self-employed (but not if you pay tax through the PAYE system) tax relief is available for any donations or gifts (minimum €250) made to charities or a wide range of not-for-profit organisations.

Loan interest relief

If you're paying interest on a loan, you may be able to claim tax relief. Various types of loan are eligible, including:

- mortgages in relation to your main home
- bridging loans
- loans taken out for business purposes
- loans borrowed to pay death duties
- borrowings used to acquire shares in your own business.

With regard to mortgage interest relief, this is now granted 'at source' which, in plain English, means that your lender will claim it on your behalf and reduce your monthly payments accordingly. You should be aware that mortgage interest relief is available on money borrowed for the purchase, repair, development or improvement of your sole or main residence situated in Ireland or in the UK. You can also claim the relief if you have to borrow money to 'purchase a residence for a former or separated spouse or a dependent relative where the accommodation is being provided by you rent-free'. The amount of relief you can claim will be determined by your personal circumstances. Only first-time mortgage holders can claim tax relief for the first seven years of the mortgage, up to a limit of €20,000 for married couples or widow(er)s or €10,000 for a single person.

Status	First-time Buyers:	Non-first-time Buyers:	First-time Buyers (new loan 2012):
Single Person	€10,000	€3,000	€3,000
Married or in a Civil Partnership/Widowed or Surviving Civil Partner	€20,000	€6,000	€6,000

	Tax Years 1–2	Tax Years 3–5	Tax Years 6–7
First-time Buyer	25%	22.5%	20%

	All years	All years	All years
Non-first-time Buyer	15%	15%	15%

Loans taken out in 2012	
First-time Buyer	25%
Non-first-time Buyer	15%

The higher limits for first-time buyers apply for the tax year in which the first mortgage interest payment is made plus six subsequent tax years. The rates of relief that are available for mortgage TRS are dependent on the status of the

The higher limits for first-time buyers apply for the tax year in which the first mortgage interest payment is made plus six subsequent tax years. The rates of relief that are available for mortgage TRS are dependent on the status of the individual, that is, whether they are first time buyers or not.

	First-time Buyer Start Year of Current Loan								
	2010 rate	2011 rate	2012 rate	2013 rate	2014 rate	2015 rate	2016 rate	2017 rate	2018 rate
2012	n/a	n/a	25%	25%	22.5%	22.5%	20%	20%	0%
2011	n/a	25%	25%	22.5%	22.5%	22.5%	20%	20%	0%
2010	25%	25%	22.5%	22.5%	22.5%	20%	20%	15%	0%
2009	25%	22.5%	22.5%	22.5%	20%	20%	15%	15%	0%
2008	22.5%	22.5%	22.5%	20%	20%	15%	15%	15%	0%
2007	22.5%	22.5%	20%	20%	15%	15%	15%	15%	0%
2006	22.5%	20%	20%	15%	15%	15%	15%	15%	0%
2005	20%	20%	15%	15%	15%	15%	15%	15%	0%
2004	20%	15%	15%	15%	15%	15%	15%	15%	0%
2003	0%	0%	0%	0%	0%	0%	0%	0%	0%

	Non-first-time Buyer Start Year of Current Loan								
	2010 rate	2011 rate	2012 rate	2013 rate	2014 rate	2015 rate	2016 rate	2017 rate	2018 rate
2012	n/a	n/a	10%	10%	10%	10%	10%	10%	20%
2011	n/a	15%	15%	15%	15%	15%	15%	15%	0%
2010	15%	15%	15%	15%	15%	15%	15%	15%	0%
2009	15%	15%	15%	15%	15%	15%	15%	15%	0%
2008	15%	15%	15%	15%	15%	15%	15%	15%	0%
2007	15%	15%	15%	15%	15%	15%	15%	15%	0%
2006	15%	15%	15%	15%	15%	15%	15%	15%	0%
2005	15%	15%	15%	15%	15%	15%	15%	15%	0%
2004	15%	15%	15%	15%	15%	15%	15%	15%	0%
2003	0%	0%	0%	0%	0%	0%	0%	0%	0%

Relief on deeds of covenant

If you make a legal commitment – known as a deed of covenant – to pay money for a period of time to someone who is aged 65 or over, or permanently incapacitated (providing the latter isn't to a son or daughter under 18) you will be able to claim the tax relief.

Pension contributions

If you're making payments into an approved personal pension scheme (here the word 'approved' refers to Revenue Commissioners' approval!), then income tax relief will be available to you at your marginal (top) rate of tax. The amount of relief is restricted to a percentage of your income. Unused allowances in any one year can be carried forward to the next. The percentage of your income that you're allowed to put, tax-free, into a pension scheme increases as you get older. For 2012 it works as follows:

- If you're under the age of 30 you can put up to 15% of your income into your pension scheme tax-free.
- If you're aged between 30 and 39 you can put 20%.
- If you're aged between 40 and 49 you can put 25%.
- If you're aged 50 and over you can put 30%.
- If you're aged 55 and over you can put 35%
- If you're aged 60 and over you can put 40%.

However, there is a cap of €115,000 on the income taken into account.

Service charges

Most of the service charges in relation to your home are eligible for tax relief at standard rate. This includes:

- charges imposed by your local authority for water, rubbish collection and/or sewage disposal
- any money you pay to an independent contractor for refuse collection
- the cost of water when arranged through a group water scheme.

If you're on PAYE, then it should be possible to arrange for your local authority to inform your tax office when they receive payment, so that it can be taken into account when calculating your income tax. If you're not on PAYE – or if your payments aren't being made to a local authority – then you'll have to keep your receipts and make a separate claim. This relief is being abolished from tax year 2012 onward.

Investment relief

Two different forms of tax incentive are available to investors. The first is 'relief for investment in corporate trades' – known generally as **BES**. The second is a relief for investment in the film industry – known as **Section 35 Investments**. Note that BES relief was extended in the 2007 Budget to 2013, and that film industry relief will cease on 31 December 2012.

Seafarer's allowance

If you are a seafarer and you're away on a voyage for at least 161 days in a tax year, then you are eligible for a special allowance of €6,350. Do note, however, that this allowance can only be offset against seafaring employment.

HOW TO MAKE THE PAY AS YOU EARN (PAYE) TAX SYSTEM WORK IN YOUR FAVOUR

Just because you're in salaried employment and have your income tax is deducted automatically using the **pay as you earn** (PAYE) system doesn't mean there aren't plenty of things you can do to keep your tax bill to a bare minimum. So, in addition to explaining how PAYE operates, this chapter also examines some of the tax-saving opportunities open to those who pay tax by this method.

THE INS AND OUTS OF PAYE

It is easy to understand why the Revenue Commissioners like the PAYE system. It allows them to collect tax as it falls due rather than once a year. But it does have two advantages for the taxpayer as well. Firstly, your employer and the Revenue Commissioners handle all the administration involved with your tax bill. If you were self-employed this could cost you thousands of euros a year. Secondly, you don't have to worry about being faced with a tax bill every year.

PAYE is operated by employers in conjunction with the Revenue Commissioners. The system is simplicity itself:

- Your employer provides your details to the Revenue Commissioners.
- Before the beginning of each tax year (usually in December), the Revenue Commissioners issue a 'Notification of Determination of Tax Credits and Standard Rate Cut-off Point'. This sets out any tax credits due to you, details your rate or rates of tax, and incorporates something called your **standard rate cut-off point** which I'll explain further in a moment.
- Using the information supplied by the Revenue Commissioners, your employer calculates how much tax to deduct from your salary.

So what is the standard rate cut-off point? Basically it's the amount of money you can earn at the standard rate – currently 20%. This is determined by your personal circumstances – whether you are married, single or widowed. You may also have allowances that are allowed at the higher rate of tax, such as a contribution to an approved pension scheme. Where this is the case, your standard rate cut-off rate will be higher.

The formula for working out PAYE is:

- The standard rate of tax (currently 20%) is applied to your gross pay up to the standard rate cut-off point for the period in question.

- Any income over and above that amount in the pay period is taxed at the higher rate (currently 41%).

- The tax payable at this point is referred to as the gross tax payable.

- Any tax credits you're entitled to are then deducted from the gross tax payable to arrive at the net tax payable.

This is probably best explained with a couple of real-life examples.

> John earns €53,000 per annum and, being married, takes all the tax credits available as he pays all the bills, the mortgage and the little luxuries. He pays tax at 20% on €41,800 and on the balance at 41%, amounting to approx. €8,000 after tax credits are applied. After payment of PRSI and USC, John's net income is approx. €40,000.
>
> Patricia, his wife, earns €26,000 and, as she has no credits, has to pay PRSI plus USC and the higher tax rate of 41% on her entire salary. Therefore, her net income is approx. €13,000 or half of her salary.

MONEY DOCTOR WEALTH CHECK

It is in your interest to keep the taxperson up to date...

If the Revenue Commissioners don't have all your personal information, they may make a mistake regarding all the different sorts of tax credits and allowances to which you are entitled. You can use the information in the previous chapter to compile a list of credits and allowances that you believe you can claim, and you should then complete a Form 12A 'Application for a Certificate of Tax Credits and Standard Rate Cut-off Point' and send it to your tax office. This form is available on request or can be downloaded from www.revenue.ie When you receive your 'Notification of Determination of Tax Credits and Standard Rate Cut-off Point' double-check that it lists all the tax reliefs you wish to claim.

EMERGENCY TAX

If your employer doesn't have the information needed in order to calculate the correct amount of tax to deduct (a 'Notification of Determination of Tax Credits and Standard Rate Cut-off Point') you will automatically be put onto PAYE emergency tax. As emergency tax only incorporates minimal tax credits, it is important, from your point of view, to contact your local tax office to resolve the situation.

GETTING YOUR TAX BACK! PAYE REFUNDS

There are various circumstances under which you may be entitled to a PAYE tax refund. For instance:

- If you become unemployed: in this situation you should write to your Inspector of Taxes and ask for a Form P50. You should complete and return this, along with Parts 2 and 3 of your Form P45 (the form your last employer should have given to you prior to you leaving).
- If the Revenue Commissioners have made an error and overtaxed you due to some factor of which they were unaware.

After the end of the tax year (31 December), your employer should give you a Form P60, which sets out the amount you earned in that year together with any tax that has been deducted. Check this form in order to make sure that all the allowances, deductions and credits to which you are entitled have been claimed. If you believe there is an error you should advise your employer and your local Inspector of Taxes in order to request a refund.

MONEY DOCTOR WEALTH CHECK

Double-check you are claiming everything

Below is a list of all the tax credits and allowances you may be entitled to (full details are to be found in the previous chapter). Why not take a moment or two to check through it now to make doubly sure that you aren't paying a cent more tax than you have to?

Tax credit	2011 (€)
Single person	1,650
Married person	3,330

Widowed person (w/o dependent children)	2,190
Widowed person (qualifying for one-parent family tax credit)	1,650
Widowed person (in year of bereavement)	3,300
One-parent family (widowed person)	1,650
One-parent family (other person)	1,650
Age tax credit (65 years plus & single/widowed)	245
Age tax credit (65 years plus & married)	490
Home carer's credit (max.)	810
Incapacitated child (max.)	3,300
Dependent relative (max.)	70
Employee's tax credit	1,650

MAKING SURE YOUR EXPENSES ARE TAX-FREE

One of the areas in which the Revenue Commissioners are extremely strict is that of **expenses** paid to employees. What they don't want is a situation where employers are disguising a benefit (effectively extra salary) in the guise of a legitimate expense. The Revenue Commissioners' guidance rules say that any expense 'must have been wholly, exclusively and necessarily incurred for the purpose of performing the duties of your employment'. (What is interesting is that if you're self-employed, the 'necessarily' criterion doesn't apply.)

So what is, and isn't, allowable? If you have to buy special equipment or clothing, for instance, it is unlikely that the Revenue will argue with your claim. By the same token, they are unlikely to take issue if you use a company-owned computer at home or claim part of your telephone bill when used for work calls. In general, what you can get away with – I mean, legitimately claim, of course, slip of the pen – will very much depend on the nature of your employment. For instance, if you work in a publishing company, any books you buy will almost certainly be allowable, as might trips to the theatre or cinema. If you're an engineer, this is unlikely to be the case!

If the Revenue Commissioners believe that you are making a claim for something that is not wholly, exclusively and necessarily incurred for the purpose of performing the duties of your employment, they will tax it! This tax is called **benefit in kind**. Your employer will be required to value the benefit and to stop tax and PRSI at source through the PAYE system. So, for example, if your employer were to send you away on a one-week holiday to recuperate from overwork, you would pay tax on the cost of that holiday as if you had been paid the extra salary.

Motor and travelling expenses

If you make a journey in your own car for business purposes, the money paid to you by your employer will not be taxable as a benefit in kind providing it does not exceed something referred to as the civil service mileage rate. If you are going to claim motoring expenses from your employer, you should keep a track of the journeys you make and the mileage actually incurred.

Sadly, you cannot claim for journeys between your home and work.

The amount you can claim under the civil service mileage rate rules varies according to whether or not you use your car in the normal course of your duties, or only occasionally. The current rates are set out in the table below:

Civil Service kilometre rates from 5 March 2009 (unchanged since)

Official Motor Travel in Calendar Year	Engine capacity up to 1,200cc (Cent/km)	Engine capacity 1,200cc to 1,500cc (Cent/km)	Engine capacity 1,501 cc and over (Cent/km)
Up to 6,437 km	39.12	46.25	59.07
6,438 and over	21.22	23.62	28.46

A chance to claim more

Some trade unions and professional bodies have negotiated special, higher, flat-rate motoring allowances for their members. For instance, teachers, nurses, journalists and building workers may all claim their special flat rate allowance tax-free – without the Revenue Commissioners questioning it. It's worth checking with your own trade union or professional body to see if such an arrangement is in place.

OTHER TAX-FREE AND TAX-EFFICIENT PERKS

Below is a list of tax-free or tax-efficient benefits that it's possible for an employee to receive.

Daily and overnight allowances

If you're working away from home your employer can pay you a daily and/or an overnight allowance to cover the cost of any expenses you may incur, such as lunch, an evening meal, accommodation, and so forth. The amount you can receive tax free depends on your salary level. The more you earn, the more you can receive tax-free. However, the longer you stay away the less you can receive. The current rates are set out in the chart below.

The Civil Service Subsistence Allowances were last reviewed in 2009:

Civil Service domestic subsistence rates from 5 March 2009

	Overnight Rates			Day rates	
Class of Allowances	Normal Rate	Reduced Rate	Detention Rate	10 hours or more	5–10 hours
A Class	€108.99	€100.48	€54.48	€33.61	€13.71
B Class	€107.69	€92.11	€53.87	€33.61	€13.71

Class	Salary
A	Excess €69,659
B	€31,159–€69,659

Free or inexpensive accommodation

If your job necessitates it, your employer can offer you rent-free or subsidised accommodation without any tax being incurred. Naturally, your residence has to be in part of your employer's business premises and there has to be a clear work-related reason for your needing to live there.

Staff entertainment

Your employer is allowed to entertain you at a reasonable cost without you incurring any benefit in kind.

Communal transport to your place of work

For instance, if your employer provides a company bus or shared taxi to bring you or from your place of employment, this is tax-free.

Presents!

Your employer can give you non-cash personal gifts providing it isn't for some reason connected with your work. However, it could be because you are retiring.

Meals

Meals, whether free or subsidised, are entirely tax-free if they're provided in a staff canteen. However, the facility has to be open to all the employees.

Lump sum payments

Lump sum payments for special reasons – such as redundancy, on account of an injury or disability, or relating to your pension scheme – may be totally exempt from tax depending on the amount and circumstances. Details relating to redundancy payments may be found in Chapter 31.

Educational fees

Any scholarship income or bursaries paid by your employer will be completely free of tax provided that the course is relevant to your employment.

Injury or disability payments

Payment made on account of an injury or disability will also usually be 100% tax-free.

Work tools

Equipment, tools, or working clothes, or anything else required to fulfil your employment will not be taxed.

Pension scheme payments

If your employer contributes to an approved or statutory pension scheme, then those contributions are also tax-free. For more details on this, see Chapter 18.

€250 bonus!

You are entitled to receive an annual, non-cash benefit of up to a value of €250 without paying a cent in tax. Many employers provide this in the form of a gift voucher, which gives the employee flexibility as to how to use it.

Health insurance

If your employer pays the cost of permanent health insurance for you, this is tax-free.

Medical cover

Your employer can also pay for your VHI or other medical expenses insurance without you being taxed on the benefit unless you're a higher rate taxpayer (when you will have to pay tax at 41%).

Season tickets

Bus, train and Luas passes are tax-free. Furthermore, the only condition is that they are monthly or annual transport passes, so they don't necessarily have to be used for work purposes.

Childcare

Crèche and childcare facilities, provided by your employer on a free or subsidised basis, will not be taxed provided that they are not privately owned.

Relocation expenses

All your home relocation expenses will be tax-free provided you are being forced to move as a requirement of your job.

Sports and recreational facilities

Sports and recreational facilities – so long as they are located on an employer's own premises – can be enjoyed tax-free by workers. This, of course, can include a company gym or health spa.

Mobile telephones

Your company-provided mobile telephone is tax-free provided it can be justified on the basis of business use. This rule also applies to the provision of computers, and even broadband access at home.

Car parking

A free car-parking space will not be taxed either – potentially a very valuable benefit indeed if you happen to work in a city centre.

Exam payments

A cash award given to you in recognition of obtaining a qualification of relevance to your job will also be treated as tax-free provided it is roughly equivalent to the expenses incurred in studying for the exam.

Membership fees

If you need to join any professional body by reason of your employment, then your subscription will be tax-free.

Health screening

If your employer insists on you having a medical check-up it will be tax-free.

Long-service presents

If you work for your company for at least 20 years they can buy you a present costing no more than €50 for each year of service, and it will be completely tax-free, a potentially €1,000 tax-free gift.

Has your employer offered you an opportunity to buy shares?

An increasing number of employees are being offered an opportunity to buy shares – directly or indirectly – in their employer's company. The tax treatment of the various different types of share schemes varies. Some offer an opportunity to save tax and others don't. You should also note that some employee share schemes won't cost you anything to participate in, whereas others will require you to make an investment. As this is a complicated area I would always suggest taking professional advice before participating. However, to give you a general idea of the different types of scheme work I have outlined the seven (!) main options below, together with a few guidance notes.

> **Approved profit share scheme.** This is probably the most advantageous scheme from an employee's point of view, as it allows you to receive shares tax-free up to an annual limit of €12,700 provided certain conditions are met. Basically, provided you hold the shares granted to you for at least three years, they will be entirely tax-free.

> **Employee share ownership trusts (ESOTs).** Employee share ownership trusts were created to run alongside company profit-sharing schemes and they work pretty much in the same way so far as the employee is concerned. One additional benefit, however, is that after ten years a one-off additional payment of €38,100 can be made.

> **Stock options.** A stock option allows you the opportunity to purchase shares in your employer's company at a pre-set price, normally within a

certain timeframe. The benefit arises if the price at which you can buy the shares is less than their market value. This does, of course, constitute a gain from your point of view, and such a gain would be taxable. Stock options are rarely tax efficient.

Share subscription schemes. If you purchase new shares in your employer's company and hold them for at least three years, then you will achieve a tax benefit. However, there is an upper limit on the amount of tax you can save and you will – of course – incur a risk, since the value of the shares you buy may fall during the period you hold them.

Save as you earn scheme (SAYE). Save as you earn (SAYE) is basically a scheme that allows you to purchase shares in your employer's company over a period of time, with the cost of those shares being deducted from your salary as it's paid. There is the potential for some tax savings here – though they are not enormous.

Share incentive schemes. Share incentive schemes and employee share purchase plans offer you an opportunity to buy shares in your employer's company, but do not normally attract much of a tax benefit.

The free gift of shares. If your employer gives shares to you, without charge, you will be liable to tax on the benefit of receiving them but you should escape PRSI.

All the different schemes outlined above have stringent conditions attached to them by the Revenue Commissioners, and I cannot over-emphasise the need to take professional advice.

REVENUE ON-LINE SERVICE (ROS)

Finally, a point to note is that the Revenue in mid-2006 extended their Revenue On-line Service (ROS) to be available to PAYE taxpayers. Once you have registered you can avail of a full suite of services, including viewing information on your Revenue record and submitting tax credit claims and incomes information. You can also carry out a range of transactions without the need to fully register for the service. To access the site and register go to www.ros.ie.

MONEY DOCTOR WEALTH CHECK

You should find out if you are eligible for any refund of tax already paid, e.g. bin allowances, rental relief, union fees, dental and medical expenses, etc., even going back as far as four years. This is particularly relevant to PAYE workers who sometimes overlook their entitlements. There are two main companies in Ireland offering tax refunds on a 'no refund – no fee' basis:

- www.taxback.com is an award-winning company that specialises in this area. To start the ball rolling, text MONEYDOCTOR to 53135 (normal SMS rates apply) and they will be in touch with you to assess your situation within 48 hours.

- www.redoaktaxrefunds.ie also specialises in tax refunds. Simply quote on their on-line request form the code MONEYDOCTOR to receive a special discount on their fees.

Better in your pocket than theirs!

23
INCOME TAX FOR THE
SELF-EMPLOYED

HOW TO REDUCE YOUR INCOME TAX BILL IF YOU WORK FOR YOURSELF

If you are self-employed – or thinking of becoming self-employed – then this chapter is essential reading. You will find out:

- how the tax system operates in relation to your earnings
- the different ways in which you can reduce your share of the tax burden
- how to avoid the unwanted attention of the Revenue whilst simultaneously making some worthwhile tax savings.

First things first

Perhaps it would be helpful to start by explaining the basic ground rules. Let's look at what is meant by the self-assessment system and preliminary tax.

SELF-ASSESSMENT SYSTEM

If you are a director in your family company or if you're in salaried employment (in other words on PAYE) but have income from other sources, you'll have to pay tax under the **self-assessment system**. Self-assessment means that you have to complete your own tax return, decide how much tax you owe, and pay it to the Revenue Commissioners at the specified time. You can, of course, get a professional accountant to do all of this for you.

The latest date by which you can complete your income tax return (**Form 11**) for the Revenue Commissioner is 31 October following the year of assessment. In other words, your 2012 tax return must be submitted no later than 31 October 2013, or mid-November 2013 if using the Revenue On-line Service (ROS).

PRELIMINARY TAX

When you submit your income tax return you must also pay something called

preliminary tax. Preliminary tax is the amount of income tax you think you're going to owe for the year in which you pay it. In other words, on 31 October 2012 your preliminary tax will be the amount of tax you think you'll owe for 2012. The amount you'll actually have to pay is the lower of either 90% of your final liability for 2012 or 100% of your liability for 2011. Let me give you an example:

> Supposing you had a good year last year, but are having a bad year this year. Last year you had to pay €10,000 tax, but this year you believe you only expect a liability of €1,000 tax. Your preliminary tax bill would, therefore, be 90% of this year's liability – or €900.
>
> Since your preliminary tax is only an estimate of the tax you owe you will, naturally, either have to pay the difference or ask for a refund. This is done at the same time. Supposing, for instance, you've paid €1,000 preliminary tax on 31 October 2011. Your final tax bill for the year, however, turned out to be €1,500. The €500 extra will fall due no later than the 31 October 2012.

In other words, on or before 31 October every year you submit a return and pay an amount on account plus the balance of the previous year's income tax. If you're owed money by the Revenue Commissioners from the previous year, then you are allowed to deduct it from the amount you're paying. This is known as **Pay and File**.

THE MYSTERY FACTOR!

As if this isn't all complicated enough, there is an added factor that makes it all even more confusing: you can choose the dates of your financial year. The tax year, of course, runs just like the calendar year, from 1 January to 31 December. However, the Revenue Commissioners will allow you to pick your own accounting period. So while your 2012 tax return could refer to the period 1 January 2012 to 31 December 2012, it could actually refer to the 12 months ending on 2 January 2012.

A quick aside about accounting dates

It may seem like a tiny detail to you – considering the enormity of being self-employed and running your own business – but your **accounting date** can have important implications. For instance, if you run a seasonal business you're unlikely to want your accounting period to end during a busy period. Also, whilst you can choose an accounting period that gives you the longest possible time to pay your tax, if you aren't good at putting money away to meet your tax liabilities all you're doing is postponing your problem and making it worse.

As hardly anyone starts a new business on 1 January, what many self-employed people do is submit their first set of accounts for a period of less than 12 months. For instance, if you started your business on 1 July you might submit your first set of accounts to cover the period 1 July to 31 December. Your second tax return would then run from 1 January the following year.

You are actually entitled to change your accounting period any time you want. However, this can trigger an additional tax charge so you need to think carefully before you do so.

MAKE YOUR PAYMENTS ON TIME... OR ELSE

The Revenue Commissioners do not take kindly to income tax returns being submitted late. They take a similar line if you fail to pay any tax you owe on the date it is due. Indeed, if you don't submit your tax return by 31 October the Revenue Commissioners will add a surcharge to your tax bill:

- a surcharge of 5% of any tax due can be imposed if you are up to two months late
- if you are more than two months late then the surcharge can rise to 10% of the tax due
- in addition to the surcharge, you will be charged interest at the rate of roughly 1% per month on any outstanding tax.

If you are going to have trouble making a tax payment, let the Revenue Commissioners know in good time. Remember, it is almost certainly cheaper to borrow the money from a bank than to suffer heavy late payment surcharges and interest.

Revenue On-line Service (ROS)

The Revenue has a service 'Revenue On-line' known as 'ROS' which has been available to self-employed taxpayers for some time. Once registered for this service ROS enables you to view your own current position with Revenue for various taxes and USC, file tax returns and forms and make payments for these taxes online in a variety of ways.

The service is highly efficient and avoids the pitfalls of postal delays when returns are being sent close to the due date.

Furthermore, self-employed taxpayers filing their annual return (**Form 11**) through ROS are given an extra two weeks approximately after the 31 October deadline to pay and file. To qualify for the extension you must:

- File your return through ROS.

- Pay preliminary tax for the current year.

- Pay income tax balance due for previous year.

- Pay capital gains tax on gains arising from 1 January to 30 September in the current year.

To register for ROS go to www.ros.ie.

MONEY DOCTOR WEALTH WARNING

Don't get on the wrong side of the Revenue

If you are self-employed or a company director, then the last thing you want is an investigation or audit by the Revenue Commissioners. You'll be pleased to discover, therefore, that it is possible to reduce dramatically your chances of being bothered by Revenue. All you have to do is follow a few very basic rules:

1   If your return is late then this increases the Revenue's interest in you. By the same token, make sure you pay the tax you owe on time.

2   Given that the Revenue Commissioners deal with every business in the country, they have a good idea about the sort of profits that you ought to be making. If you consistently appear to be making less than the industry average, they may decide to take a closer look.

3   A low salary or low drawings may make them suspicious as well. They'll be wondering if you're earning cash and not declaring it.

4   Incomplete returns. If your tax return has not been completed correctly, you are simply asking for trouble.

5   **Discrepancies.** The Revenue Commissioners are not idiots, and if
     there is a discrepancy between, say, your VAT return and your
     annual tax return, eyebrows will be raised and questions will be
     asked.

6   **Erratic turnover** figures. If your company or business seems to do
     well one year, and not the other, your inspector may decide to look
     a little closer.

7   Ownership by an **offshore entity**. If the Revenue Commissioners
     notice that your shareholders are located in a tax haven – or if they
     see that you are doing a lot of business with a tax haven – this is
     bound to set off alarm bells.

The basic rules are **stay on top of your paperwork** and **pay your tax on
time**, and you are much, much less likely to suffer the bother and
expense of a Revenue investigation.

DO YOU NEED TO REGISTER FOR VAT?

You only have to register for **value added tax** (VAT) if your sales are in excess
of certain amounts. The amounts are:

- €37,500 per year if you provide services
- €75,000 per year if you provide goods.

Once you're registered for VAT you must charge it on all your invoices but –
looking on the bright side – you can reclaim any VAT you pay out on business
expenses (other than those for entertainment or motoring). Once registered,
you will need to keep proper VAT records and complete a return every two
months.

Don't forget your PRSI

If you are self-employed you will have to pay PRSI contributions of 4% of your
gross income. For more information about PRSI see Chapter 5.

AND ANOTHER THING

If you are operating your self-employed business from home, remember that it
is now also a business premises and that you should advise your insurance

company. In most cases, this is unlikely to affect your insurance premium – but it is important that you are covered if equipment is stolen or damaged, or if a business visitor has an accident while on your premises.

Incidentally, if you do use your home as business premises, then you can claim some of the running costs as expenses against your annual tax bill. Do bear in mind, however, that if you pay yourself 'rent' this may have capital gains tax implications when you come to sell your home. This is because although there is no capital gains tax on a principal residence there could well be a liability on a business premises.

Self-employment comes in many forms

The term 'self-employed' refers specifically to people who are:

- in business as a 'sole trader'
- in partnership with one or more other people.

Many people who work for themselves actually do so as a 'contractor' working on a regular basis for someone else. You should be aware that if you work for an employer for more than eight hours a week you are entitled to a contract of employment. Such a contract would give you all sorts of benefits such as the right to holidays, the right not to be dismissed unfairly, minimum notice and so forth. On the other hand, as a contractor, you aren't protected under employment legislation and must – of course – make your own tax arrangements.

Many self-employed people find it is worth their while to form a limited company and to trade in this way. The advantages of running a limited company include:

- limited financial risk
- ability to make more generous pension contributions to your retirement fund
- possible tax benefits.

However, don't rush into forming a company without taking legal and accounting advice.

WORKING OUT YOUR PROFITS

When you are self-employed you pay income tax on what the Revenue Commissioners refer to as **taxable profits**. Your taxable profits are your gross income (the total amount you make) less any expenses which are allowed for income tax purposes. So, if you earn a total of €20,000 a year and have expenses of €5,000, your taxable profits will be €15,000 a year.

EXPENSES

So what expenses are allowable against your profits? In some ways it is actually easier to consider what expenses the Revenue Commissioners will definitely *not* allow:

- any money you spend which is not '**wholly and exclusively**' for the purpose of your business. For example, if you buy a suit for work the Revenue Commissioners would say that it isn't 'wholly and exclusively' for business purposes. If you're considering any sort of major expenditure as part of your business, and you're not sure if it will be allowable, it's well worth checking with either the Revenue Commissioners or your accountant first
- **entertainment**. With the exception of entertaining your staff, the provision of accommodation, meals, or drink for your customers is not allowable. Indeed, if you take a client out to dinner not only will the expense be disallowed but you may also suffer benefit in kind tax yourself
- any sort of **personal expenses**
- money spent on **improving your business premises**. This said, money spent renewing or repairing your business premises is allowable.

So what *can* you claim? Let me give you an example. Imagine that you are a chef who has opened his or her own restaurant. Here are some of the expenses that you could legitimately claim against your profits:

- rent
- wages paid to employees
- interest paid on business loans
- other property expenses including electricity, gas, water, rubbish disposal and so on
- furniture

- equipment for the kitchen
- linen, tableware, glasses, and related items
- travel, stationery, telecommunications, postage and advertising
- cookery books
- buying trips overseas to source produce not only for your restaurant but – perhaps – because you plan to go into the import and wholesale business
- ingredients
- uniforms for yourself and staff
- wine
- other beverages.

You might also argue that you needed to eat in your competitors' restaurants for research purposes. The real point is: if you can show you had to spend the money to run your business, then it is almost certainly an allowable expense.

A WORD ABOUT CAPITAL EXPENDITURE

Many businesses require special plant, machinery or equipment. When you buy this, it is referred to as **capital expenditure**. Such expenditure will be allowed as a business expense. However, not all at once. Since December 2002, 12.5% of the cost is allowed as an expense each year. So if you spend, say, €1,000 on a photocopier you can claim €125 a year as a cost against your income for the following eight years. This is one of the reasons why many people who are self-employed opt to lease rather than purchase certain items.

OTHER TAX-SAVING POSSIBILITIES

There are a number of different ways in which someone who is self-employed can hope to reap a tax advantage. These include:

- claiming for business expenses that would be disallowed for someone who was employed
- by taking advantage of the special rules regarding pension plans
- by using the self-assessment system to delay the payment of tax.

24
TAX AND PROPERTY

PROPERTY INVESTOR? HOW TO ENSURE YOU KEEP YOUR TAX BILL TO A MINIMUM

From a tax perspective, property is just about the most complicated investment you can make, which is why I have devoted this short chapter to the subject. The reason it is complicated is that:

- If you make a profit on the rent, you will have to pay income tax.
- If you make a profit when you sell the property, you will have to pay capital gains tax.
- There are all sorts of expenses you can claim against your profits and it is important to make sure you claim all of them.

The benefits of investing in property are huge, especially if you have been a property investor since the early 1980s or you are starting afresh in 2013.

THE TAX ADVANTAGES OF PROPERTY INVESTMENT

There are several generous tax advantages to be had from property investment including:

- In the current climate of low capital gains tax, should you sell the property at a profit you will only have to pay tax at a rate of 30%.
- You can currently earn up to €10,000 a year in rent tax-free from the letting of a room in your own principal private residence.
- All the normal personal allowances are available to you, if you haven't already used them against other income.
- The Revenue Commissioners will allow you to set a surprisingly wide range of expenses against your rental income, thus helping to keep your income tax bill to a minimum.

A WORD OF WARNING

It is worth bearing in mind that rental income is treated in the same way as self-employed income. As a result, it may have the effect of pushing you into the higher tax bracket (in other words, 41% tax plus 5% PRSI and USC). Many people wrongly believe that they will reduce their tax liability by holding property through a limited company. This is not the case, because:

- The rate of **corporation tax** on rental income is 25%.
- Undistributed investment and rental income in a **close company** is liable to a further tax charge of 20%. (A 'close' company is one that is controlled by five or fewer shareholders or is controlled by any number of shareholders who are directors.)
- The effective corporation tax rate can be as high as 40%.

TAX INCENTIVES

Over the last few years, there have been two property tax incentives you could have availed of:

1 Capital allowances in relation to **industrial buildings**. The term 'industrial buildings' includes not just factories but nursing homes, crèche facilities, and even – in certain cases – holiday cottages.

2 Tax incentives to **designated areas.** These designated areas are to be found in run-down parts of Cork, Dublin, Galway, Limerick and Waterford. The idea was to encourage urban renewal. The best known of these tax incentives was the '**Section 23**' relief in respect of expenditure on the construction, conversion or refurbishment of residential property in certain inner-city areas.

'GENEROUS' EXPENSES

Below is a list of the expenses that can normally be deducted from your rental income for tax purposes:

- any rates you have to pay on the property
- any rent (such as ground rent) that you have to pay on the property
- interest paid on money borrowed to acquire or improve the premises. Note that since 7 April 2009 this has been restricted to 75% of the interest paid

on loans relating to residential investment property. This restriction does not apply to non-residential property.

- the cost of anything you supply to your tenant that isn't covered by their rent. For instance, if you pay for the electric light in the hallways, or for the lawns to be mown, it is an allowable expense
- the cost of any maintenance, repairs, insurance or management/PRTB fees
- a capital allowance of 12.5% a year on the value of any fixtures, fittings or furniture you have purchased specifically for the property. In plain English, this means that if you buy furniture for the flat you can write it off over an eight-year period.

Do note that where your costs exceed the income from your rental property, the loss you incur may only be offset against future rental income. In other words, you can't use a loss from property investment to reduce – say – the tax you pay on your monthly salary.

25
TAX AND THE COMPANY CAR

HOW WORKING MOTORISTS CAN DRIVE DOWN THEIR TAX BILL

There was a time, in the distant past, when being provided with a company car was a genuine perk. Not only were there major tax advantages but also there was the additional benefit of not having to purchase, maintain or run a vehicle oneself. However, as the table below shows, it may not in fact be to your advantage any more to have a company car.

Civil Service motor kilometric rates from 5 March 2009

Official Motor Travel in a calendar year	Engine capacity		
	Up to 1,200cc (cent/km)	1,200cc to 1,500cc (cent/km)	1,501 cc and over (cent/km)
Up to 6,437 km	39.12 cent	46.25 cent	59.07 cent
6,438 km and over	21.22 cent	23.62 cent	28.46 cent

Nowadays, however, company cars are liable for PAYE, USC and PRSI. The amount of tax you have to pay is linked to the value of the car and the amount of mileage you do. For instance, if you do less than 15,000 miles a year you will be taxed as if you had received a cash amount equivalent to 30% of the 'original market value' of the car supplied. This calculation does not change even if the car you drive is second hand. Keep in mind, though, that if you do a very high annual business mileage, the amount of tax drops substantially. For instance, if you do more than 30,000 miles a year, you only have to pay the cash equivalent of 6% of the 'original market value'. Let's look at a real-life example:

> Your company provides you with a car worth €30,000 and your business mileage is less than 15,000 a year. You will be taxed as if you had received 30% of €30,000 – in other words, €9,000 of extra salary a year. Assuming that you're paid monthly, you will be taxed on an extra €750 per month – in other words, one-twelfth of the €9,000 benefit you are considered to have received.

The cost of this can be brought down if you contribute towards the cost of the car and also pay for your own private fuel.

HOW TO SLASH THE COST OF YOUR BENEFIT IN KIND

It is possible to reduce your **benefit in kind** charge to a flat 20% providing the following conditions are met:

- You spend 70% or more of your time away from your place of work.
- Your annual business mileage is between 5,000 miles and 15,000 miles.
- Your average working week is more than 20 hours.

To have any hope of reducing your benefit in kind tax bill, it is very important that you maintain a logbook detailing all your business trips and make it available, if required, to your Inspector of Taxes.

Another clever way to cut your benefit in kind

If, for some reason, the car is not available to you for a period the amount of tax will be reduced. For instance, supposing you gave the car back to your employer for one month a year, you would reduce your tax liability by one-twelfth.

SHOULD YOU HAVE A COMPANY CAR AT ALL?

For many people, the benefit in kind tax is so high that it makes better sense to use their personal car for business and take a mileage allowance instead of a company car. One benefit of this is that if you only receive the civil service kilometric rates (see previous page), any money paid to you by your employer will be completely free of tax.

If you're entitled to a company car, and forgo it, you may also find yourself better off. As the table below shows, this will be particularly true if you do a relatively low business mileage each year.

Car costing €20,000 and over 1500 cc

Kilometres per year	40,000	30,000	20,000	10,000	5,000
Depreciation	€6,500	€5,500	€4,000	€3,000	€3,000
Petrol	€8,000	€6,000	€4,000	€2,000	€1,000
Insurance	€1,000	€1,000	€1,000	€1,000	€1,000

Road tax	€350	€350	€350	€350	€350
Service/repairs	€2,000	€1,200	€750	€300	€300
Total running costs	€17,850	€14,050	€10,100	€6,650	€5,650
Mileage claims at civil service rates*	€13,384	€10,508	€7,662	€4,816	€2,953
Net running costs	€4,496	€3,542	€2,438	€1,834	€2,697
BIK **	€1,200	€2,400	€4,800	€6,000	€6,000

* First 6,437 miles at 59.07 cent per mile and balance at 28.46 cent per mile.
** Benefit in kind calculation.

Note: USC applies to the benefit in kind.

Cost	Mileage	BIK %	BIK
€20,000	5,000	30	€6,000
€20,000	10,000	30	€6,000
€20,000	15,000	30	€6,000
€20,000	20,000	24	€4,800
€20,000	25,000	18	€3,600
€20,000	30,000	12	€2,400
€20,000	40,000	6	€1,200

100% TAX-FREE MOTORING!

There is one way in which you can enjoy a company car with absolutely no tax liability whatsoever. Any car included in a **car pool** will be tax-free provided all of the following conditions are met:

- The car is available for use (and is actually used) by more than one employee and isn't ordinarily used by any one such employee to the exclusion of the others.

- Private use by any employee is incidental to business use.

- The car is not normally kept overnight at, or in the vicinity of, any of the employees' homes.

Finally, if you work for your own company or are self-employed, bear in mind the cost of running a 'business' car will be further reduced by capital allowances. As with other capital expenditure, you're allowed to write off the cost for tax purposes over a period of eight years. So if you purchased the car for €10,000, you can set an allowance of €1,250 per year against your tax bill.

26
CAPITAL GAINS TAX

DON'T PAY A PENNY MORE CAPITAL GAINS TAX THAN YOU HAVE TO

Just because **capital gains tax** – at a flat rate of 30% – is much cheaper than it used to be (at its peak it was 40%) it doesn't follow that you want to pay any more of it than you have to.

Capital gains tax planning is not easy even though, ironically, the rules relating to it have been much simplified. Nevertheless, there are still some useful allowances and exemptions which do make it possible to reduce, delay, and – in some instances – completely avoid this tax. As you'll discover in this chapter.

HOW THE TAX WORKS

If you buy something for one price and then sell it at a higher price or, for that matter, give it away when it is worth more than you paid for it, then the Revenue Commissioners consider that you have made a 'capital gain' and may, therefore, be liable for tax.

MONEY DOCTOR WEALTH CHECK

Indexation relief

If you owned whatever you have sold prior to 31 December 2002 – good news – before 1 January 2003 something called **indexation relief** was applied to all possible gains and this has the effect of reducing tax liability. Indexation relief was, essentially, an allowance designed to take account of inflation. As such, it meant that only gains over and above the rate of inflation were liable for tax. You can still apply indexation relief to assets held prior to 31 December 2002.

BASIC CAPITAL GAINS TAX PLANNING

Below is a list of the main ways in which capital gains tax can be reduced or avoided:

- It may seem a bit dramatic, but if you **move abroad** prior to making a disposal of your assets (in other words selling them), you will not be liable for any Irish capital gains tax. The only exception to this is if you're selling Irish property or mineral/exploration rights. Obviously, you would want to be selling a fairly major asset to make it worth becoming non-resident. For further information about becoming non-resident see Chapter 29.

- The **first €1,270** made as a capital gain in each tax year is tax-free.

- You do not have to pay capital gains tax from the **sale of your principal residence**, including up to one acre of land. However, if you sell your home for development, then you will be taxed on the profit attributed to the 'development value'.

- If you've **bought a home for a dependent** relative (this would include a relative who was unable to look after themselves, a widowed mother, and so forth) then any gain you make on the sale of the property would be free of tax.

- If you **give a house site** to a child who then builds his or her private residence on it, providing that site is not worth more than €500,000, no tax will be due.

- There is no capital gains tax on bonuses from **post office** or **state savings schemes**, or from the disposal of **government stocks**.

- You don't have to pay tax if you sell an asset with a '**predictable life**' of less than 50 years – for instance, if you sold a car or a horse at a profit.

- If you **hand your business** (including a farm) to a member of your family on retirement, there will be no capital gains tax liability either. This is called 'retirement relief'.

- You can dispose of a '**moveable, tangible asset**' worth €2,540 or less without paying capital gains tax.

- Capital gains tax is not applicable to any **winnings** from gambling, the lottery, or competitions.

- Any benefits from **life assurance** policies or **deferred annuities** are tax-free.

- If you transfer something to your **spouse** there is no capital gains tax charge.

Incidentally, the retirement relief not only applies when you pass an asset to a member of your family. Providing you're aged over 55, and have owned the farm or business for more than five years, if you sell that farm or business for a sum that is less than €750,000 you won't have to pay capital gains tax. If you sell the asset for more than €750,000 you will pay a reduced level of capital gains tax. In Budget 2012, a new incentive relief from CGT was introduced for the first 7 years of ownership for properties bought between Budget night and the end of 2013, where the property is held for more than 7 years.

The relief will apply to all new property, whether residential or non-residential. The relief will not apply if a property is sold within 7 years of its acquisition. If it is sold more than 7 years after acquisition and a gain is made on the sale, relief will be given for the initial 7-year holding period. For example, if the property was bought in January 2012 and sold in January 2022, the property would have been held for 10 years, so $\frac{7}{10}$ of any gain will be relieved from CGT and $\frac{3}{10}$ is taxable.

ONE MORE USEFUL WAY TO REDUCE YOUR BILL

If you incur expenses relating to the item you are selling – or if you have improved it in some way – then you may be able to claim them against your tax bill.

For instance, supposing you purchased an investment property and added an extra bedroom to the attic. The cost of doing this could be deducted from the sale price, thus reducing your tax liability.

27
CAPITAL ACQUISITION TAX

DON'T ALLOW YOUR GIFTS AND INHERITANCES TO BE TAXED UNNECESSARILY

The purpose of capital acquisition tax is to tax gifts and inheritances – and the purpose of this chapter is to ensure that your gifts and inheritances aren't taxed unnecessarily!

There are two key ways to lessen the effect of capital acquisition tax (which operates at a flat rate of 30% on benefits taken on or after 7 December 2011):

1   Make sure that the value of what you're leaving or giving falls below the tax-free threshold that is available.

2   Make sure that what you're leaving or giving is excluded completely from the tax. As there is a long list of excluded benefits, this is not as hard as it may seem.

TAKE FULL ADVANTAGE OF THE TAX-FREE THRESHOLDS

There are all sorts of gifts and inheritances that the government feel it would be unfair to tax. Or, to be more accurate, they feel it would be unfair to tax them unless the amount involved was fairly substantial. What we are talking about here are gifts and inheritance made to members of your immediate family and other people who are close to you. The tax-free allowances that apply are referred to as tax-free thresholds. I am afraid the tax-free threshold system is not straightforward but I'll do my best to summarise its key features.

Essentially, there are three different groups. The first applies to your closest relatives, the second to your slightly more distant relatives, and the third to everyone else. The thresholds are personal to the recipient, not to the donor (known legally as the disponer). For instance, for the current year the total amount a child can receive as gifts and/or inheritances is €250,000 from a parent. So providing the amount a child inherits from either of his or her parents is beneath this figure, he or she will pay no tax on it. Where it gets complicated is in the case of – say – nieces and nephews, who may receive bequests from a number of uncles and aunts. Anyway, below are the current thresholds:

Group 1: Children. €250,000 where the recipient is a child, or a minor grandchild of the benefactor, if the parent is dead. In some cases, this threshold can also apply to a parent, niece or nephew who has worked in a family business for a period of time. The threshold is also available if a parent receives an inheritance from a child. And foster children may also receive this amount providing they were maintained by and resided with the foster parent for a successive period of five years while under the age of 18.

Group 2: Close relatives. €33,500 where the recipient is a brother, sister, niece, nephew or linear ancestor/descendant of the benefactor or where the gift is made by the child to the parent.

Group 3: Everyone else! €16,750 in all other cases.

In other words, as an individual you can receive €250,000 from a parent, a total of €33,500 from uncles and aunts, and an additional €16,750 from friends or other more distant relatives without incurring any tax.

The rates indicated apply from 7 January 2011.

FIVE COMPLETELY TAX-FREE CATEGORIES

Five different categories of gift or inheritance are excluded completely for purposes of capital acquisition tax. They are:

1   Any gift or inheritance made between spouses.

2   Any inheritance received from a deceased child which was originally given to that child by one or other of their parents.

3   Up to €3,000 worth of gifts or cash in any single calendar year.

4   Irish government stock when given to a non-Irish domiciled beneficiary. There are conditions attached to this – the main one being that the person receiving it must hold it for at least six years after receiving it. The legal definition of 'non-Irish domiciled' is complicated, but essentially it means someone who wasn't born in Ireland or who hasn't married someone born in Ireland.

5   Your family home. Again, there are certain conditions. It should be your
    principal private residence (or the recipient's principal private residence);
    the recipient should have been living in the home for the three years prior
    to the transfer; and the recipient should not have an interest in any other
    residential property. Furthermore, the recipient mustn't sell the home for
    at least six years.

As you will see from the list above, with a bit of careful planning it is possible
to take the main family home and other assets out of one's estate for
inheritance tax purposes.

TWO USEFUL WAYS TO AVOID CAPITAL ACQUISITION TAX

Because the government knows it would be unfair to include **farms** and
business assets in the capital acquisitions tax net, both can be given away or
bequeathed with only minimal tax liability.

The rules are written so that someone who wished to reduce or avoid
capital acquisition tax could, in fact, with a little foresight transfer their
assets into either a business or a farm and see them escape tax. As you can
imagine, the rules governing these two tax loopholes are complex, so I will
only summarise them below. It would be unwise (to say the least) to attempt
to take advantage of these tax breaks without consulting a professional
accountant and/or solicitor.

FARMS

With regard to farms, 'agricultural assets are valued at only 10% of their true
market value when calculating a liability for capital acquisitions tax'. Farm
assets, in this instance, include not just land but buildings, woodland,
livestock, bloodstock, and machinery. The recipient of the farm must be a
'farmer', which means that at least 80% of his or her assets are farm assets.
You must also hold onto the assets for at least ten years to avoid any claw-
back of tax.

A farm may, of course, also be considered a family business, and the
Revenue Commissioners very generously allow them to be taxed as such for
capital acquisition tax purposes, if it means a lower tax bill in the hands of the
recipient.

BUSINESSES

So what are the rules regarding **business** assets? Once again, the primary condition is that the recipient must hold them for at least ten years after the transfer. The business itself must be Irish. Most businesses qualify, including property, unquoted shares, buildings, land, and even machinery. However, businesses whose 'sole or main business is dealing in land, shares, or securities' are not covered by this loophole. The transfer of a business by way of gift or inheritance is not entirely tax-free under these circumstances, but the assets will be assessed at just 10% of their market value.

Incidentally, keep in mind that the person giving away or bequeathing either farm or business assets need not have owned them for very long. In the case of a gift it should be five years, but in the case of death it need be only two years.

28
LOVE, MARRIAGE AND LOWER TAXES

EXTRA TAX BENEFITS FOR THOSE WHO ARE MARRIED

Billy Connolly, one of my favourite comedians, famously said: 'Marriage is a wonderful invention, but, then again, so is a bicycle repair kit.' However, unlike a bicycle repair kit, marriage has some very tasty tax benefits attaching to it. And in this chapter I will explain how you can take advantage of them.

MARRIAGE BRINGS GREATER FLEXIBILITY

The first big benefit of being married is that you get to choose how you are taxed. The options open to you are:

Joint assessment. This means that you will be taxed as one unit and allowed some tax concessions not used by one spouse to be transferred to the other.

Separate assessment. This is very like joint assessment except that all the available allowances are split evenly between you and your spouse.

Single assessment. This is where you and your spouse decide to be treated as if you were two single people for tax purposes.

Why this flexibility of benefit? Basically, you can choose to be taxed in the way that will produce the greatest possible tax advantage given your personal circumstances.

Under joint assessment and separate assessment, some unused allowances can be passed between husband and wife. This is particularly beneficial in the case of a two-income couple where one spouse earns more than another. Under normal circumstances, the Revenue Commissioners will assume that you wish to be taxed under joint assessment, and will calculate your tax liability accordingly. However, it is worth checking that you are taking full advantage of all the allowances and tax credits open to you, as the Revenue Commissioners may not be fully aware of your financial situation.

The only circumstances under which most people might wish to be taxed under the single assessment system is where they are separated.

What is interesting is that on a combined salary of, say, €55,000 a couple is likely to save over €1,000 by being taxed under the joint assessment system over and above what they would pay under the separate or single assessment system.

OTHER TAX CONCESSIONS MADE TO MARRIED COUPLES

A number of other generous tax concessions are made to married couples, including:

- Assets may be transferred between husband and wife without being subject to capital gains tax.

- Any capital losses made by one spouse may be used by the other spouse to reduce a capital gains tax bill.

- Any gifts or inheritances given by one spouse to another are completely free of capital acquisition tax.

- Any money received by yourself or your spouse from a life assurance policy (providing you or your spouse were the original beneficial owners) will be completely tax-free.

- Married couples do not have to pay stamp duty when they transfer assets from one to another.

EVEN BETTER NEWS IF YOU'RE MARRIED AND SELF-EMPLOYED

If you are self-employed or run your own business, by employing your spouse, you may be able to save up to €5,000 a year in tax. To make this saving, the total amount of income you and your spouse earn each year must be at least €70,800. It doesn't, by the way, all have to come from your own business. Your spouse can earn up to €25,000 and you can still gain a tax benefit.

The reason why the tax saving can be made is the fact that a two-income family can take advantage of a €65,600 standard rate band as opposed to the €41,800 band available to a single-income family.

The best way to illustrate this is with a real example:

One income			Two incomes		
Income		€75,000	Income		€75,000
€41,800 @ 20%		€8,360	€65,600 @ 20%		€13,120
€33,200 @ 41%		€13,612	€9,400 @ 41%		€3,854
Total tax before tax credits		€21,972	Total tax before tax credits		€16,974
Tax credits			**Tax credits**		
Married person	€3,300		Married person €3,300		
PAYE	€1,650	€4,950	PAYE	€1,650	€4,950
Tax payable		€17,022	Tax payable		€12,024
	Tax saving	€17,022 − €12,024 = €4,998			

MONEY DOCTOR WEALTH CHECK

Turn your children into a tax advantage

If you're self-employed, and if you have children, you may be able to avoid tax on up to €16,500 per child a year. This is because your children are entitled – like anybody else – to avail of tax credits. Of course, the child must actually be doing the work for which they are paid – and it may be necessary for you to register as an employer for PAYE and PRSI purposes – but given the tax saving this has to be worth it! However, the child may have to pay PRSI and USC of €870 and you as the employer will be liable for the employer's PRSI contribution.

29
TAX FOR THE EX-PAT

TAX PLANNING TIPS IF YOU'RE LIVING AND WORKING ABROAD

What happens to your tax position if you decide to live abroad? Much depends, of course, on where you go, what you do, and how long you're away. If, for instance, you move to a country with much lower rates of tax than we have here in Ireland, you could make a substantial saving. Since there are over 130 different tax jurisdictions in the world, it's obviously beyond the scope of this book to look at all the different possibilities. However, in this chapter I can, at least, explain how your Irish tax situation will be affected by a move overseas.

IT'S ALL ABOUT RESIDENCY AND DOMICILE

Every country in the world has its own rules about whom it taxes and under what circumstances. In some countries it's all about whether you **reside** there for legal purposes. This may have absolutely nothing to do with the amount of time you actually spend in the country. For instance, you can be tax-resident in Malta (thus taking advantage of a very liberal tax regime) but not set foot on the island from one end of the year to the other. Other countries have more complicated rules that are not only linked to your residence but also to your **domicile**, a rather complicated legal concept. Put simply, it is considered to be *the country that you call your natural home*. When you're born you usually have the same domicile as your father. If you marry, or move abroad for a long time, then your domicile may change.

Here in Ireland your tax liability will be determined by *both* your resident status and your domicile. Just to make things more complex, we have two types of residence. You may be **ordinarily resident** or simply **resident**.

You will be viewed as being resident here for tax purposes in the current tax year if:

- You spend 183 days or more in the state.
- The combined number of days you spend here in the current tax year and the number of days you spent here in the last tax year exceeds 280. In

applying this two-year test, a period of less than 30 days spent in Ireland in a tax year will be ignored.

Incidentally, the term 'day' really refers to whether or not you were in the country on the stroke of midnight.

Once you've been in Ireland for **three** consecutive tax years you are considered to have become ordinarily resident. You stop becoming ordinarily resident in Ireland once you've left the country for three consecutive years.

WHAT HAPPENS WHEN YOU MOVE ABROAD?

Assuming that you are resident, ordinarily resident, and domiciled in Ireland – what happens when you decide to move abroad on a permanent or, at least, long-term basis?

The year you leave Ireland you will still be considered resident. However, the year after your departure you will not be considered resident. Since this could lead to a very unfair situation – where you're taxed in two countries simultaneously – the law says that:

- As soon as you depart Ireland you may apply to be granted **emigrant status**, which means that your earnings outside Ireland after that date will be ignored for Irish tax purposes.

If you move to a country that has a **double taxation agreement** with Ireland, then you won't be expected to pay tax on the same money twice.

A MONEY-BACK OFFER: TAX REBATES

If you leave a job in Ireland and move overseas to work, you may well be entitled to a **tax rebate**. In fact, you can claim a rebate going back for up to four years. The reason you get this rebate is that under the PAYE system your various tax credits and allowances are spread out over an entire year. Under these circumstances, if you leave your job and move abroad halfway through the year, you'll only ever see the benefit of half your tax allowances and credits. You won't, however, be given this rebate automatically, though you may apply for it before you've even left the country.

WHAT IS YOUR TAX STATUS?

So, what is your tax status? There are four different possibilities:

1 If you are resident and domiciled in Ireland then you pay Irish tax including income tax on your Irish income and on your worldwide income.

2 If you are resident in Ireland but not domiciled here, and if you haven't lived here for at least three years (in other words you are not ordinarily resident in Ireland), then you pay Irish income tax on your Irish and UK income, and on any foreign income paid to you in Ireland. In other words, foreign income (unless it comes from the UK) that you don't deposit in an Irish bank or spend in Ireland escapes Irish tax.

3 If you are ordinarily resident in Ireland, but not resident here for a particular tax year, then your tax status changes dramatically. In theory you're liable to Irish income tax on your whole worldwide income. However, employment or income which you earn wholly abroad (plus an extra €3,810) will be ignored for tax purposes. Furthermore, you may be able to take advantage of double taxation agreements to further reduce your tax bill.

4 If you are not resident, or ordinarily resident – in other words, if you haven't lived in Ireland for at least three years – then your only liability to Irish tax is on Irish income.

Budget 2010 introduced a **Domicile Levy**. From 1 January 2010 certain individuals who are Irish citizens and Irish domiciled in a tax year will pay a levy of €200,000. Specifically the levy will apply where the individual has:

- Irish located property greater than €5 million,
- worldwide income in excess of €1 million, and
- an Irish income tax liability less than €200,000.

The Finance Bill clarified that Irish property is all property located in Ireland but does not include shares in a trading company or a holding company that derive the greater part of their value from subsidiary trading companies.

The individual's Irish income tax liability for the year will be allowed as a credit in arriving at the amount of the domicile levy for that year. The levy will apply irrespective of where they live or where they are tax resident.

YOUR PERSONAL TAX CREDITS AND RELIEFS

What happens to all your personal tax credits and allowances if you cease to be resident in Ireland? The answer will be determined by the source of your income, and your resident status.

GET PROFESSIONAL HELP!

In the excitement of moving abroad, many people omit to take professional advice on their tax position, and end up with an unexpected tax bill or – just as bad – missing an opportunity to claim back tax they've already paid. The Money Doctor's advice to anybody moving abroad is get professional tax help sooner rather than later.

THE MONEY DOCTOR SAYS...

If you are living abroad, or lived abroad, you may be entitled to a tax refund. To start the process, simply text MONEY DOCTOR to **53135** and you will be contacted by tax refund specialists taxback.com.

30
SPECIAL TAX ADVICE FOR FARMERS

We city folk have an idyllic view of farming life – sun-drenched fields, wholesome food, healthy lifestyle, happy people. There is all that, but there is also the everyday issue the farming community face that we all face – tax. Tax is and always has been a thorny issue on both sides of the fence. Some city folk may think that farmers don't pay enough and farmers might say that they should be given special status because of the importance of their role in Irish heritage – not to mention the produce they yield from Irish soil. Being married to a farmer's daughter, I tend to agree with the latter!

If you are a farmer, you need to consider a number of areas:

- income tax
- capital acquisitions tax
- capitals gains tax
- VAT
- stock relief
- compulsory disposal of livestock
- capital allowances
- milk quotas
- stamp duty
- farm consolidation relief
- leasing of farm land.

Let's look at them all in more detail now.

INCOME TAX

The Finance Act allows for a **deferral of tax** on FEOGA income. This is the European Agricultural Guidance and Guarantee Fund, support through funding from the Common Agricultural Policy. (FEOGA are the French initials!) However, you must meet certain conditions:

- You must be a farmer in receipt of payments under the EU single payments scheme for farmers and certain terminated FEOGA scheme payments.

- You must not be availing of farm averaging.

The provision allows payments received under terminated FEOGA schemes to be disregarded for tax purposes in 2007, and instead to be deemed to arise in three equal instalments in 2007, 2008, and 2009. If you cease to farm during this period, any untaxed payments will fall to be taxed in the year the farming stopped. Once agreed to go this route, it cannot be changed.

CAPITAL ACQUISITIONS TAX

A gift/inheritance of land, buildings and other agricultural property (e.g. machinery and livestock) may be reduced by 90% of its market value for gift/inheritance tax when received by a qualifying farmer as long as:

- the farmer is domiciled in Ireland
- 80% of the market value of the property after taking the gift/ inheritance consists of agricultural property.

However, do keep in mind that this relief is lost if the assets are disposed of within a six-year timeframe, without being replaced within one year of sale, or within a period of six years in the case of a sale or compulsory acquisition made on or after 25 March 2002. Make any claims for agricultural relief on Form I.T.41.

Gifts or inheritances of agricultural property qualify for business relief (where the relevant criteria are met) in circumstances where it fails to qualify for agricultural relief. This reduces the market value of the gift/inheritance by 90%. Again, business relief will be clawed back if the assets are disposed of within six years, without being replaced.

Before you receive a gift of farm assets, make sure that 80% of your personal assets are agricultural assets after you have received the gift.

CAPITAL GAINS TAX

Retirement relief means that a disponer (the person who is giving the legacy, generally the mother or father), can hand over land to a child without capital gains tax liability for that child. However, the conditions are:

- The disponer must be over 55 years of age.

- She or he must have used the business assets for at least ten years prior to handing over to the disponer's child.

You should also note these other key points:

- Periods of ownership of a deceased spouse may also be included.

- 'Child' includes anyone who has worked substantially on a full-time basis for five years before the handover.

- Where proceeds do not exceed €750,000, relief on the disposal can be given to an unconnected person. There is marginal relief exceeding this amount.

In addition, land that has been let for up to five years prior to a compulsory purchase order being made will qualify for retirement relief if it was used for farming for ten years prior to the letting.

Note that a farmer who participates in the EU 'Early retirement from farming scheme' by leasing the land qualifies for the relief. Therefore, while it is called 'retirement relief', you don't actually have to retire to qualify for this relief!

VAT

- A flat rate of 5.2% applies to supplies of agricultural goods or services.

- If you engage in any other services and your turnover exceeds €37,500 in a calendar year, normal VAT rates will apply – this includes the farming itself.

- Keep in mind that if you are a flat rate (5.2%) farmer, you can also reclaim this VAT on any expenditure incurred in the construction or improvement of farm buildings, farm structures, fencing, drainage and land reclamation.

- VAT on farm vehicles (vans, pick-up trucks but not passenger vehicles) can also be reclaimed.

- VAT on diesel is also reclaimable.

STOCK RELIEF

Stock relief is a basic relief for first-time farmers (who meet certain required criteria) whereby they can reduce their taxable trading profit by 100% of the increase in their farming stock at the end of their trading year over their farming stock at the beginning of that year. The 2009 Budget extended this relief to 31 December 2010. The existing 25% general stock relief for farmers was also extended to this date.

COMPULSORY DISPOSAL OF LIVESTOCK

There is a special relief for farmers (individuals and companies) in respect of profits resulting from the **disposal of livestock** due to statutory disease-eradication measures.

You can have tax on profits spread over four consecutive annual instalments *after* the year in which the profits arise or spread equally over the four years including the year in which the profits arise.

This relief extends to all animals and poultry.

CAPITAL ALLOWANCES

Relief is available for farmers who have:

- incurred expenditure on necessary pollution-control measures
- who have a **Farm Nutrient Management** plan in place.

The maximum allowed is €63,500. This scheme has been extended to 31 December 2010 with the Finance Act 2005 shortening the write-off period to three years in respect to expenditure incurred after 1 January 2005.

MILK QUOTAS

Capital allowances are available to farmers incurred in purchasing a milk quota. The period for write-off is seven years – 15% for the first six years and 10% for the seventh year. **Do note that capital allowances may be claimed by a farmer who leases a milk quota from a relative and who later purchases that quota.**

STAMP DUTY

Essentially a tax on buying or transferring property or land, this duty payable is restricted to half for related bequests (e.g. giving your son your farm) but to young trained farmers this duty is nil. There are clawbacks whereby within five years of receiving a stamp duty relief, the proceeds of that disposal of the property are not reinvested within one year in other land.

FARM CONSOLIDATION RELIEF

This is another type of stamp duty relief for exchanging farm land between two farmers to consolidate each other's holding. There are a number of conditions attached to this relief and you should consult your accountant for more advice on this.

LEASING OF FARM LAND

If you are over 40 and you lease your farm land, you are eligible for income tax exemption subject to certain thresholds – bear in mind the lease income of the husband and wife are treated separately for the purpose of the relief, whether jointly assessed or not.

In January 2007, a new exemption of €20,000 per annum was introduced for leases of 10 years or more duration. This measure was subjected to clearance with the European Commission under state-aid rules.

PART 9

WHEN THE LAST THING YOU WANT TO THINK ABOUT IS MONEY

This section of the book offers advice and information relating to five highly sensitive subjects:

- *redundancy*
- *separation*
- *divorce*
- *the death of a loved one*
- *personal insolvency and bankruptcy*

In each of these situations, of course, the last thing you'll want to think about is money. And yet, unfortunately, each of these difficult experiences has important financial implications.

31
REDUNDANCY

TOP TIPS, INCLUDING ADVICE ON YOUR RIGHTS SHOULD YOU EXPERIENCE REDUNDANCY

Whether you have opted for redundancy because of the financial benefits it offers you, or whether it was thrust upon you, it is vital that you know your rights and that you can make sure that you come out of it in as strong a financial position as possible. In this chapter I will explain your rights and offer general advice on making the most – from a money perspective – of the situation.

BACKGROUND BRIEFING ON 'REDUNDANCY'

The term 'redundancy' applies to a very specific situation, so the first thing you must do is find out whether or not you are covered by the relevant legislation. Essentially, in order to be eligible for a redundancy payment, you must:

*   be aged between 16 and 66
*   have been working for at least eight hours a week for your employer
*   have at least 104 weeks (in other words, two years) of continuous service for the same employer.

Redundancy can only exist when an employee is dismissed because:

*   The employer is no longer undertaking the business activity which necessitated employing you.
*   The employer is moving the location of the business.
*   The employer has decided to carry on business with fewer employees, or to carry out work in some different manner.

Voluntary redundancy – also known as 'voluntary parting' – is where an employer wants to lose members of staff and asks for volunteers for redundancy. If you do volunteer, you will automatically become entitled to a

statutory lump sum payment. Note that employers must give you at least *two weeks' notice* before making you redundant, and notice must be given using the specific form – **Form RP1** – at that time.

HOW MUCH ARE YOU ENTITLED TO?

The law is very precise about the amount of money an employer must pay you if you are to be made redundant. It is calculated as follows:

- You should receive two weeks' pay for each year of employment continuous and reckonable between the ages of 16 and 66.

- You should also receive an equivalent of one week's normal pay.

However, there *is* an upper limit. No matter what your salary, one week's pay will never be more than €600.

WHAT HAPPENS IF THE EMPLOYER DOESN'T PAY UP?

There are many situations where employers either don't – or can't – make the lump sum redundancy payment. For instance, the employer may be inefficient, insolvent, or even dead. Under these circumstances, it may be possible to receive a payment from the government. To pursue this, contact the:

> Department of Jobs,
> Trade and Employment
> Davitt House, 65A Adelaide Road
> Dublin 2

or contact your local FÁS office.

WHAT'S THE TAX SITUATION?

Depending on your circumstances, and the amount of money being paid, your redundancy lump sum may or may not be liable to tax. It will be totally exempt from tax if the payment was made:

- under the Redundancy Payments Acts of 1987–1991

- as a result of injury or disability

- from an approved pension scheme.

Even if your lump sum isn't entirely tax-free, you may be able to claim an extra tax-free amount. How much you can claim will be the highest of the three different exemptions outlined below. Where you are receiving a larger sum, it is likely to become taxable. Under these circumstances, you can either treat it as income in the year in which you receive it, and have it taxed as such, or else you can take advantage of something called **top slicing relief**, which works by calculating your average rate of tax for the five years prior to the tax year in which you received a lump sum.

Do note that it is often possible to reduce your tax bill on a redundancy lump sum by using it to make an additional voluntary contribution to a pension scheme (see Chapter 18).

CLAIMING TAX RELIEF ON A REDUNDANCY PAYMENT

You can claim tax relief under one of these three exemptions:

Basic exemption. You can receive up to €10,160 as a lump sum together with an additional €765 for each complete year of service without paying a cent of tax.

Increased exemption. The tax-free sum you are entitled to receive may be increased by €10,000 to a maximum of €20,160 (plus the additional €765 for each complete year of service) if you haven't made a claim for an increased exemption amount in the previous ten years, nor received a tax-free lump sum under an approved pension scheme.

Standard capital superannuation benefit (SCSB). This is a way for those with a long service record to receive a higher tax-free sum. The SCSB formula involves taking your average salary over the past three years, multiplying it by the number of years of service, dividing it by 15, and deducting any tax-free lump sum paid, or due, from a pension scheme.

Let me give you an example:

Peter, aged 65, has given 44 years service to his company. His average salary over the last three years was €47,500. If you multiply this by 44 (the number of years service), you would get a total of €2,090,000. Then divide it by 15, giving you a total of €139,333.33 tax-free.

THE MONEY DOCTOR SAYS...

If you have been working for an employer for a sufficiently long period of time to entitle you to a redundancy payment, then there is no doubt in my mind that it's worth seeking professional help to ensure that you not only optimise that payment but that you pay the least possible amount of tax on the benefit. There may also be an opportunity to claim 'Top Slicing' relief on any taxed element of a redundancy payment.

32
SEPARATION

THE FINANCIAL CONSEQUENCES OF SEPARATION

Sadly, no book dealing with personal finances is complete without chapters covering separation and divorce. First of all, it's worth pointing out that from a legal perspective the breakdown of a marriage actually has three separate stages:

1   When a couple make the decision to **live apart**.

2   When a couple seek a **legal separation**.

3   When a couple seek a **judicial separation**.

In this chapter I will explain the consequences and issues surrounding a separation, and in the next chapter I will explain what happens as a result of a divorce.

The implications of living apart

Living separately from your husband or wife does not in any way alter the legal status of your marriage. For example, you don't automatically lose your Succession Act entitlements (see next page for further details) if you are separated from your spouse. However, do note that if a spouse is found guilty of **desertion** or **bad conduct**, they might well be deemed by a court to have forfeited these rights.

WHAT HAPPENS WHEN YOU 'LIVE APART'?

The financial effects of **living apart** can be summarised as follows:

*   In the case of a **temporary** or **short-term** separation, there will be no alteration in the income tax situation and you can still elect for joint, separate or single assessment.

*   If the separation is considered to be **permanent**, then the husband and wife will be assessed for income tax under the **single assessment system**. The only situation where this really alters is if there are legally enforceable

maintenance payments being made. In some circumstances, these will be tax deductible to the payer, and taxable in the hands of the recipient; in other circumstances, they will be ignored for income tax purposes.

- With regard to **capital gains tax**, a temporary separation will make no change in either spouse's tax status. In the event of a permanent separation, any transfer of assets that are connected with the separation itself will remain capital gains tax free. However, other transfers will become taxable and unused capital gains tax losses will no longer be permitted.

- Couples who live apart continue to be exempt from **capital acquisitions tax** on the transfer of assets between each other.

- **Life assurance proceeds** continue to be tax-free – providing the beneficiary was originally named in the policy as such.

Couples who are separated continue to enjoy exemption from stamp duty when transferring property between each other.

WHAT HAPPENS WHEN YOU GET A 'LEGAL SEPARATION'?

A **legal separation** (often referred to as a 'Deed of Separation') is a voluntary agreement made between a husband and wife who have decided to live apart on a permanent basis. Interestingly, it does not change the *legal* status of a marriage. Its purpose is really to resolve the key financial and, where relevant, child-custody arrangements. Under normal circumstances, a legal separation makes provision regarding two key financial matters:

- any maintenance payments to be made by one spouse for the benefit of the other spouse and/or their children

- any desired change regarding rights under the Succession Act 1965.

With regard to **Succession Act rights**, these only change if altered legally by the Deed of Separation. However, on becoming legally separated, many people alter their wills to account for the new circumstances.

From an **income tax** perspective, a legal separation is no different from a married couple simply deciding to live apart. Thus, if the separation is likely to be permanent and legally enforceable maintenance payments have been agreed, most couples decide to opt for separate assessment. If this happens, then **maintenance payments** are ignored for income tax purposes.

While the income tax situation may be relatively straightforward in the first year of separation, in subsequent years it may become slightly trickier. This is because a number of different factors come into play, including:

- voluntary maintenance payments, whether made to a spouse or for the benefit of a child

- legally enforceable maintenance payments, whether made to a spouse and/or child

- interest relief on mortgage repayments

- single-parent credits.

PRSI and **USC** may be payable on maintenance payments, depending on whether the separated couple have opted for single or separate assessment.

Keep in mind that – in most circumstances – there is a tax benefit to legally enforceable maintenance payments. This is because they are tax deductible for the spouse paying them but will not, necessarily, be large enough for the recipient to have to pay tax on them.

The situation regarding capital gains tax, capital acquisition tax, and stamp duty do not alter if you become legally separated as opposed to simply living apart.

WHAT IS A JUDICIAL SEPARATION?

If a couple cannot agree to a legal separation, one of them may apply to the courts for a judicial separation. In this case, instead of a voluntary arrangement regarding the marital assets, maintenance and so on, the court will make a number of Ancillary Orders, which are legally enforceable.

From a financial perspective, there is little difference between a legal separation and a judicial separation. There is one area, however, where a judicial separation is more like a divorce, and this is with regard to pension benefits. Under the Family Law Act of 1995, if a judicial separation takes place, a spouse's pension benefits will be treated in one of three different ways:

1 **Earmarking** may occur. This means that when a pension becomes payable, a share of it is earmarked for the other spouse.

2 **Pension-splitting** results in the pension benefits being split on a pre-set formula between the two spouses.

3 **Offsetting** whereby the spouse with pension rights may be entitled to keep them in exchange for something else. For instance, the spouse with pension rights might give up all entitlement to a family home.

Keep in mind that a decree of judicial separation does *not* affect the legal status of a marriage – it merely means that a husband and wife no longer have to live together. The key difference between a judicial separation and a divorce is that a judicial separation will not allow either party to re-marry.

THE MONEY DOCTOR SAYS...

Sadly, many separating couples take legal but not financial advice. I strongly recommend a thorough review of your finances both before and after separation.

You should consider every aspect of your finances – life cover, income protection, critical illness cover, borrowings, savings, investments and (especially) pension plans.

Given that after a separation both parties are likely to be managing on a lower income, it is also important to work out a new monthly budget. Contact consultancy@moneydoctor.ie

---

33
DIVORCE

THE FINANCIAL CONSEQUENCES OF DIVORCE

Although a great deal has been written about the legal, emotional, religious, moral and logistical aspects of divorce, there are very few sources of reference relating to the *financial* consequences of ending a marriage.

The financial consequences will, of course, vary considerably depending on a variety of factors including:

- each partner's age
- the income of each partner
- whether or not there are any children
- whether or not there is a family home
- other joint and individually held assets
- the pension entitlements for each partner
- the health of each partner
- whether or not any life assurance is in place for one or other partner
- whether or not they both live in Ireland.

Decisions over whether or not the family home should be sold, or concerning maintenance payments are legal rather than financial and, therefore, outside the scope of this book.

If you are divorced, whatever settlement was reached – whether voluntary or decided by the courts – you need to now re-consider and review your financial planning.

In this chapter, then, I look at the key issues facing a newly divorced person, and I make a number of specific suggestions relating to your personal finances.

THE IMPORTANCE OF BUDGETING

There is no doubt that divorce is expensive. Leaving aside the legal costs, both husband and wife are likely to find themselves now having to fund two homes where, previously, they only had to pay for one. By the same token, other assets are likely to be depleted:

- Extra life cover may become necessary.
- All sorts of living expenses will increase.
- You may be required to start or increase retirement savings.

In addition, the emotional strain of divorce is often such that people become somewhat reckless about their spending and borrowing habits. If you do find yourself in this unfortunate position, my advice is that – at the earliest possible moment – you sit down and work out a **new budget**.

If you would like assistance with this, I would refer you to my website (www.moneydoctor.ie) where you will find a free, online monthly budget planner.

HOW YOUR SITUATION WILL HAVE CHANGED

Once you are legally divorced, your financial position in relation to succession, tax, pensions, insurance and social welfare will all have changed:

- Your **succession rights** will automatically be lost. However, if you have made any specific bequests in your will to your former spouse, they will stand unless you change your will or make a new one.

- In terms of **income tax** your position is broadly the same as if you were simply legally separated (see Chapter 32). The main thing to remember is that if there are legally enforceable maintenance payments, then you can usually opt to be taxed either under the single assessment or separate assessment systems. Under the single assessment system, maintenance payments are tax deductible for the person paying them, and taxable for the person receiving them. If you decide to be taxed under the separate assessment system, then maintenance payments will be ignored for income tax purposes.

- Any transfer in assets that is made because of the divorce will be **capital gains tax** free. Do note however that after that point transfers will no longer be exempt from capital gains tax.

  Any transfer of assets or gifts that take place as a result of the divorce settlement are exempt from **capital acquisition tax**. As with capital gains tax, once you are divorced, the spouse exemption for capital acquisitions tax no longer applies.

MAKING PROPER PENSION PROVISION

Pension rights can be a very important part of the financial arrangements resulting from a divorce. Indeed, for many married couples, their pension rights can be as valuable, if not more valuable, than the family home. For this reason, I advise you strongly to take expert advice when you separate.

In fact, the law recognises the vital importance and value of pension rights – as a result, spouses are *not allowed* to arrange a **pension adjustment** order between themselves. Only a court of law has the right to decide what happens to pension rights after a couple separate or divorce.

Deciding on the value of the pension is not easy. It will depend on the beneficiary's salary, type of pension scheme, level of contributions, prescribed benefits, years of service, and scheme performance.

A court will not necessarily make any decision regarding pensions if it believes that the rest of the agreed settlement is fair to both parties. However, there are three things concerning pension benefits that divorcing couples should be aware of:

1   A court can make orders about the pension benefits of either spouse.
2   Normally any decisions about pensions will be made at the time of the divorce, but if this doesn't happen, either spouse can go back to court for a **pension adjustment order** at any time during the lifetime of the pension scheme member.
3   A court can order that part of a pension is paid to either a spouse or to a dependent child.

THE MONEY DOCTOR SAYS...

If you are getting divorced, do not rely solely on the services of a solicitor – call in one or more financial professionals to help with financial planning, tax planning and pension planning. I cannot stress how important it is to do this at the earliest possible opportunity. Email consultancy@monetdoctor.ie

34
COPING WITH BEREAVEMENT

WHAT TO DO ABOUT THE MONEY SIDE OF THINGS WHEN SOMEONE CLOSE DIES

When somebody close to you dies, tax and other financial matters are obviously the last thing on your mind. If there are dependants involved, however, it may be necessary to tackle such matters with a degree of urgency. Even if dependants aren't involved, there is a legal obligation for the personal representative to carry out certain responsibilities within a reasonable period of time.

Making and executing a will, especially after purchasing a property, is probably the most important legal task a person should perform. Despite that fact, very few people during their lifetime actually execute a will. Many of us have a psychological or emotional difficulty addressing thoughts of a will, or with meeting a solicitor or other persons to instruct the drafting of a will and then executing it. These aversions are very understandable as nothing can be as stressful or as morbid as planning for one's own death. However, as anybody who has been touched by bereavement knows, creating a will during one's lifetime will in fact minimise the grief and distress felt by surviving relatives.

A will also guarantees that the affairs of a deceased person will be dispensed with and distributed far more urgently than someone who dies either without having made a will (intestate) or with an invalid will, thereby minimising stress for surviving loved ones.

A SHORT LIST OF DEFINITIONS

Below you'll find a plain English definition of the different legal terms and expressions that are used to sort out the affairs of someone who has died.

The administrator. Where the deceased hasn't appointed a personal representative (in his or her will), the person looking after the financial situation is known as an administrator.

The beneficiary. A beneficiary is someone who inherits either part or the whole of the deceased's estate.

The deceased. The 'deceased' refers to the person who has died.

The estate. The 'estate', or the 'deceased's estate' is made up of all the assets that the deceased person owned. This includes bank accounts, property, jewellery, stocks and shares, furniture, and so on.

The executor. If the deceased has written a will, he or she will have appointed an executor to ensure that his or her wishes are carried out. Many people appoint several executors, and it is normal for the personal representative to be one of them.

Intestate. If the deceased did not write a will, they are said to have died 'intestate'. The word 'intestacy' refers to the situation where no will exists. What happens to the assets where there is no will is set out in the 1965 Succession Act.

The personal representative. The personal representative is the person ultimately responsible for sorting out and finalising the deceased's affairs.

The Succession Act. This piece of legislation sets down the requirements for a valid will. Under Irish law, a spouse and children are legally entitled to a certain share in the property of a deceased parent or spouse – whether a will has been made or not. As it currently stands, if there are children then the spouse's share, by legal right, is at least one-third of the estate. Where there are no children, the spouse is entitled to at least one-half of the estate.

The trustee. If there is some reason why some or all of the deceased's assets cannot be distributed immediately to the beneficiaries, then the will may provide for certain assets or property to be held 'in trust'. This situation might arise, for example, if the deceased was leaving something to someone who was under the age of 18. The person whose responsibility it is to look after such property or assets is called the trustee. Many people appoint more than one trustee in their will.

The will. This is the legal document in which the deceased set out his or her wishes regarding his or her assets.

WHEN THERE IS A WILL

If there is a valid will, the following rules apply:

- On the death of a **married person with no children**, their surviving spouse is entitled to one-half of the deceased's estate.
- On the death of a **married person with children**, their surviving spouse is entitled to a one-third of the deceased's estate.
- The spouse is legally entitled to the appropriate share, regardless of the actual terms of the will. The fact that the parties may have lived apart for many years does not of itself affect their entitlements under the Act.

WHEN THERE IS NO WILL OR NO VALID WILL

In these circumstances, under the Succession Act 1965, the following rules apply:

- On the death of a **married person with no children**, the surviving spouse is entitled to the entire of the deceased's estate.
- On the death of a **married person with children**, their surviving spouse is entitled to two-thirds of the deceased's estate and their children are entitled to the remaining one-third.
- If a **single person or widowed person passes away** without having made a valid will, their next of kin will be entitled to inherit their estate as outlined in the Succession Act 1965.

THE RIGHT OF THE SPOUSE TO INHERIT

A spouse, i.e. somebody who is legally married to another person, is entitled to share in the estate of that person on death regardless of the will made by that person prior to their death.

If a person has made a will and passes away, regardless of what is mentioned in that will (e.g. entire estate left to a third party), the spouse is entitled to one-half of the deceased's estate if there are no children.

If a person has died having made a will with a spouse and children, the spouse is entitled to one-third of the deceased's estate.

The spouse is also entitled to a portion for their own benefit of the family home, namely the place where the husband and wife normally resided prior to the death of a spouse.

However, note that the right to apportion the family home should not exceed the legal right share (i.e., one-half if there are no children; one-third if there are children of the spouse to share in the estate of the deceased).

In order to explain this element of the law more clearly, it may be useful to give an example:

> Mr and Mrs Murphy are legally married. Mr Murphy makes a will. They have no children and live in a house which is registered in Mr Murphy's sole name.
>
> Mr Murphy dies and when his will is read it appears that under his will he has left everything to charity.
>
> The value of Mr Murphy's estate is €2 million. Regardless of the will of Mr Murphy, his spouse is entitled to:
>
> - The family home *and*
> - One-half of the share of Mr Murphy's estate to include the family home.
>
> If in this example, Mr and Mrs Murphy had children, but the facts were exactly the same, Mrs Murphy would be entitled to only one-third of the value of the estate (to include the family home).

STATUS OF CHILDREN UNDER A WILL

If a party dies leaving children and no surviving spouse, these children will be deemed to be the next of kin of the deceased and entitled to share in the estate of the deceased.

However, they are only entitled to share in the estate of the deceased because they are the next of kin of the deceased for legal purposes.

It is a common misconception that an individual has an obligation to their children to leave a portion of their estate to them. Unlike a wife or husband (spouse), children over the age of eighteen have no right to share in the estate of their parents and rank as a beneficiary to the estate of a parent purely in their position as next of kin.

A child (again over the age of 18) of a deceased person who has been disinherited in a will may challenge this will in the courts on very strict legal grounds to the extent that the parent **failed during their lifetime to make proper provision for the child.**

Just because a child has a right to challenge the will of a parent, this does not mean that the parent has an obligation under law to leave anything to that child in their will. Irish children beware!

Confusion often arises because spouses have certain rights in the estate of a deceased person by virtue of the fact that they were married to the deceased, plus the fact that children often share in the estates of deceased persons not because they are children, but because they are legally the next of kin of the deceased. In other words, a party may make a will during their lifetime wherein they endeavour to disinherit their spouse and children. Once he or she has passed away, the spouse has an automatic right to share in the estate despite what is in the will but the children do not have such automatic right. However, if a party dies without making a will, the children may share in the estate of the deceased person by virtue of the fact that they are the next of kin.

NON-MARITAL CHILDREN

The status of children born to an individual outside marriage is exactly the same as children born inside marriage.

For example, a couple may have never married but have three children. If one of them does not make a will and passes away, the partner will not be entitled to any share in the estate of the deceased, but rather the children as next of kin will be entitled to a share. In this example, if the deceased had made a will leaving everything to the surviving partner and the children over the age of 18, the children have no right to share in the estate of the parent who has passed away.

The matter becomes even more complicated in the following example:

A married couple have three children. One party to the marriage has a fourth child outside of the marriage with another party. This parent passes away without making a will: all four children as next of kin are entitled to a proportionate share in the estate of the deceased parent.

NON-MARITAL RELATIONSHIPS

Non-marital partners have no right to share in the estate of a deceased partner. For example, a man and woman may have lived together all their lives as husband and wife (often referred to as a common-law husband or wife) and the male partner passes away without having made a will.

The surviving partner has no right to share in the estate of the deceased

and the estate will be inherited by the next of kin of the deceased person, e.g. parents, brother or perhaps even children.

Accordingly, one can envisage the situation whereby a man and woman live together as husband and wife for thirty years and have three children but never marry. One party to the relationship passes away without having made a will and the surviving party is entitled to no benefit in the estate of the deceased. Instead, the estate passes to the children of the couple as the next of kin, legally speaking, of the deceased person.

THE ROLE OF THE PERSONAL REPRESENTATIVE

When someone dies, it usually becomes clear fairly quickly whether he or she has left a will. If they have, then this will list one or more executors, one of whom will be appointed as the **personal representative** of the deceased.

If a personal representative has not been appointed in the will, or no valid will is in existence, then the courts will appoint an administrator to act as a personal representative (usually the next of kin).

It is the personal representative's or administrator's responsibility to finalise the deceased's affairs. The administrator or executor is usually referred to as the personal representative. The personal representative should within a reasonable period of time collect the deceased's assets, pay any debts and distribute the remaining assets to the beneficiaries.

Obtaining the Grant of Representation

The primary obligation of the personal representative is to obtain a **Grant of Representation**. If somebody has died with a will, they will be entitled to a **Grant of Probate**, and if somebody has died intestate (without a will), they will be granted a **Grant of Representation**.

The grant is made by the Probate Office, which is an office of the High Court. If the application is made for the grant in Dublin, one applies to the Probate Office in the Four Courts. Outside of Dublin, every County Hall or Registrar will have a Probate Office. Only somebody with a valid will may apply for probate. If somebody has died with an invalid will or no will, the personal representative applies for administration rights called **Letters of Administration.**

Commonly, regardless of the status of the will and the estate of the deceased person, somebody is said *to apply for Probate* even if they are applying for a **Grant of Administration.**

The Grant of Representation (i.e., Grant of Probate or Letters of Administration) is an Order from the High Court which allows the party to whom the grant is issued to deal with the affairs of the deceased person. It is effectively a Court Order or an authority from the Court for this person to step into the shoes of the deceased person and carry out the wishes of the deceased person if there is a will or alternatively, deal with the estate as per the law of the land if there is no will.

A Grant of Representation allows the personal representative to execute documents for the sale of property, the lease of property and the remortgage of same, for the transfer of property to other members of the family who may inherit under the will or the law, to close bank accounts, transfer money and discharge debts.

In order to obtain the grant, clearance must be sought from the Revenue Commissioners.

The importance of notifying the tax office

Prior to obtaining the Grant of Representation from the Probate Office, the Personal Representative must settle the deceased's **tax affairs**. Furthermore, before financial institutions can release money, the personal representative must apply to the Capital Taxes Office of the Revenue Commissioners for something called a **Letter of Clearance** – effectively stating that all taxes have been paid to date or are in the process of being paid. Without this Letter of Clearance from the Revenue Commissioners, banks, building societies, credit unions, insurance companies and other financial institutions are prohibited by law from releasing any monies other than those:

- held in a current account lodged or
- deposited in the joint names of the deceased and another person or persons.

The only exception to this is money that is being held in the joint names of the deceased and his or her surviving spouse.

Furthermore, the application to the Revenue Commissioners will also contain details of the beneficiaries to the estate of the deceased person.

A Personal Representative must obtain a Grant from the Probate Office to deal with the affairs of the deceased person. The Probate Office will not release such a Grant until such time as the **Tax Clearance Certificate** or **Letter of Clearance** from the Revenue Commissioners has been delivered which does not just address the tax affairs of the deceased but also the tax affairs of the beneficiaries to the estate.

What the personal representative could be liable for

If the personal representative makes payments or passes assets to the beneficiaries of the estate without paying any outstanding tax liabilities, he or she will be liable to pay the tax out of his or her own pocket. By the same token if, as personal representative, you fail to claim a tax rebate due to the deceased, then the beneficiaries will be entitled to come after you for this money.

If the deceased was an employee, there may be a PAYE tax rebate due. This can be arranged by asking the deceased's employer to send a Form P45 to the tax office. If, on the other hand, the deceased was self-employed, you will need to file an outstanding income tax return and business accounts to the deceased's tax office. Don't forget that you may also need to deal with outstanding VAT and PRSI matters.

Before the Probate Office can process the application for the Grant of Representation, they will require a certified Revenue Affidavit from the Capital Taxes Office. It is the responsibility of the personal representative to provide the Revenue Commissioners with a Revenue Affidavit. The Revenue Affidavit requires the personal representative to supply:

- full details of the deceased's assets and liabilities
- information about assets passing outside of the will
- details of the beneficiaries and the value of the benefits taken.

How the assets are passed on

The deceased's assets will be passed on to the beneficiaries in one of three different ways:

1   Assets left by will pass to the beneficiaries in accordance with the terms of the will.

2   If there is no will, assets that would otherwise have passed by will instead pass by special laws laid down by law.

3   Assets may also pass outside of the will or intestacy.

The benefits of Joint Ownership

Regardless of the law in relationship to intestacy or the will drafted by an individual, the **Rule of Joint Ownership** is extremely important. Joint Ownership effectively takes precedence over either the law or the will.

Under law, two parties or more can own property in two ways. They can own it as **Tenants in Common** or by **Joint Tenancy**. I do not propose to set out in depth details of the differences between Joint Tenancy and Tenants in Common as this is a very particular legal issue, but it is important that the concept be understood – particularly in relation to any post-death planning.

When two parties or more are said to own property as Tenants in Common, they are said to own shares in that property. For example:

> Mr Murphy and Mr Smith buy a house as **Tenants in Common**. They own a half share each. On the death of either person, their share is passed on to that person's devisees or heirs, either by will or by intestate succession.

If in our example given above, Mr Murphy and Mr Smith buy a property and own the same as **joint tenants**, they do not own shares in the property but rather they own the property jointly.

If Mr Smith were to die, Mr Murphy would be the surviving/remaining owner of the property and would be deemed to automatically inherit the property. If, for example, Mr Murphy, Mr Smith and Mr Jones were to purchase a property as **joint owners** and Mr Smith were to pass away, Mr Murphy and Mr Jones would be the surviving joint owners. If Mr Jones were then to pass away Mr Murphy would be the remaining owner of the property.

The relevance of Joint Ownership is extremely pertinent, particularly in relation to family financial planning. If a husband and wife have bank accounts in joint names, they do not own shares in this bank account but rather they own the bank account jointly. If the husband or wife pass away, the surviving spouse is said to be the surviving or remaining owner of the property, i.e., the bank account.

The same concept applies to all property, including the family home. If a family home is held in joint names, neither the husband nor wife own a share of the property but rather own the property jointly. If one party passes away the other is deemed to be the surviving owner of the property.

Regardless of the law or any will made, if property is held jointly it cannot be severed.

HOW IS IT THAT ASSETS CAN PASS OUTSIDE OF THE WILL OR INTESTACY?

This is best explained by an example. The deceased may have taken out a life insurance policy or pension scheme where the beneficiaries have been named. Under these circumstances, the insurance or pension company would pay the beneficiaries directly without any reference to the will or estate.

THE MONEY DOCTOR SAYS...

- Sorting out the financial dealings of someone who has passed on is an emotional business. Help whoever will be looking after your affairs by making a proper will and keeping a file somewhere containing all your financial documents.

- Many parties believe that there is no necessity to make a will as they are happy to allow their spouse or their next of kin inherit as per the Succession Act Rules. However, a will should *always* be made – this means that the estate is distributed more quickly and also distributed in accordance with your wishes – there may be relatives, next of kin or bequests you may want to acknowledge. Remember it is also a simple process – you will need two independent witnesses (who cannot gain from the will) and a nominated person to execute your wishes (executor/executrix), then date the will and sign it.

- It is extremely important if you are involved in a non-marital relationship to ensure that you have proper wills drafted to ensure inheritance for your surviving partner and your or their children.

- It is also important to take professional and perhaps legal advice in relation to the drafting and execution of a will especially where there are complications. Many homemade wills can be ineffective and can often lead to further confusion after death. Remember: the bulk of wealth in Ireland is in property – to convey the transfer of ownership, a solicitor will be required to effect same.

- One other reason for making a will is you can direct who is your Personal Representative and who is charged with the responsibility of dealing with your affairs after your death. This way, you will avoid any application to the Courts to appoint somebody who is inappropriate for that purpose.

- Many people apply to the Revenue Commissioners and the Probate Office to be appointed as the Personal Representative of the deceased themselves. Both the Revenue Commissioners and the Probate Office are extremely co-operative when dealing with members of the public. Again, depending on the complexity of the estate, legal accounting and financial advice should be sought prior to contact with these offices.

- Ensure that all family and marital property is held jointly, including the family home – it is better for all concerned.

- If involved in a non-marital relationship, both partners should ensure that all property is held *jointly* as the death of one partner will ensure the other partner inherits, which is denied under law or via the will.

35
PERSONAL INSOLVENCY AND BANKRUPTCY

Since 2006, property prices have dropped by up to 70% and personal debt has risen to unprecedented levels. In some cases, the personal debt has arisen from day-to-day living costs and/or maintaining debt repayments – a vicious circle. Stories of families paying their mortgage rather than putting food on the table abound. With debt levels and mortgage arrears on the increase, several legislative initiatives have been launched to help people with arrears and those for whom the only option is bankruptcy.

The term 'bankrupt' comes from two Latin words: *bancus*, meaning the bench on which moneylenders used to ply their trade in the markets many years ago, and *ruptus*, meaning broken; a moneylender would break his bench once he ran out of money or could not pay back his creditors.

Very simply, when you do not have income to service your debt, and you have no assets to sell in order to repay that debt, then your creditor can bring you to court and have a 'judgment' served against you. This effectively means:

- The judgement stays there against your credit record with the Irish Credit Bureau (www.icb.ie – for €6 you can order your own credit report).
- If you repay what is owed, a 'satisfaction' is registered, but the judgment is recorded and remains on your credit history for life.
- Borrowing again from a financial institution or creditor with a judgment against you is extremely unlikely.
- When you cannot or are unwilling to repay, the final procedure is bankruptcy.

Declaring bankruptcy in Ireland was not only regarded as a slight on your character, but you were also banned from running a business or borrowing, at least in your own name, for 12 years. That is, until now.

In the UK, there are 50,000 bankruptcies every year, while in the US, it is over one million annually! In the UK, the Insolvency Act 1986 brought into effect a real, workable alternative to bankruptcy proceedings known as Individual Voluntary Arrangements (IVAs). This process – in which Court involvement is limited – has been greatly simplified and ensures a cheaper, more expeditious distribution of the debtor's assets to his creditors than under bankruptcy. It also provides greater flexibility to both debtor and creditor alike, and offers a possibility of reviving a previously unsuccessful business. It offers the debtor an opportunity to come to some arrangement with his creditors and to continue in business, which is not possible in the event of bankruptcy. The arrangement must be implemented by a supervisor, who is usually a licensed Insolvency Practitioner, accountant or solicitor and who is usually empowered to realise the debtor's assets and distribute the proceeds amongst the creditors in the priority set down by law. Bankrupts are discharged after 12 months in the UK from all debts worldwide.

Bankruptcy is defined as a law for the benefit and relief of creditors and their debtors in cases where the latter are unable or unwilling to pay their debts. Essentially, it is a procedure whereby the assets of an individual debtor are distributed equitably among his creditors. The procedure is instigated either by the debtor himself filing for his own bankruptcy, or by an aggrieved creditor petitioning the Courts.

One of the new Irish legislative changes saw the proposed reduction of the period for automatic discharge from bankruptcy down from 12 years to 3 years through the Personal Insolvency Bill published in June 2012. Minister for Justice Mr Alan Shatter stated on the launch that 'This Bill does not relieve solvent debtors of their responsibility to meet their contractual obligations.'

The reform of Ireland's bankruptcy laws was a condition of the EU/IMF bailout agreement, and the three-year discharge period is in line with recommendations made by the Law Reform Commission (LRC) in 2010.

The last five savage years have changed all government thinking on debt. First of all, the lenders and the Central Bank recognised the need to help borrowers, especially those with home loans. With over 10% of all home mortgages in arrears of 3 months or more, steps had to be taken to lighten the load of the hard-pressed borrower. As Taoiseach Enda Kenny stated, 'It's not your fault'; house prices dropped by up to 70% as unemployment rose to 14.8%. Even if properties could be sold, householders were staring at massive deficits they were unable to repay – plus, of course, they still had to live somewhere.

THE MORTGAGE ARREARS RESOLUTION PROCESS (MARP)

The first initiative was the **Mortgage Arrears Resolution Process (MARP)**, a system for helping mortgage holders with their arrears, introduced in December 2010.

The Central Bank's Code of Conduct on Mortgage Arrears (CCMA) sets out the framework that lenders *must* use when dealing with borrowers in mortgage arrears or in pre-arrears. It requires lenders to handle all such cases sympathetically and positively, with the objective at all times of helping people to meet their mortgage obligations.

Under the CCMA, lenders must operate a MARP when dealing with arrears and pre-arrears customers.

The 5 steps of the MARP are summarised below. They are

1 *communication*
2 *financial information*
3 *assessment*
4 *resolution*
5 *appeals*

Where a borrower co-operates with his or her lender, the lender must wait at least 12 months from the date the case is treated as a MARP case – namely, 31 days after arrears first arise – before seeking to repossess.

If these 5 steps have been exhausted, and the lender intends to repossess your home, they must then adhere to the MARP rules governing repossession proceedings.

Communication

A mortgage arrears problem arises as soon as you fail to make a full mortgage repayment or make only a partial mortgage repayment on the date it is due.

If the arrears remain outstanding 31 days from this date, the lender must inform you in writing of the status of the mortgage account. This letter must include full details of the payment(s) missed and the total amount now in arrears. It must also explain that your arrears are now being dealt with under the MARP; the importance of cooperating with the lender; the consequences of non-cooperation; and the impact of missed repayments/repossession on your credit rating. You should also receive an information booklet on MARP and contact details for The Money Advice and Budgeting Service (MABS).

For as long as you are in arrears, the lender must give you a written update of the status of your account every 3 months.

If no alternative payment scheme is arranged and your state of arrears continues to a third consecutive month, you should be warned of the possibility of legal action, which could lead to repossession and the likely costs involved.

Financial information

Lenders must provide a Standard Financial Statement (SFS) to obtain financial information from a borrower who is in arrears or in pre-arrears so that they can assess your financial position and identify the best course of action. The Central Bank has developed a standard format for this, and since 1 July 2011, all lenders must use this SFS, together with a guide to its completion. When providing the financial statement, the lender must ensure that the borrower understands the MARP. They must tell you about the availability of independent advice (from MABS, for example) for help in completing the SFS.

The lender must pass the completed SFS to its Arrears Support Unit (ASU) for assessment.

You may be required to provide supporting documentation to verify the information in the SFS.

Assessment

The lender's Arrears Support Unit must assess the completed SFS and examine the borrower's case on its individual merits. The ASU must base its assessment of your case on your full circumstances. These include your personal circumstances; overall indebtedness; information provided in the standard financial statement; current repayment capacity; and previous payment history.

Resolution

The lender must explore all options for alternative repayment arrangements. These options must include:

- an interest-only arrangement for a specified period
- an arrangement to pay interest and part of the normal capital element for a specified period

- deferring payment of all or part of the usual repayment for a period
- extending the term of the mortgage
- changing the type of the mortgage, except in the case of tracker mortgages
- capitalising the arrears and interest, and
- any voluntary scheme to which the lender has signed up, e.g. Deferred Interest Scheme.

The lender must not require you to change from an existing tracker mortgage to another mortgage type as part of any alternative arrangement being offered.

When the lender is offering an alternative repayment arrangement, they must give you a clear written explanation of the arrangement. As well as the basic details of the new repayment amount and the term of the arrangement, the lender must explain its impact on the mortgage term, the balance outstanding and the existing arrears, if any.

The lender must give details of the following: how interest will be applied to your mortgage loan account as a result of the arrangement; how the arrangement will be reported to the Irish Credit Bureau and the impact of this on your credit rating; and information on your right to appeal the lender's decision, including how to submit an appeal.

The lender must also advise you to take appropriate independent legal and/or financial advice. The lender must monitor the arrangement on an ongoing basis and formally review its appropriateness for you at least every 6 months. This review must include checking with you as to whether your circumstances have changed since the start of the arrangement or since the last review.

IF AN ALTERNATIVE ARRANGEMENT IS NOT AGREED

It may not be possible for you and your lender to agree on an alternative repayment. If the lender is not willing to offer you an alternative repayment arrangement, they must give their reasons in writing. If they do offer an arrangement, you may choose not to accept it. In both of these cases, the lender must inform you in writing about other options, including voluntary surrender, trading down or voluntary sale, and the implications for you of each option. They must also inform you of your right to make an appeal to their Appeals Board about the ASU's decision, the lender's treatment of your case under the MARP, or their compliance with the requirements of the CCMA. The lender must also inform you that the 12-month moratorium on taking legal action will no longer apply to your case if you do not make an appeal.

IF YOU BREACH AN ALTERNATIVE ARRANGEMENT

If you cease to adhere to the terms of an alternative repayment arrangement, the lender's Arrears Support Unit must formally review your case, including the standard financial statement, immediately.

Appeals

The lender's Appeals Board will consider any appeals that you submit and will independently review the ASU's decision, the lender's treatment of your case under the MARP and the lender's compliance with the requirements of the CCMA.

The lender must allow you a reasonable period to consider submitting an appeal. This must be at least 20 business days from the date you receive notification of the ASU's decision.

The Appeals Board will be made up of three of the lender's senior personnel who have not yet been involved in your case. At least one member of the Appeals Board must be independent of the management team and must not be involved in lending matters.

There must be a written procedure for handling appeals, to include points of contact, timescale, etc.

Repossession proceedings

The lender must not apply to the courts to commence legal action for repossession of your property until every reasonable effort has been made to agree an alternative arrangement. If you are cooperating with the lender, they must wait at least 12 months from the date your arrears were classified as a MARP case (31 days after the first missed repayment) before applying to the courts.

Your property may be repossessed either by voluntary agreement or by court order. Even if court proceedings have started, the lender must still try to maintain contact with you to seek an agreement on repayments, and must put legal proceedings on hold if agreement is reached.

The lender must explain to you that, if the property is sold and the sale price does not cover the amount you owe, you are still liable for the rest of the amount you owe.

If your property is repossessed and sold, the lender must write to you promptly with the following information:

- any balance outstanding on your mortgage loan account
- details and amount of any costs arising from the disposal which have been added to the account
- interest rate to be charged on any remaining balance.

Having gone through the above process, and perhaps through no fault of your own, you may be one of the many who simply lack the wherewithal to maintain your commitments. The old saying 'you can't get blood from a stone' now rings true for many who would be happy to divest themselves of any assets that could repay their debts. Unfortunately, these assets, even if sold, may not repay these debts.

PERSONAL INSOLVENCY BILL 2012

In January 2012, the government announced plans to launch the Personal Insolvency Bill later in the year to address the outdated bankruptcy laws and to allow dignity back into debtors' lives by creating closure on debts they are unable to repay via a non-judicial process.

Under the proposals unveiled by Justice Minister Alan Shatter and published on 29 June 2012, the new Personal Insolvency Service will be established to process three separate types of non-judicial arrangement. But how will they work in practice?

Debt Relief Notice (DRN)

This will provide for the forgiveness of unsecured debt (such as an overdraft or credit card debt) under €20,000 for debtors with little or no capacity to pay off debts – described as 'no assets, no income'. The debtor will apply to the Insolvency Service, which will examine the income and outgoings of the applicant and decide whether a DRN is appropriate. If granted, a 3-year moratorium period will apply during which creditors cannot pursue action against the debtor for the debts covered by the DRN. At the end of the 3-year moratorium period, the applicant is discharged from the debts. Applications for a DRN must be submitted on behalf of the debtor by an authorised approved intermediary body such as MABS.

This approved intermediary would:

1. Advise the debtor as to their options and the qualifying requirements.
2. Assist in the preparation of the necessary Prescribed or Standard Financial Statement (SFS), which must be verified by means of a statutory declaration, plus include any other required documentation.
3. Transmit the debtor's application to the Insolvency Service to have a DRN approved if the qualifying criteria are met.

General conditions of application for a DRN

- Debtors would have qualifying debts of €20,000 or less.
- Debtors would not be eligible where 25 per cent or more of the qualifying debts were incurred in the 6 months preceding the application.
- Debts qualifying for inclusion in a DRN are most likely to be unsecured debts: e.g. credit card, personal loan, catalogue payments, etc.
- Debtors will have a net monthly disposable income of €60 or less after provision for 'reasonable' living expenses and payments in respect of excluded debts (if any).
- Debtors would hold assets (separately or jointly) to the value of €400 or less. There is an exemption from the asset test for essential household appliances, tools, etc., required for employment or business and one motor vehicle up to value of €1,200.
- Debtors must act in good faith and cooperate fully.
- Debts excluded from a DRN include: taxes, court fines, family maintenance payments and service charges arrears.

After the Insolvency Service has received the application, and is satisfied with same, they shall issue a certificate to that effect and furnish the certificate and supporting documentation to the court. The court then will consider the application and, if satisfied, issue the DRN and notify the Insolvency Service, which in turn notifies the approved intermediary and the creditors of the issue of the DRN and registers it in the Register of Debt Relief Notices.

During the DRN period, creditors may not initiate or prosecute legal proceedings or seek to recover payment for a debt or recover goods or contact the debtor.

The DRN period lasts for 3 years from date of issue. At the end of the DRN period, (and subject to no other action) the DRN terminates and the qualifying debts are discharged and the debtor will be removed from the Register of Debt Relief Notices.

Only one DRN per lifetime is permitted, and it must not fall within 5 years of the completion of a Debt Settlement Arrangement (DSA) or Personal Insolvency Arrangement (PIA). There is a restriction on the debtor from applying for credit over €650 during the DRN supervision period without informing the creditor of his/her status.

The debtor must inform the authorised intermediary and the Insolvency Service of any material change in financial circumstances. So as not to reduce the incentive to seek and obtain employment following approval of a DRN, there is provision for the debtor to repay a portion of the debts in circumstances where his/her financial situation improves. These circumstances include the receipt of gifts or windfalls over €500, such as from a Lotto win, or where the debtor's income has increased by over €250 per month. The debtor will transmit funds to the Insolvency Service to be paid on an equal basis to the listed creditors.

Should a debtor make repayments totalling 50 per cent of the original debt, the debtor will be deemed to have satisfied the debts in full, the DRN will cease to have effect and the debtor will be removed from the Register and all of the debts will be discharged.

Debt Settlement Arrangement (DSA)

This provision also covers unsecured debt, but is concerned with debts *above* €20,000. In this case the Insolvency *Service* would design a plan in which the debtor would pay a specified amount to creditors over a 5-year period, with a possible agreed extension to 6 years, after which the debts would be discharged. The creditors would be required to approve the DSA agreement.

The application for a DSA must be made through a Personal Insolvency Practitioner (PIP) appointed by the debtor. The PIP must:

1. Advise the debtor as to their options in regard to insolvency processes
2. Assist in the preparation of the necessary Prescribed or Standard Financial

Statement (SFS) which must be verified by means of a statutory declaration, plus any other required documentation.

3. Apply to the Insolvency Service for a **Protective Certificate** in respect of the preparation of a DSA if the qualifying criteria are met. A joint application is permitted where the particular circumstances might warrant such an approach. The debtor must normally be resident in the State or have a close connection to it. Only one application for a DSA is permitted in a lifetime.

Certain debts are excluded from the DSA, including Court fines in respect of a criminal offence. In addition, certain other debts are also excluded, such as family maintenance payments, taxes, local authority charges and service charges, unless the relevant creditor agrees otherwise. In addition, any debt that would have a preferential status in bankruptcy will also have a preferential status in a DSA.

The Insolvency Service, if satisfied as to the application, shall issue a certificate to that effect and furnish the certificate and supporting document-ation to the court. The court will consider the application and, subject to the creditors' right to appeal, if satisfied, issue the Protective Certificate and notify the Insolvency Service. Once such an approval is granted, the Protective Certificate is registered in the Register of Protective Certificates and a 'stand-still' period of 70 days applies to permit the PIP to propose a DSA to the listed creditors. That period may, on application to the court, be extended for no more than a further 40 days. The PIP will inform the creditors of the issue of the Protective Certificate.

The effect of the issue of the Protective Certificate is that the creditors may not initiate or prosecute legal proceedings or seek to recover payment for a debt or recover goods or contact the debtor. The rights of secured creditors are unaffected.

A DSA proposal does not require the debtor to dispose of or cease to occupy their principal private residence (their home) where appropriate. If the DSA proposal is accepted (by 65% in value of the creditors present and voting) it is binding on all creditors. The PIP shall inform the Insolvency Service who shall then transmit the agreement to the relevant court for approval. If satisfied, and if no objection is received by it within 10 days, the court shall approve the DSA and notify the Insolvency Service, which will register it in the Register of Debt Settlement Agreements, whereupon it comes into effect. The PIP will then administer the DSA for its duration.

The Insolvency Service has *no* role in the negotiation and agreement of a DSA.

While there is provision for a wide range of repayment options, the default position unless otherwise agreed is that creditors be paid on an equal or proportionate basis. Conditions attach to the conduct of the debtor during the DSA. There is provision for an annual review of the financial circumstances of the debtor, and the agreement could, if necessary, be varied or terminated. On the termination or failure of the DSA, a debtor could risk an application for adjudication in bankruptcy.

At the satisfactory conclusion of the DSA, all debts covered by it are discharged.

Personal Insolvency Arrangement (PIA)

This arrangement is designed to cover both secured and unsecured debt, and will be appropriate if the Insolvency Service concludes that a 5-year DSA would not be sufficient to make the debtor solvent. Under this provision, a portion of the unsecured debt would be written off and the remainder repaid over a 6–year period, possibly extended to 7 years. The secured debt, a mortgage for example, would also be written down, and its repayment period extended, reducing the repayments further. The creditors would also be required to approve the PIA and, should the debtors' financial circumstances improve over the course of the PIA, they are obliged to notify the Insolvency Service.

The application for a PIA must be made through a Personal Insolvency Practitioner (PIP) appointed by the debtor. The PIP must:

1. Advise the debtor as to their options in regard to insolvency processes. A debtor may only propose a PIA if he or she is cash-flow insolvent (i.e. unable to pay his or her debts in full as they fall due) and there is no likelihood within a period of 5 years that the debtor will become solvent.
2. Assist in the preparation of the necessary Prescribed or Standard Financial Statement (SFS), which must be verified by means of a statutory declaration and any other required documentation.
3. May apply to the Insolvency Service for a Protective Certificate in respect of the preparation of a PIA, if the qualifying criteria are met, (which includes cooperation with the secured creditor in respect of the debtor's principal private residence, under a mortgage arrears process approved or required by the Central Bank.) A joint application or an interlocking PIA is permitted

where the particular circumstances might warrant such approach. The debtor must normally be resident in the State or have a close connection. Only one application for a PIA is permitted in a lifetime.

Certain debts are excluded from the PIA, including Court fines in respect of a criminal offence. In addition, certain other debts are also excluded, such as family maintenance payments, taxes, local authority charges and service charges, unless the relevant creditor agrees otherwise. In addition, any debt that would have a preferential status in bankruptcy will also have a preferential status in a PIA as with the DSA.

The Insolvency Service, being satisfied as to the application, shall issue a certificate to that effect and furnish the certificate and supporting documentation to the court. The court will consider the application and, subject to the creditors' right to appeal, if satisfied, issue the Protective Certificate and notify the Insolvency Service.

Once such approval is granted, the Protective Certificate is registered in the Register of Protective Certificates and a 'stand-still' period of 70 days applies to permit the PIP to propose a PIA to the listed creditors. That period may, on application to the court, be extended for no more than a further 40 days. The PIP will inform the creditors of the issue of the Protective Certificate.

The effect of the issue of the Protective Certificate is that the creditors may not initiate or prosecute legal proceedings or seek to recover payment for a debt or recover goods, enforce security or contact the debtor.

A PIA proposal does not require the debtor to dispose of or cease to occupy their principal private residence where appropriate. There are certain specific protections for secured creditors, including a 'claw-back' in the event of a subsequent sale of a mortgaged property where the mortgage has been written down.

If the PIA proposal is accepted, it is binding on all creditors. A PIA must be supported by at least 65% (it was 75% originally) of all creditors voting at the creditors meeting (based on the value of the total of both secured and unsecured debt owed to those voting creditors) and more than 50% of secured creditors voting (based on the lesser of value of the security underpinning the secured debt or the amount of that debt) and 50% of unsecured creditors (based on the amount of the debt).

The PIP shall inform the Insolvency Service of the agreement, and the Service will then transmit the agreement to the relevant court for approval.

If satisfied, and if no objection is received by it within 10 days, the court shall approve the PIA and notify the Insolvency Service will register it in the Register of Personal Insolvency Arrangements and it comes into effect. The PIP will then administer the PIA for its duration.

Conditions attach to the conduct of the debtor during the PIA. There is provision for an annual review of the financial circumstances of the debtor and the agreement could if necessary be varied or terminated. On the termination or failure of the PIA, a debtor could risk an application for adjudication in bankruptcy.

The Insolvency Service has *no* role in the negotiation and agreement of a PIA.

At the satisfactory conclusion of the PIA all unsecured debts covered by it are discharged. Secured debts are only discharged at the conclusion of the PIA, if and to the extent, specified in the PIA. To the extent that they are not provided for in the PIA, all other debt obligations will remain.

Bankruptcy

The Bill also provides for a number of amendments to the Bankruptcy Act 1988 to provide for a more enlightened, less punitive and costly approach to bankruptcy. These amendments will continue the reform of bankruptcy law begun in the Civil Law (Miscellaneous Provisions) Act 2011. The main new provisions are as follows:

- A creditor bankruptcy summons:
  - The new minimum amount for a creditor or combined non-partner creditors petition for bankruptcy is €20,000. (The current limits are €1,900 for a creditor and €1,300 for combined non-partner creditors).
  - Fourteen days' notice must be provided to ensure that a bankruptcy summons is not brought prematurely by a creditor, so as to allow the debtor to consider other options such as a Debt Settlement Arrangement (DSA) or a Personal Insolvency Arrangement (PIA).
  - Presenting a petition for bankruptcy: the creditor must prove for a debt of more than €20,000 (the current limit is €1,900). Where a debtor presents a petition, they must:
    - swear an affidavit that they have made reasonable efforts to make use of alternatives to bankruptcy, such as a Debt Settlement Arrangement or Personal Insolvency Arrangement;

❑ present a statement of affairs, which must disclose that their debts exceed their assets by more than €20,000.

- Adjudication of a creditor's petition for bankruptcy: the court will be required to consider the assets and liabilities of the debtor and assess whether it may be appropriate to adjourn proceedings to allow the debtor to attempt to enter into a Debt Settlement Arrangement or Personal Insolvency Arrangement.

- Excepted articles: the maximum value of household furniture or tools or equipment required by a bankrupt for a trade or occupation is increased from the current level of €3,100 to €6,000.

- Avoidance of fraudulent preferences and certain transactions made before adjudication in bankruptcy: the current time period of 1 year is extended to 3 years.

- Avoidance of certain settlements: the time periods in regard to certain voluntary settlements of property made before adjudication in bankruptcy is extended from 2 years to 3 years.

- Discharge from bankruptcy: the following new provisions will apply:

  ◆ The automatic discharge from bankruptcy after 3 years from the date of adjudication (reduced from the current 12 years).

  ◆ Bankruptcies existing for 3 years or more at the time of commencement of the Act will be automatically discharged after a further six months have elapsed, this latter time to allow for any creditor objection.

  ◆ The bankrupt's unrealised property will remain vested in the Official Assignee in Bankruptcy after discharge from bankruptcy and the discharged bankrupt will be under a duty to cooperate with the Official Assignee in the realisation and distribution of such of his or her property as is vested in the Official Assignee.

  ◆ The Official Assignee or a creditor may apply to the court to object to the discharge of a person from bankruptcy. The grounds for such an objection are that the debtor has failed to cooperate with the Official Assignee or has hidden or failed to disclose income or assets. The court may suspend the discharge pending further investigation or extend the period before discharge of the bankrupt up to a maximum of 8 years from the date of adjudication.

  ◆ The court may order a bankrupt to make payments from his or her income or other assets to the Official Assignee for the benefit of his or her creditors. In making such an order, the court must have regard to the reasonable living expenses of the bankrupt and his or her family. The court may vary a bankruptcy payment order where there has been a material change in the circumstances of the discharged bankrupt. Such an order must be applied for before the discharge from bankruptcy and may operate for no more than 5 years.

There are no prohibitions contained in the Bankruptcy Act 1988 with regard to restrictions on the nature of employment or profession of a person adjudicated bankrupt. Such prohibitions, where they exist, are contained in sectoral legislation, e.g. in the Electoral Acts in regard to membership of Dáil Éireann or in contracts of employment, e.g. in the legal profession.

Regulation of Personal Insolvency Practitioners

The Bill in Part 5 provides for an enabling provision in regard to the regulation of Personal Insolvency Practitioners (PIPs). However, a definitive approach to the regulation of PIPs, be they members of the legal or accountancy professions or other qualified persons, awaits final decision. Consultations will continue between the Departments of Finance and Justice and Equality and the Central Bank in that regard, and will likely be the subject of a legislative proposal at a later stage.

APPENDIX 1
THE MONEY DOCTOR'S JARGON
BUSTER

Have you ever noticed that with most contracts, the writing becomes smaller as you read through it and the jargon becomes indecipherable? Financial institutions in particular have nurtured their reputation for being as obtuse, confusing and ambiguous as possible in their use of the English language. All you have to do is look at a loan offer and you will see what I mean. *Caveat emptor* and all that, but the caveats, while no doubt valid and necessary, are never fully explained. Therefore, it is hugely important in the first instance to know what some of these words and phrases mean – in plain English. In this appendix, I explain many of these financial terms.

If you would like to see any specific jargon that is not covered in this year's edition explained in *next year*'s edition, please write to me at jlowe@moneydoctor.ie.

ACCIDENT INSURANCE
An insurance policy that pays out a lump sum if you suffer an injury. For instance, you might receive €20,000 for the loss of a limb, or €50,000 for the loss of your sight.

ADDITIONAL VOLUNTARY CONTRIBUTIONS (AVCs)
Extra payments that you make in addition to the normal pension contributions (or premiums) that you or your employer already make if you are a member of an employer pension plan. AVCs help to boost the value of your pension fund or can be used to contribute to a tax-free lump sum on retirement. You can claim tax relief on AVCs up to certain limits, as long as you earn an income.

ADMINISTRATION FEE
A fee paid to a financial services provider for a service or product.

ALLOCATION RATE

The percentage of your money used to buy units in a pension or investment fund. For example, if you invest €100, and €2 goes towards charges and set-up costs, then your allocation rate is 98%.

ANNUAL EQUIVALENT RATE (AER)

This shows what the interest on a savings account would be if the interest were compounded and paid out on a yearly basis. This can be used as a basis of comparison for savings plans that may be of less than or greater than 12 months duration. See also Compound Annual Return.

ANNUAL PERCENTAGE RATE (APR)

The way in which lenders express the rate of interest and charges they're making. You should always compare annual percentage rates before taking out any loan, and you should bear in mind that there are different ways of calculating the cost of any debt.

ANNUITY

A fixed amount of money paid to you as an income for a particular length of time. The length of time may be the rest of your life (lifetime annuity) or for a set period (temporary annuity). You buy an annuity using a lump sum of money. Once you've purchased it you cannot get your original capital back, and you are locked in to the income agreed at the outset.

ANNUITY RATE

Compares how much an investment will pay you each year with the size of the lump sum required to buy it.

APPROVED MINIMUM RETIREMENT FUND (AMRF)

A type of personal pension fund in which the capital may not be reduced below a fixed limit before age 75.

APPROVED RETIREMENT FUND (ARF)

A personal retirement fund – after you make provision for an AMRF if necessary – where you keep your pension invested in a lump sum after retirement. Withdrawals that you make from this fund in order to give yourself an income are taxable.

ASSETS

Physical items such as land, or intangible items such as goodwill, that are owned by a company or a person. Asset Finance is a loan secured by that asset, whether it is a car, boat, helicopter, etc.

AVERAGE CLAUSE

This refers to a condition included in some home insurance policies that limits what you can claim if you are under-insured, e.g. if the contents of your home are worth €50,000, but you insure them for €25,000, you are under-insured by 50%. If your contents are damaged, destroyed or stolen, the most you will receive from your insurance company is 50% of the claim on your loss.

BALLOON PAYMENT

A reference to one large final payment due at the end of a loan agreement, such as car finance or other short-term loans. It is used to keep monthly payments lower throughout the duration of the loan, but must be paid to complete the agreement and to allow you to become the owner of the goods at that point.

BEAR MARKET

A falling stock market; the opposite of a bull market.

BENEFIT STATEMENT

A statement giving details of your pension plan, which your pension provider must supply you with annually.

BID–SPREAD OFFER

Refers to an investment charge and to the difference between the buying and selling price of a unit in an investment or pension fund on any given day. A typical bid–spread offer would be 5%; this means that if you invest €1000 in a pension or investment fund, its value would be €950 (€1000 less 5%) if you withdrew the funds immediately. The buying and selling prices of these units in a fund depend on the value of the assets in the fund, sometimes referred to as the underlying assets.

BOILER ROOMS

In financial circles, this is the name given to unauthorised and unscrupulous

investment companies that use high-pressure sales tactics to sell worthless or
high-risk shares, foreign currency or other 'investments' to unsuspecting
investors. Once bought, these shares are impossible to offload or sell.

BOND
A certificate of debt raised by individuals, companies or governments; in other
words, a way for them to borrow money. Bonds can have a fixed date of
repayment or a variable one. The dividend (i.e. the payment or return you
receive for investing in the bond) is known as the coupon.

BULL MARKET
A prolonged rise in the stock market; the opposite of a bear market.

BUY-OUT BOND
A fund into which you can transfer your employer pension fund if you leave or
change job.

CAPITAL
In essence, the total resources you have, or the amount you have available to
invest, or the amount you originally invested.

CAPITAL GAINS TAX
A tax on the increase in value of assets during your period of ownership. Once
an asset is purchased, if the value increases from day one, it is said to have
made a Capital Gain. Governments the world over tax this gain so that they
can share in your good fortune.

CHARGE CARD
A plastic card that enables a customer to purchase goods or services to be
charged to a current account or store account. Charge cards are subject to a
credit limit and _must_ be cleared in full regularly – every month if there is an
outstanding balance. No interest charges are applied.

COLLATERAL
Usually, assets such as property or investments that a lender will accept as
security for a loan, which can be easily converted to cash in the event of the
loan not being repaid.

COMMISSION
A payment to a sales person or adviser, usually based on the value of the sale from the supplier of the product.

COMPOUND ANNUAL RETURN (CAR)
This is a measure of the rate of return on a deposit or investment and it enables you to make a direct comparison between various savings schemes.

COMPOUND GROWTH
The process by which interest-bearing savings grow. If, for example, you invest €10,000 in a deposit account attracting 5%, at the end of the year, you will have a balance of €10,500.

CONTRACTS FOR DIFFERENCE (CFDs)
The **Futures & Options** market is a mechanism for buying a small percentage of a commodity or share ownership now, with a maturity date upon which you must then pay the full price. Essentially, you are betting that the price will be lower or higher on that date. CFDs do not have a maturity date, but if the contract goes below 80% of the original price at the time of purchase, the difference is called in at that point.

CONVEYANCING
A legal term for the process of transferring ownership of a property from seller to buyer and carried out by a solicitor.

CORPORATE BOND
A fixed-interest bond raised by a company. See **Bond**.

COST OF CREDIT
The full cost of borrowing money that shows the difference between the amount you borrow and what you will have repaid at the end of the loan period, plus any other extras such as valuation fees.

CREDIT CARD
A plastic card from a credit card company that makes funds available to you to an agreed limit. The monthly bill – you can receive over 30 days free credit – must be paid within a certain time, or be subject to an interest charge if only

the minimum is paid. This minimum amount is less than 5% of the total bill, but because of some credit card company interest rates, it can take you over 11 years to repay this debt if you are only repaying the minimum balance each month.

CREDIT HISTORY

Your repayment history on all loans with the front-line credit institutions – all 42 members – in Ireland is tracked by the Irish Credit Bureau based in Newstead, Clonskeagh, Dublin 14. Lenders will use this information to assess your credit worthiness. Missed payments stay on record for 5 years while a judgment (in which you are successfully sued in court by a creditor whom you owe money) is there for life. Guard your good name!

CREDIT INSURANCE

Sometimes called payment protection insurance, this insurance covers the monthly cost of a debt for a limited period (usually a year) if you can't work because of illness or unemployment. For instance, you might take out credit insurance to cover your mortgage payments.

CREST

CREST is the electronic settlement system used to buy and sell shares on the London and Irish stock market exchanges. CREST also offers investors the opportunity to hold their shares in electronic form in their own name through personal membership.

CRITICAL ILLNESS INSURANCE

This insurance pays out a lump sum if you're diagnosed with or suffer from any of a list of life-threatening conditions. For instance, if you have a heart attack or cancer you would receive a pre-agreed amount of money. This is also referred to as serious illness insurance.

CURRENT ACCOUNT MORTGAGE

A mortgage – linked to your bank current account – that allows you to vary your monthly payments. By over-paying each month you can save yourself a substantial amount of interest and shorten the length of your mortgage by many years. On a daily basis the balances of your mortgage and current accounts are aggregated and interest is calculated on the net balance. Also known as a flexible mortgage.

DEBT CONSOLIDATION

Putting all or some of your short-, medium- and long-term loans into one single loan to reduce your monthly outlay and help cash flow. Consolidating once can be a good idea, especially if you can then hive some of the saving into a deposit or investment account. You should only ever consolidate once.

DEFAULT

A term used to describe a situation in which you have failed to pay some or all of the instalments due on a mortgage or loan.

DEFINED BENEFIT PENSION PLAN

A type of pension plan in which your income on retirement is related to your final salary and the number of years you have worked for your employer. An example would be an annual pension of 66% of your final salary on retirement after 40 years service.

DEFINED CONTRIBUTION PENSION PLAN

With this type of pension plan, your income on retirement is not related to your final salary, but depends on the value of the pension fund accumulated during your working life. If your and your employer's contributions are invested in a pension fund that has not performed, that is your tough luck. Most DC plans were dropped by the bigger employers during the early 2000s.

DEPOSIT INTEREST RETENTION TAX (DIRT)

A tax on interest earned on deposits with the Irish financial institutions. The current rate is 20%, and it is deducted directly from gross interest and passed on to the Revenue Commissioners.

DEPRECIATION

A loss in value of certain assets, such as a car or a machine, over time.

DERIVATIVES

Financial contracts that gamble on the future prices of assets; secondary assets, such as options and futures, which derive their value from primary assets such as currency, commodities, stocks and bonds. The current price of an asset is determined by the market demand for and supply of the asset; however, the future price of an asset typically remains unknown. A week or a month in the future, the asset's price may increase, decrease, or remain the same. Buyers and sellers often like to hedge their bets against this uncertainty about future price by making a contract for future trading at a specified price. It is this contract – a financial instrument – that is known as a derivative.

DISCOUNT RATE MORTGAGE
A mortgage with an interest rate that is kept at a set percentage below the standard variable mortgage rate for an agreed period. Borrowers must make sure that the difference between the normal and discounted rates of interest is not being added to their outstanding loan, which could dramatically increase the overall cost of the mortgage.

DIVIDENDS
The distribution of part of a company's profits to shareholders; the money you earn for investing in shares, and it can be paid in cash or shares.

EMERGENCY FUND
Money you set aside in some reasonably accessible form such as a bank or building society account, which can be drawn upon in the event of some unforeseen need for funds.

ENDOWMENT MORTGAGE
A mortgage in which your monthly payments consist entirely of the interest on the amount you've borrowed, whilst the loan itself gets paid off using the proceeds of an endowment insurance policy.

ENDOWMENT MIS-SELLING
In the 1980s and 1990s, thousands of endowment mortgages were sold with endowment policies that didn't grow in value sufficiently to repay the lump sum borrowed. In other words, borrowers found themselves unable to pay off all of their mortgages. This crisis continues as borrowers who took out endowment mortgages come to the end of their mortgage terms.

ENDOWMENT INSURANCE POLICY
An investment-type insurance policy that pays out a single amount on a fixed date in the future, usually to repay a mortgage or when the policy holder dies, whichever comes first.

EQUITY
The net value of a property minus the balance of any remaining mortgage.

EQUITY RELEASE
A scheme whereby you make use of some of the equity (the difference between the value of a property and the loan borrowed against it) in your home, by way of remortgage or top-up for refurbishment or other investment purposes.

ESTATE
The assets of a person who has died.

ESCALATION
An automatic and regular increase in pension over successive years, either at a fixed rate or linked to inflation.

EURIBOR
The **Eu**ro **I**nterbank **O**ffered **R**ate is the interest rate at which eurozone banks will lend to each other. There is a separate rate for each lending period (a lending period can be from one week up to 12 months). Euribor rates may affect the interest rate your bank offers you. These rates change every day, depending on quotes from a representative panel of banks. It is *not* the same as the ECB rate, which is set by the European Central Bank, so the standard variable mortgage interest rate can be decidedly different to an ECB tracker rate – talk to your financial adviser to learn more.

EUROPEAN CENTRAL BANK (ECB)
This is the Central Bank for the eurozone countries. Its main purposes are to maintain the value of the euro by means of keeping prices stable and controlling inflation in the member states. It sets the interest rates for the zone, which in turn influence domestic interest rates.

EXCHANGE TRADED FUNDS (EFTs)
An investment fund that tracks the shares of a particular stock market index, such as the top 20 shares quoted in the Irish Stock Exchange. The fund itself is also quoted and traded on the stock market. Entry and exit to EFTs can also be cheaper and better administratively, as you do not have to buy 20 separate share holdings, for example.

EXIT PENALTY

Also referred to as an **exit charge** or **early encashment charge**, this is a penalty applied by financial institutions for cashing in an investment before its specified maturity date.

EXIT TAX

A tax on the profit made on an investment. On the maturity of that investment or when you have decided to cash it in, you are taxed 23% (the standard rate of tax, currently 20%, plus 3% government levy) on the profit of that investment.

FINANCIAL ADVISER

A person or firm offering advice about investments, insurance, mortgages and other financial products. See the note on the Financial Regulator below.

FINANCIAL REGULATOR

The body charged with policing the Irish financial services industry – that is all banks, building societies, credit unions, insurance companies, stockbrokers, financial advisers and intermediaries. Formerly the Irish Financial Services Regulatory Authority.

FIXED RATE MORTGAGE

A mortgage with an interest rate set at a particular level that does not vary during an initial set period. At the end of the period, the rate reverts, usually to the normal variable rate for that lender.

FIXED TERM DEPOSITS

A deposit account into which you put your money for a fixed time and at a fixed interest rate. Any withdrawals before the fixed period expires will usually attract a penalty.

FUTURES AND OPTIONS

A **future** or **forward contract** is formed when both the buyer and the seller are committed and legally obliged to exchange the underlying asset when the contract matures. An **option**, on the other hand, is a contract that gives its owner the right, but not the obligation, to buy or sell the underlying asset on or before a given date at the agreed-upon price. Both these contracts are time-bound.

HOME INCOME PLAN

A scheme, usually set up by an insurance company, which offers income to the elderly by releasing some of the value tied up in their homes.

HOME REVERSION SCHEME

A scheme that provides extra capital or income once you're retired: you sell part of your home, but retain the right to live in it until you die (or both you and your spouse have died if it's a joint scheme). The amount raised can either be kept as a lump sum or used to buy an annuity, which would provide a monthly income.

HOSPITAL CASH PLAN

This policy will pay out a lump sum in specified circumstances – for instance if you have to go into hospital, become pregnant, and so forth.

INCREASING TERM INSURANCE

Life insurance where the amount of cover and the cost increase automatically during the term, either by a set percentage each year or in line with inflation. One of the benefits is that the extra you pay assumes that your state of health is still the same as it was when you originally took out the policy, even if it has in fact deteriorated.

INDEMNITY BOND

A type of insurance policy that, in the event of your home being repossessed by your lender as a result of failure to repay the mortgage, insures the lender against the risk of taking a loss usually over 80% of the original value of the property on its subsequent sale. Some lenders will charge you for the costs of this indemnity Bond.

INDEX LINKING

A method whereby the benefits of your investment, life assurance or house insurance policies are increased annually to keep pace with inflation. Your premiums will also increase proportionately each year.

INFLATION

The term used to describe how rising prices cause the purchasing power of your money to decrease. At one point we suffered very high levels of inflation in Ireland, when prices increased by as much as one-sixth a year. In recent years, inflation has been pretty much under control but, worryingly, has been on the rise again in the last 2 years. Note that when inflation rises, so do interest rates – hence the steady rate increases of the last 24 months.

INTEREST
The money charged by a lender to a borrower, and the amount of money an investor earns from his or her investments. Here are two short examples: if you borrow €100 and you have to pay an annual interest rate of 20%, it means you have to pay the lender €20 per year. If, on the other hand, you invest €100 and receive interest of 5%, this means that the amount you will receive is €5 a year.

INTEREST-ONLY MORTGAGE
Similar to an **endowment mortgage**. Basically, you only pay interest during the term of the loan. Normally, the amount that would go to repaying capital is instead transferred to a savings scheme that should on maturity have grown sufficiently to repay the loan. In this case, there is no investment planned but the loan reverts at a future point to a Capital and Interest loan (called the Repayment or Annuity Loan) or if you have negotiated a 40-year interest-only loan, the amount borrowed is repaid, by whatever means, at the end of the term.

INVESTOR COMPENSATION SCHEME
Introduced in 1997, this is a guarantee from the government to protect eligible consumers and investor savings up to €20,000 per person/entity in any Irish bank, deposit-taker or authorised investment firm should that credit institution or firm fail or collapse. The government's Deposit Protection Scheme guaranteeing €100,000 per person in every Irish financial institution has replaced the ICS.

IRISH CREDIT BUREAU
A credit reference agency that maintains information about individual borrower's credit history. With 95 credit institution members, one missed payment stays on record for 5 years, while a **judgment** (a formal decision by a court of law that you owe money) remains forever. Any loan application will always result in an ICB enquiry. You can check your own credit for €6 by writing to them at Newstead, Clonskeagh, Dublin 6. Guard your good name!

JOINT LIFE INSURANCE
Life insurance that covers two people's lives (usually husband and wife) and pays out a lump sum when either one or both has died. A 'first death policy' will pay out when one of the people covered has died, whereas a 'last survivor policy' pays out only when both of the people covered have died. This type of life insurance is useful as a way of paying off a mortgage or meeting some other liability. The 'first death' policy is the cheaper of the two, while the most expensive is a **dual life policy,** which pays out on both lives irrespective of who dies first.

JUNK BOND
A high-yield corporate bond issue with a below-investment rating (BB or lower) that became a growing source of corporate funding in the 1980s. They are the lowest quality bonds and since they are speculative and risky, they potentially have a greater yield or return, and are generally issued by corporations of questionable financial strength or without proven track records.

LETTER OF OFFER
Usually a letter from your mortgage lender setting out the amount or loan offer they are willing to lend you and listing the requirements and conditions attaching to the loan before the funds can be released.

LIFE ASSURANCE
An insurance policy that pays out a lump sum on the death of the insured. The policyholder is not necessarily the insured, e.g. a wife could make her children the beneficiaries of an insurance policy on her husband's life.

LIQUIDITY
In simple terms, this refers to the availability of cash – as opposed to assets tied up in long-term investments – to meet any sudden demands.

LOADING
A charge added to an insurance premium because of some specific risk factor such as the health of an individual looking for life cover insurance.

LOAN TO VALUE (LTV)

Shows the relationship between the value of your home and the amount of your mortgage, expressed as a percentage. Thus, if your home is worth €500,000 and you owe €250,000 the LTV is 50%.

MARKET VALUE REDUCTION (MVR)

A reduction in the value of your investment that your life insurance company may apply when you withdraw some or all of your investment except at certain times.

MORTGAGE

This is a loan secured against the value of your home or property. A legal term in French meaning 'dead pledge', a mortgage is essentially a contract between a lender and a borrower. It obliges the lender to make money available to the borrower, and obliges the borrower to repay the loan over a specified period of time.

MORTGAGE PROTECTION ASSURANCE

A form of life assurance tailored to provide enough cover to pay off your mortgage in the event of your death. The policy will be set up to run for the same term of years as your mortgage, but the level of cover will decrease in line with the decreasing balance of your mortgage, so the more you repay on the original amount borrowed, the less you have to 'cover' on the balance. The premiums are fixed for the full term of the policy.

MORTGAGE REPAYMENT PROTECTION INSURANCE

A special policy designed to cover your mortgage payments for a limited period – usually not more than two years – if you can't work due to an accident, illness or unemployment.

NATIONAL TREASURY MANAGEMENT AGENCY (NTMA)

The government agency that manages the national debt and administers the national pension fund. It also administers a fund into which unclaimed money from dormant bank accounts is transferred.

NET DISPOSABLE INCOME (NDI)

One of the two methods used by lenders to determine how much money can be borrowed by an applicant. Your monthly take-home pay (that is, after tax and deductions) is used to allow up to c. 35% in financial commitments (mortgage, car loan, personal loan, etc.). This leaves the other 65% disposable income for food, clothing, living and luxury expenses. Under certain circumstances, this could be as high as 50%. The other method of calculating your borrowing eligibility is called the Salary Multiplier. Again, as a rule of thumb, your income is multiplied by 4.5 times for a single applicant or twice 4.5 times for joint applicants. If there are no loans outstanding or other financial commitments, the NDI system may give you a greater borrowing eligibility.

NEGATIVE EQUITY

Unfortunately, this phrase has been in common use in Ireland since the summer of 2008, and is used to described the situation when an asset – especially a home – falls below the value of the loan (or loans) taken out to buy it. In other words, suppose you have a house worth €200,000 and your mortgage is for €220,000; your negative equity would be €20,000.

NET WORTH

What someone is really worth financially, found by adding up the value of all your assets and then deducting the total of all your debts. Suppose you have a house, car, and other possessions worth €150,000 and mortgages and loans to the value of €100,000; your net worth would then be €50,000.

NO-CLAIMS BONUS

The reduction you receive on your home or motor insurance, based on the number of years you have not made any claims on that insurance.

OVERDRAFT

When more money is paid out of your current account than you have paid in, your account is said to be in *overdraft* or that you have *overdrawn your account*. Your bank must normally approve such overdrafts in advance, and when they do, it is generally up to an agreed limit. If you do not have advance permission, your account may still be allowed to overdraw, but you will be penalised by paying a surcharge on top of the already excessive overdraft interest rate, plus referral fees and possibly unpaid charges will apply.

PAY-RELATED SOCIAL INSURANCE (PRSI)

A contribution toward the cost of social welfare and pension benefits, payable by employers, employees and the self-employed. It is calculated as a percentage of your earnings and only up to a certain limit.

PERSONAL RETIREMENT SAVINGS ACCOUNT (PRSA)

Introduced in 2002, a **P**ersonal **R**etirement **S**avings **A**ccount is a **pension** plan that provides a regular income on retirement plus a lump sum tax-free amount and available through banks and assurance companies. It is regarded as more flexible and cheaper to maintain than the traditional personal pension plan.

RATE OF RETURN

The amount of money you make from an investment, worked out by adding together any capital appreciation and any income you have received, expressed as a percentage. When people refer to the 'real' rate of return, they mean the figure after it has been adjusted for inflation.

RENEWABLE TERM INSURANCE

Life insurance that includes a guarantee that you can take out a second-term insurance policy at the end of the original term. Your rights will not be affected by any change in your health.

RE-MORTGAGING

The process of repaying one loan with the proceeds from an existing property by taking out a new consolidated loan with a different lender using the same property as security. Generally, an additional amount of borrowing would be added to the existing debt in a remortgaging situation.

REPAYMENT MORTGAGE

A mortgage that has monthly payments to repay both the capital and the interest on the loan over a stated term.

SECURED LOAN

A loan that is supported by an asset that guarantees repayment of a loan. Mortgages are normally secured by the property being offered as security.

SECURITY
Assets such as title deeds of a property, life policies or share certificates used as support for a loan. The lender has the right to sell the security if the loan is not repaid according to the terms of the mortgage agreement.

SERIOUS or SPECIFIED ILLNESS INSURANCE
See **Critical Illness Insurance**. This form of assurance pays out if you are diagnosed with one of a number of serious illnesses that are specified in the policy schedule.

SHARES
Literally, a share in the ownership of a business. Different types of shares will carry different types of benefits; some may allow you to vote, while others may allow you a share of the company's profits in the form of **dividends**.

SHORT SELLING
The selling of a stock (equities or shares in a company, commodities) that a person does not own in the hope of profiting from buying the stock back at a lower price. This is also called **shorting**. This was banned virtually worldwide in September 2008.

STAMP DUTY (PROPERTY)
A tax you pay to the government when buying a property that is applied on a sliding scale depending on the property's value. There are a number of exemptions, including first-time buyers. With shares the stamp duty is 1%, **and there is also stamp duty** on credit cards (€30 up to 2008) and cash cards or Laser cards (€5).

SURRENDER VALUE
The amount of money an endowment policy yields when it is cashed in before reaching maturity.

TAX AVOIDANCE
Legal tax planning that takes full advantage of the tax laws to minimise your tax liabilities.

TAX EVASION
Illegal tax planning that requires breaking the law. If, for example, you get paid in cash and don't declare it on your tax form, then you are engaging in tax evasion.

TERM ASSURANCE
A life insurance policy which pays out a fixed sum on the death of the policy-holder within a fixed number of years (the 'term' of the policy).

TIED AGENT
A salesperson who sells products and services on behalf of one company. The financial advice of tied agents is neither impartial nor independent.

TRACKER MORTGAGE
A mortgage where the margin (i.e. the profit to the lender), is set (or 'tracked') at a fixed percentage above the ECB interest rate for the duration of the loan term.

TRUST
A trust is a legal entity, like a company, or a person for that matter. It allows assets by one set of people – the beneficiaries – to be managed and run by other people, known as 'trustees'. Trusts are a useful way of protecting your loved ones while saving tax at the same time.

UNIT TRUST
Investors pool their money into a fund, which in turn invests in a number of different companies. Unit trusts are a good way to spread your risk because they allow you to diversify without having to buy lots and lots of different shares.

UNSECURED LOAN
A loan that is not supported by any asset to guarantee repayment of the loan. Personal unsecured loans can include car loans, overdrafts, holiday and short-term personal loans.

VALUATION
Either a report by a registered valuer on the value of a property that is

required when applying for a mortgage, or an estimate from a fund manager of the value of the assets in your investment or pension fund.

VARIABLE RATE MORTGAGE
A mortgage that permits the lender to adjust its interest rates periodically, but generally on the back of interest rate rises around the globe and in particular those rates from the European Central Bank that are pertinent to Ireland.

WHOLE-OF-LIFE POLICY
A type of life insurance policy that, as its name implies, provides cover for your whole life and pays out on your death, providing the policy is still on force. Premiums are not fixed and will be reviewed (upwards) at regular intervals. Policies also have an encashment value.

WITH-PROFITS POLICY
An insurance policy that offers a policy-holder a share of any surplus in the insurance company's life insurance and pension profits from the business.

APPENDIX 2
LEARN TO SPEAK THE LANGUAGE

A QUICK GUIDE TO THE MOST IMPORTANT 'PERSONAL FINANCE' TERMINOLOGY

One of the first things about finance that puts people off is the language. The moment an expert starts to bandy around terms like 'dividend', 'yield', 'compound interest' and 'net present value' it can all start to sound very intimidating.

Like every other area of life, finance has a specialised language. It has its own jargon. Jargon is actually very useful – we need precise terms that are clearly defined so that there is no confusion about what is being said. On the other hand, if you don't understand what the jargon means, you are automatically at a disadvantage. This is something which I believe many financial institutions use to confuse their customers. After all, customers who don't understand something are hardly in a position to ask awkward questions – or to compare value for money.

In this appendix then we will look at four important terms used in personal finance. Never again will you be dependent on someone else to explain any of the following to you:

1   Percentages.
2   The difference between **capital** and **income**.
3   Compound interest.
4   Gearing.

Please note that other terminology you may find useful is explained in the 'Jargon Buster' section on www.moneydoctor.ie.

PERCENTAGES MADE EASY

You are not alone

If you aren't entirely comfortable with percentages you are not alone. In a survey designed to test graduates on their knowledge of percentages, only 8% could calculate a percentage accurately, and only 19% actually understood what a percentage was. In other words, more than eight out of ten people with a third-level education were completely at sea when it came to one of the key mathematical concepts used in personal finance. Under the circumstances, is it any wonder that the majority of people struggle to sort out their money matters?

What is a percentage?

The word 'percentage' literally means 'parts per 100' – *cent* being the Latin word for 100. Because percentages always deal with parts per hundred, they allow you to compare things that would be very difficult to compare otherwise. They are particularly useful when it comes to choosing a loan or deciding on the relative worth of different investment opportunities.

How to work out percentages

You calculate the percentage by turning your numbers into a fraction, dividing it out and then multiplying by 100.

Imagine that you have three apple trees and you want to know which one of the trees produces the highest number of good – as opposed to rotten – apples. When you harvest the apples from each tree you keep a note of the total number of apples picked and the number of apples that have to be thrown away. Your note looks like this:

Tree	Apples on tree	Apples spoiled
A	750	150
B	550	88
C	670	101

Clearly, from the above figures, it isn't easy to gauge which is your best tree. However, if you express the figures in percentage terms it will immediately become obvious.

On Tree A, 150 out of the 750 were rotten. So your calculation would look like this:

$$\frac{150}{750} \times 100 = 20 \text{ per cent}$$

If you were using a calculator you would key it in like this:

150 ÷ 750 = 0.2 x 100 = (answer 20)

For Tree B, 88 apples out of the 550 were rotten, so the calculation would be like this:

$$\frac{88}{550} \times 100 = 16 \text{ per cent}$$

For Tree C, 101 apples out of the 670 were rotten, so the calculation would be like this:

$$\frac{101}{670} \times 100 = 15 \text{ per cent}$$

Converting the numbers to percentages allows us to make a fair comparison between the 'performance' of the apple trees. So, 20% of the apples on Tree A were rotten; 16% of the apples on Tree B were rotten; but just 15% of the apples on Tree C were rotten – making it the best-performing apple tree in the orchard!

It is hard enough comparing apple trees with apple trees – but even harder to compare apple trees with – say – orange trees. This is where percentages come in so useful. By giving everything a base of 100, we can compare things which aren't alike in other ways.

Now let's put percentages into context – you are told the yield in a property you wish to buy is 6% while the internal rate of return (IRR) is 11%. The first element, the yield, is the return or rental income in proportion to the cost of the property excluding stamp duty and costs.

For example, an investment property costing €300,000 with a rental income of €18,000 per annum will give you an initial rental yield of 6% per annum. Capital growth on the property is expected over the next few years and just taking the first five years of ownership together with the yield, the combination is called the Internal Rate of Return (IRR) and is generally in excess of the initial yield. If in five years' time the property is worth €450,000 the returns would be:

- Growth = 50% (five years)
- Annual rental yield = 6%
- IRR = 16% per annum (on an un-geared investment and before tax).

MONEY DOCTOR WEALTH WARNING

Don't trust your calculator!

Don't always believe the answer the calculator gives you. Why not? Because the tiniest slip of your finger could give you a completely wrong answer without you being aware of it. Here are five things you can do to avoid calculator error:

1 Estimate your answer before you begin a calculation.

2 Do every calculation twice.

3 Know your calculator.

4 Don't be overawed by your calculator.

5 Hang on to common sense and what you know.

THE VITAL DIFFERENCE BETWEEN CAPITAL AND INCOME

All money is not equal

One of the most important financial concepts to understand is the difference between capital and income. Capital is something – it could be money, a property, shares or some other investment – that generates an income for whoever owns it. A good way to remember the difference is to think of a fruit tree. The tree itself is the 'capital'. The fruit it produces is the 'income'. You continue to own the tree (capital) and it continues to bear fruit (income) every year. Your wage or salary is the income which comes from the capital of your labour – hence, the expression 'human capital'. Money is not just money – it is either capital or income.

And then there is 'interest'

When you own capital and it produces an income you have a number of choices:

- You can hold on to the capital and spend the income.

- You can hold on to the capital, add the income to it, and generate even more income.

- You can dispose of some or all of the capital and thus reduce the income you receive.

Let's use the example of chickens and eggs! You have some hens (capital) which lay eggs (income). You can do one of three things:

1   You can hold on to the chickens (capital) and eat the eggs (income).

2   You can hold on to the chickens (capital) and leave the eggs to hatch into more chickens (more capital) that in turn will produce even more eggs (income) for you.

3   You can eat your chickens (thus eating into your capital) and thus reduce the total amount of eggs (income) you receive.

There are lots of different names for the income produced by capital. In the case of property, for instance, it is called 'rental income'. In the case of a cash deposit in a bank it is called 'interest'.

THE MIRACLE OF COMPOUND INTEREST

A financial concept that can make or break you

When you are earning it, it has the power to make you very rich. When you are paying it, it has the power to make you very poor. Albert Einstein described it as 'the greatest mathematical discovery of all time'. It is the reason why banks, building societies, credit card companies and other financial institutions make so much profit from lending money. And it is the reason why ordinary investors can make themselves rich simply by doing nothing. It is the fiendishly simple concept of 'compound interest'.

Compound interest in one easy lesson

Perhaps the easiest way to understand compound interest is to look at a hypothetical example. Imagine that you have €1,000 and that you invest it in a savings account which pays interest at a rate of 10% per year. At the end of one year you will be entitled to €100 interest. If you withdraw this interest but leave your capital, at the end of the second year you will be entitled to another €100 interest. Supposing, however, that you don't withdraw the interest but leave it to 'compound'. At the end of your first year your €1,000 is worth €1,100. At the end of your second year you will have earned €110 interest, meaning that your original €1,000 is worth €1,210. Put another way **your interest is earning you more interest**.

You will sometimes see the initials **CAR** in relation to interest. This is the **compound annual rate**... in other words it is the amount of interest you will receive if you keep adding your interest to your capital in the way I have just described.

Now let's look at a real example:

According to research, the Irish stock market has produced an annual average return of 14% since 1989. At this rate, if you invested €1,000 today it would be worth €3,700 in less than ten years.

Still not impressed? How much do you think your money would grow by if, at the age of 25, you had started saving €100 a month (that's €25 a week) for just 10 years at the same return? €15,000? €18,000? You are not close. At the age of 35 your money would be worth €25,000. Better still, at the age 65 your money would be worth €1.5 million!

No wonder lenders love you

When you **borrow** money, compound interest is working against you. Supposing, for instance, you borrow €5,000 on a credit card at an interest rate of 15% – which isn't high by today's standards. The credit card company allow you to make a minimum payment of 1.5% each month. After two years, you will still owe approx. €4,700, having made repayments of €1,750, of which €1,450 has been swallowed up in interest. Work out for yourself how long it will take you to pay off the full debt!

Compound interest is your greatest enemy and your greatest ally. When you are in debt, it works against you. But when you have money to invest you can make compound interest really work for you.

GEARING

Allowing other people to make you rich

Using borrowed money to buy an asset is called **gearing**. If you can make it work in your favour, gearing can dramatically boost your profits. For instance:

Supposing you buy a €200,000 apartment using a €40,000 deposit and a €160,000 mortgage. After one year the apartment is worth €240,000. It isn't just that you have made a €40,000 profit – you've actually doubled the €40,000 you originally invested. In other words, you've achieved a 100% gain in just 12 months.

Even if you deduct the mortgage interest you've had to pay for the year you've owned your apartment – you have still done very well. However, what goes up can also come down. In the UK between 1987 and 1989 house prices fell by around one-third. If this happened to someone selling an apartment they bought for €100,000 using an €80,000 mortgage they would not only have seen their €20,000 deposit wiped out they would owe an additional €13,333 (the difference between the mortgage of €80,000 and the €66,666 you would get for the apartment). When this happens it is called being in 'negative equity'.

> Gearing is the easiest and most effective way of increasing the potential profit from any investment. It is also the most effective way of increasing the potential loss, something every investor contemplating gearing would be well advised to remember.

There is a commonly held view that owning property is a one-way bet. But in the recent history of many European countries there have been periods when residential property prices fell. In fact, over the long term the Irish stock market has outperformed Irish property. Furthermore, it is vitally important to diversify your investments – thus spreading your risk.

> Many people re-mortgage their homes in order to have a deposit with which to buy a second investment property. This can be very sensible. However, if you have an existing mortgage on your home it might make more sense to pay that off first and then to invest in another area – such as the stock market. It very much depends on your circumstances.

Without gearing, most of us would never be able to own our own homes. It also allows us to make other, highly lucrative investments. Nevertheless, you should think carefully before you embark on any investment that requires you to borrow money. You want to make sure that the investment is going to earn you more than the loan is going to cost you.

THE MONEY DOCTOR SAYS...

- It is well worth your while to practise calculating percentages, as these are the most common way of comparing both investment and lending products.

- If you are trying to remember the difference between capital and income think of an apple tree. The tree is your capital and its annual crop of fruit is your income.

- Compound interest can make you rich and it can make you poor, too. In the case of an investment it is the process whereby the interest you earn from something is added to the capital to produce even more interest. In the case of a loan it is the process whereby the interest you owe is added to the capital making it harder to get out of debt.

- Gearing allows you to buy an asset with borrowed money. There is no better way to achieve dramatic investment returns but, remember, it can work the other way, too.

- You'll find a full explanation of all the most commonly used financial expressions and terms in the 'Jargon Buster' at www.moneydoctor.ie.

APPENDIX 3
DECISION TREES

What to do about your pension arrangements if you are self-employed

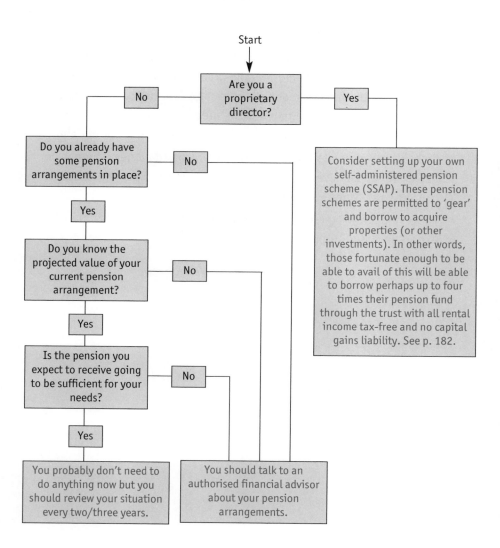

What to do about your pension arrangements if you are an employee

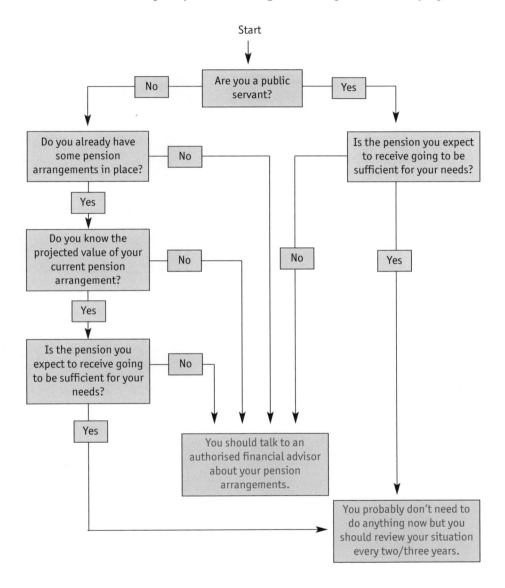

How to generate a regular income from a lump sum

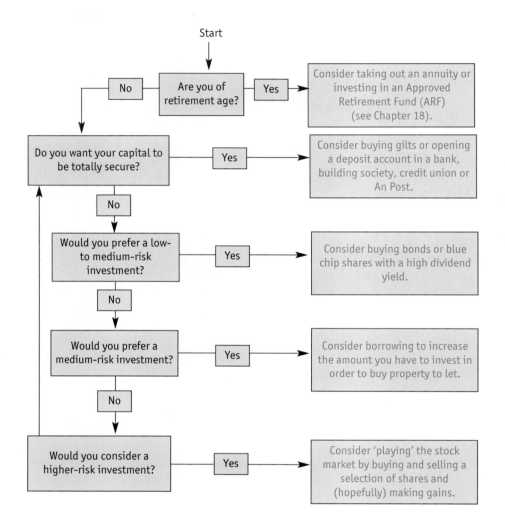

Investment options at retirement for the self-employed

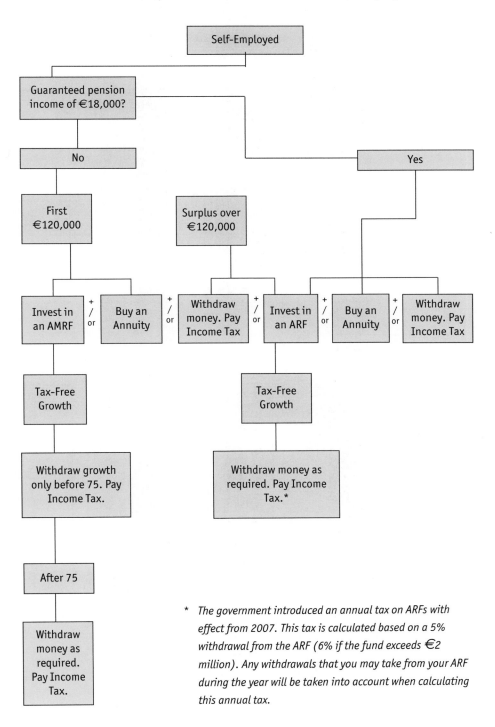

* The government introduced an annual tax on ARFs with effect from 2007. This tax is calculated based on a 5% withdrawal from the ARF (6% if the fund exceeds €2 million). Any withdrawals that you may take from your ARF during the year will be taken into account when calculating this annual tax.

How to create a financial plan

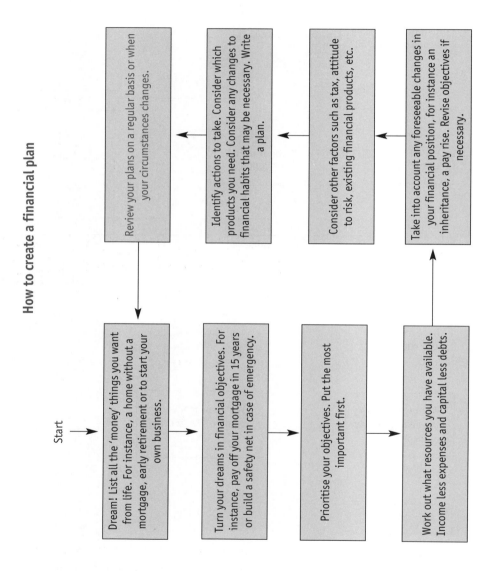

Start

Dream! List all the 'money' things you want from life. For instance, a home without a mortgage, early retirement or to start your own business.

Turn your dreams in financial objectives. For instance, pay off your mortgage in 15 years or build a safety net in case of emergency.

Prioritise your objectives. Put the most important first.

Work out what resources you have available. Income less expenses and capital less debts.

Take into account any foreseeable changes in your financial position, for instance an inheritance, a pay rise. Revise objectives if necessary.

Consider other factors such as tax, attitude to risk, existing financial products, etc.

Identify actions to take. Consider which products you need. Consider any changes to financial habits that may be necessary. Write a plan.

Review your plans on a regular basis or when your circumstances changes.

Do you need life cover?

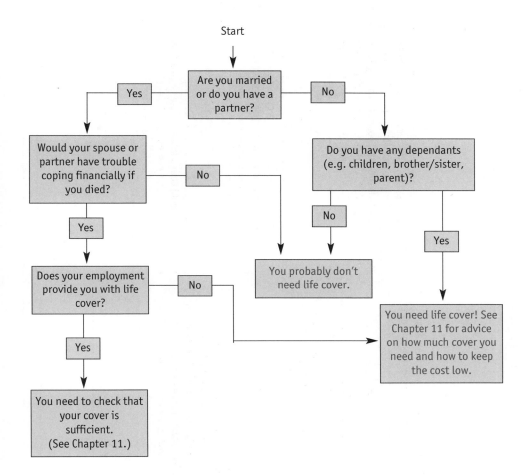

Do you need income protection insurance?

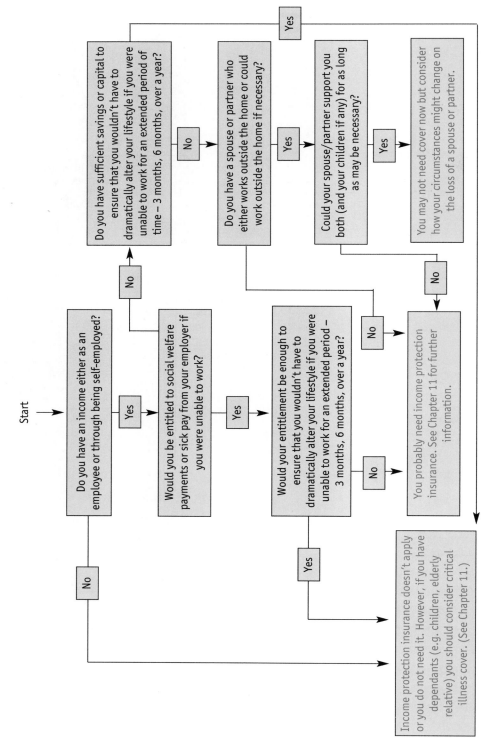

Do you need private medical insurance?

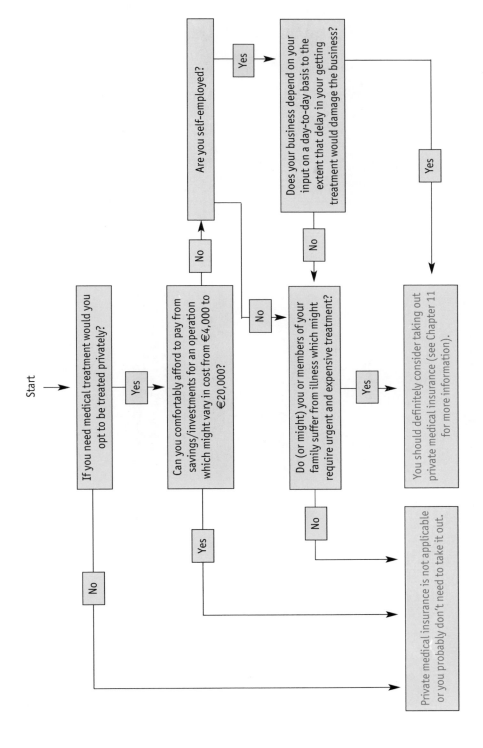

How to maximise the value of regular saving

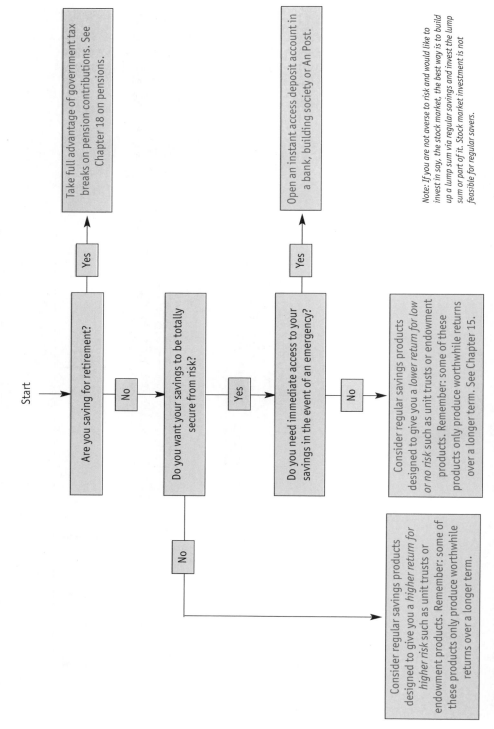

Start

Are you saving for retirement?

Yes → Take full advantage of government tax breaks on pension contributions. See Chapter 18 on pensions.

No

Do you want your savings to be totally secure from risk?

Yes → Do you need immediate access to your savings in the event of an emergency?

Yes → Open an instant access deposit account in a bank, building society or An Post.

No → Consider regular savings products designed to give you a *lower return for low or no risk* such as unit trusts or endowment products. Remember: some of these products only produce worthwhile returns over a longer term. See Chapter 15.

No → Consider regular savings products designed to give you a *higher return for higher risk* such as unit trusts or endowment products. Remember: some of these products only produce worthwhile returns over a longer term.

Note: If you are not averse to risk and would like to invest in say, the stock market, the best way is to build up a lump sum via regular savings and invest the lump sum or part of it. Stock market investment is not feasible for regular savers.

Inheritance on intestacy (no will in existence)

The diagram below outlines how your assets will be distributed under the Terms of the 1965 Succession Act, should you die without a valid will.

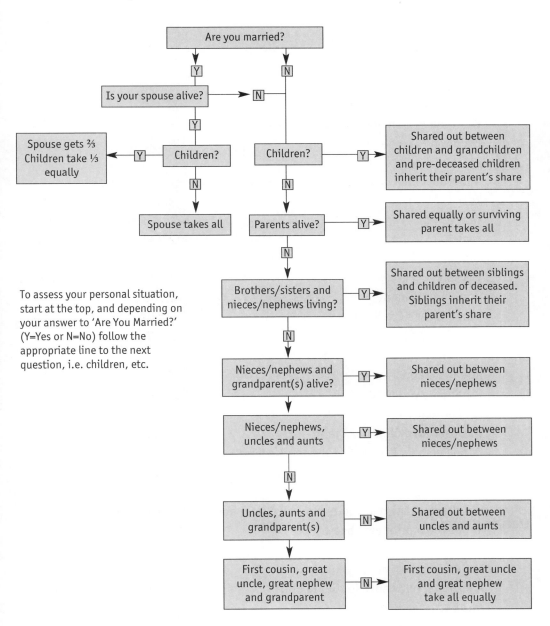

To assess your personal situation, start at the top, and depending on your answer to 'Are You Married?' (Y=Yes or N=No) follow the appropriate line to the next question, i.e. children, etc.

APPENDIX 4
TAX RATES AND CREDITS

Tax Credits @ 20%	BUDGET 2012	2011
Personal Tax Credits	€	€
Single Person	1,650	1,650
Married (assessed jointly)	3,300	3,300
Widowed Person in year of bereavement	3,300	3,300
Widowed Person – no children	2,190	2,190
Additional allowances for widowed persons in the years after bereavement		
Year 1	3,600	3,600
Year 2	3,150	3,150
Year 3	2,700	2,700
Year 4	2,250	2,250
Year 5	1,800	1,800
One-Parent Family	1,650	1,650
Home Carer's Credit (max.)	810	810
PAYE Tax Credit	1,650	1,650
Age Tax Credit		
(a) Single/Widowed	245	245
(b) Married	490	490
Incapacitated Child Tax Credit	3,300	3,300
Blind Person's Tax Credit (one spouse blind)	1,650	1,650
(both spouses blind)	3,300	3,300

Bin charges: the maximum allowance claimable if eligible is still €400 per annum on a prior year basis.

Tax allowances @ marginal rate		
Additional Allowance for Guide Dog	825	825
Incapacitated Person –		
Allowance for Employing a Carer (max.)	50,000	50,000

Exemption Limits	2012	2011
(being abolished over a four-year period from 2011)	€	€
Single/widowed 65 years of age or over	18,000	18,000
Married 65 years of age or over	36,000	36,000
Additional for Dependent Children		
1st and 2nd child (each)	575	575
Each subsequent child	830	830
Marginal Relief Tax Rate	40%	40%

Tax Rates and Tax Bands	2012	2011
Personal Circumstances	€	€
Single/widowed without dependent children	€32,800 @ 20% Balance @ 41%	€32,800 @ 20% Balance @ 41%
Single/widowed qualifying for one-parent family tax credit	€36,800 @ 20% Balance @ 41%	€36,800 @ 20% Balance @ 41%
Married couple (one spouse with income)	€41,800 @ 20% Balance @ 41%	€41,800 @ 20% Balance @ 41%
Married couple (both spouses with income)	€41,800 @ 20% (with an increase of €23,800 max.) Balance @ 41%	€41,800 @ 20% (with an increase of €23,800 max.) Balance @ 41%

Note: The increase in the standard rate tax band is restricted to the lower of €23,800 or the amount of the income of the spouse with the lower income. The increase is not transferable between spouses.

Universal Social Charge (USC)

Income €0 to €10,035 per annum	0%
€10,036 per annum	2%
€10,037 to €16,016	4%
In excess of €16,016 per annum	7%
Over €100,000 (self-assessed income only)	10%

NB Employers are now expected to collect this tax on a cumulative basis from 1 January 2012.

APPENDIX 5
TAX COMPUTATION TEMPLATE

	Example		Enter your figures	
Taxable Income	€	€	€	€
Gross income		40,000		
Add: Benefit in kind		1,000 +		+
		41,000		
Deduct: Pension contributions		(2,000) −		−
Total taxable income	A	*39,000*		
Tax payable				
Tax				
32,800 (41,800 married) @ 20%		6,560		
39,000−32,800=6,200 @ 41%		2,542		
Tax before tax credits		*9,102*		
Deduct: Tax credits				
Personal credit				
(3,300 married)	1,650			
PAYE credit				
(each PAYE employee)	1,650	(3,300) −		−
Total tax after credits	B	*5,802*		
Income after tax	A−B	33,198		
Deduct: Universal Social Charge				
7% of gross income		(2,800) −		−
Deduct: PRSI				
4% of gross income		(1,600) −		−
Net income after tax, social charge and PRSI		28,798		

APPENDIX 6
THE MONEY DOCTOR'S ANNUAL
BUDGET ACCOUNT*

Description	Monthly/quarterly	Total
Electricity		€
Home heating (oil/gas)		€
Telecoms (land/mobile/broadband)		€
TV licence/cable TV		€
Household insurance (contents)		€
Car insurance/tax/service/fuel		€
Food/drink/eating out/cinema/concerts		€
School fees/uniform and sportswear; extracurricular school costs		€
Alarm/security		€
Repairs/cleaning/waste/garden		€
Health insurance/medical expenses (incl. dentistry)		€
Christmas and birthday expenses		€
Mini breaks/holidays		€
Clothes/footwear		€
Club subscriptions/donations		€
Other		€
Totals		

* Does not include mortgage and loan repayments, life assurance or pension costs.

When you have totalled your expenditure, divide by 12 and that is the amount you have to provide monthly. All other costs (e.g. capital expenditure, new washing machine, TV, etc.) must be found outside of this budget.

THE MONEY DOCTOR'S STUDENT MONTHLY BUDGET

Category	Totals	
	Weekly	Monthly
Rent		€
Home heating (oil/gas)		€
Mobile		€
Books		€
Course materials		€
Printing/Photocopying		€
Commuter expenses (Bus/Train/DART/Luas)		€
Food		€
Household items/toiletries		€
Medical expenses/dentistry		€
Clothes		€
Gym/club subscriptions		€
Movies/theatre/concerts		€
Other (pubs, clubs & incidentals)		€
Loans		€
Total		

When you have totalled your expenditure, multiply by 12 and that is the money you have to provide annually. All other costs (e.g. holidays, buying iPods, etc.) must be found outside of this budget.

APPENDIX 7
MONEY DOCTOR SERVICES

Providence Finance Services Limited, trading as **Money Doctor**, was founded on 1 December 1999 with the intention to tell, not sell. The company is fully regulated by the *Central Bank of Ireland* and has built an enviable reputation of providing professional, independent and transparent advice with no bias for any one financial supplier, and delivered through a first-class service and administrative back-up.

This is the **company mission statement**:

> As an independent financial advisory company for debt management, insurance, savings, pensions and investments, *Money Doctor* aspires to give clients the best financial advice, service and after care in the most transparent, honest and professional manner. We are always at your service.

Now you can avail of a number of services from Money Doctor for yourself:

THE MONEY DOCTOR PERSONAL FINANCE CONSULTATIONS

Face-to-face, on the phone or by email, one 20-minute Money Doctor consultation is the same price as a visit to your local GP.

- You pay €65 up front for 20 minutes (credit card or cheque paid prior to the consultation)
- A Fact Find is emailed to you, which you complete and return to Money Doctor prior to the consultation. This details your financial circumstances and is compulsory for all financial advisers so that appropriate solutions, action plans, recommendations and strategies can be found for their clients.
- Book the appointment for specific issues and a complete financial makeover. First meetings can take 40 minutes and cover:
  - Budget planning: how to set and meet your goals
  - Evaluation of your debt management

- ◆ Savings: are you getting the best rates and terms?
- ◆ Investments: understanding and appraising them
- ◆ Life and health cover: are you over-insured? Do you have no insurance at all? Are you paying too much? Get all the facts.
- ◆ Income protection: is it worth it? Do you need it? Is it better than serious illness cover?
- ◆ Pensions and retirement planning: know the end game and what's in store for you on retirement. Are you saving enough for your retirement? Are you maximising your pension tax relief?

- Following the consultation, you will receive a comprehensive email with all the relevant documents, fact sheets, templates and a plan to sort your finances.
- Each further visit or contact will elicit a fee of €65 per 20 minutes for additional face-to-face or telephone consultations, similar to a GP.

Paying for advice

When you seek independent and authorised financial advice and do *not* pay a fee, you should ask two questions:

1. How is the adviser earning income?
2. If the *only* way the adviser can earn income is to sell you a product, your second question has to be, 'Does the adviser have a vested interest with that product?'

The benefits

With the Money Doctor, you receive unbiased, impartial information together with a wealth of financial experience. Money Doctor tells, not sells, and covers a wide variety of personal finance topics, from where to find the best and safest deposit and mortgage rates, whether to fix your interest rates, investment advice, how to deal with credit card debt, negative equity, personal debt, pensions and investments, redundancy, separation and divorce, life and health cover, general insurances, budgeting and tax credits and allowances.

We analyse the A-to-Z of your finances from top to toe, and we can then implement any actions you may require arising from consultations.

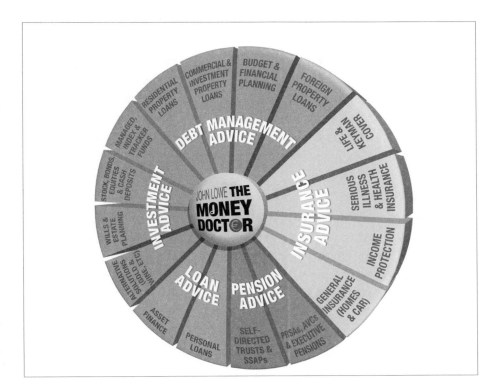

The Wheel of Services includes the Money Doctor's EAR – a three-step process to managing your debts. EAR is an acronym for

- **Evaluation** of your financial situation, strategizing solutions, costing €150 per hour.
- **Action** that helps you to get your strategy moving, such as helping to complete the intimidating and mandatory 12-page Standard Financial Statement that all lenders require, costing €150 per hour.
- **Representation**, where we act for the borrower in dealing with creditors, lenders, the courts, etc., at €250 per hour.

For further information, please contact consultation@moneydoctor.ie or call (01) 2785555.

MONEY DOCTOR EMPLOYER—EMPLOYEE SEMINARS

Seminar: 'Surviving the Recession: Simple Steps to Transform Your Finances'

In 2011, Money Doctor launched an employer-sponsored seminar for the benefit of hard-pressed employees, empowering them to structure and budget their own finances, slash living costs, and reduce and manage their debt while maximising their savings and investments.

How the Money Doctor can help

John Lowe, author of the *Money Doctor* guides and one of Ireland's best-known personal finance gurus, is offering employers the opportunity to support and improve the financial education and well-being of their employees, and in so doing, further contribute to the bottom line of their own company with greater loyalty and productivity from their employees.

The Employee seminar package

- One-off seminar or series of seminars covering all aspects of personal finance and planning – 1-hour duration to include a Q&A session at any time to suit employer or employee.
- One-to-one financial counselling on site also available if required.
- Fact sheets, templates and action guides on a credit-card-sized CD disc given to all employees after the seminar.
- Latest *Money Doctor* guide offered to all employees at a discount price – 'A terrific book that you can dip in and out of – and written in a very user-friendly way' – Gay Byrne.
- Presented in person by John Lowe and his team.
- Complete turn-key package that is very cost-effective.

Benefits to the employer

Research suggests that a well-executed workplace financial education programme is likely to reap great rewards as:

- a practical and inexpensive way to help staff with one of their greatest worries: their personal finances.
- a cost-effective way of boosting staff loyalty.

- highly topical, and demonstrates employers' understanding of what is important to their employees.
- the cornerstone of a family-friendly employment policy.
- helping to reduce stress-related absenteeism. €793m is lost per annum, 3.5% or 8 working days per year – that's 12 million days every year (source: Small Firms Association). This study found that back pain/injury and stress were the principal reasons for being absent.
- helping to reduce employee turnover rates (this can be calculated in monetary terms).
- increasing employee productivity and competitiveness.
- increasing contributions to the company pension scheme.

Benefits to the employees

With the recession showing its teeth, helping staff to better manage their money and look forward to the future has to be a major driver to attend this presentation funded by their employer. This is what they will learn:

- How to plan, set budgets and meet financial goals
- Coping with and managing debt quickly and easily
- How to cut down banking bills
- Savings and investments: find the best deals and maximise returns
- Life and health cover: what you should have and what you should drop
- Pensions: all you ever wanted to know but didn't have the time to ask
- Insuring your possessions the right way
- Fact sheets on
  - Top 100 money-saving tips
  - Tax refund processes
  - Tax rates and tax credit entitlements
  - Budgeting including templates

There is a Q&A after each seminar, with the Money Doctor team on hand to answer any immediate queries employees may have.

These seminars will help to change employee behaviour patterns that negatively affect job performance while at the same time building their assets and reduce their debt. Employees will also far better appreciate the employer-provided benefits, and the seminars may even increase their ability to retire early or at least on time.

Everyone knows the real challenges that businesses are experiencing in the current economy, and most employees are willing to work with employers to ensure the survival of the business.

Whether in terms of job satisfaction, motivation, morale, perceived stress levels or job security, for employers in survival mode, it is important to recognise the value of a fully focused workforce to the eventual recovery of their business.

Reduced incomes, levies, increased living expenses, servicing immediate household debt and concerns about the future value of pensions and savings are causing sleepless nights for a large portion of the population.

We are experiencing a huge increase in enquires from stressed, anxious and worried people seeking help from the Money Doctor because they feel they have lost control of their lives as the economic recession grinds on, as unemployment numbers rise and as financial security appears to be evaporating. What employees need is sound, independent, impartial financial advice in plain English from someone they feel they can trust to bring financial stability and options to their lives.

While most surveys have been carried out in the US and the UK, it would be fair to say that Ireland's employees would be even more affected than our overseas brethren:

- Workers' financial stress may hurt productivity (*USA Today*)
- Poor personal financial planning behaviours breed productivity-inhibiting stress for roughly 15 percent of US workers (Dr E. Thomas Garman)
- Job stress leads to increased absenteeism, tardiness and desire to quit (*Journal of Occupational and Environmental Medicine*).
- One in four of American workers are seriously financially distressed, causing negative impacts to individuals, families and employers (Dr E. Thomas Garman)
- Employee financial education is a critical component of employee wellness programmes

The cost of each seminar will depend on location and numbers. For a seminar series, economies of scale will also apply, but in the first instance please contact seminars@moneydoctor.ie or call (01) 278 5555.

Employee well-being programmes

There are a number of employee well-being or assistance programmes currently available in the State. These programmes cover mainly counselling services, are based on-site and designed to assist:

1. organisations to address productivity issues.
2. employees to identify and resolve personal concerns, including bullying in the workplace, health, marital, family, alcohol, drug, legal, emotional stress or other personal issues that may affect job performance.

However, very few address what can be a trigger for many of these issues –
   the employee's personal finances

Large state budget deficits and fiscal policies have led to significant cuts in health and social welfare, levies on income and rising living costs. Employees and business management now have to work smarter with their time and money.

   Money Doctor has developed a complete personal financial education and counselling support programme for companies to help their staff cope with their company and personal issues at minimal cost to the employer and no cost to the employee.

   From the company point of view, our fees are fully tax-deductible. Our services can also be specifically tailored to the needs of your organisation, and delivered with a responsive and compassionate approach.

The Money Doctor Well-Being Programme

All staff members are given the opportunity to avail of the Money Doctor Well-Being Programme via a staff conference given by the Money Doctor himself, via webinar or email in collaboration with the employer.

   Our Welcome Pack for each employee provides an in-depth overview of our well-being services, outlining the process, its total confidential nature and explaining our 'telling not selling' philosophy. By opting for the programme, each employee receives:

- Three consultations per annum:
  - Firstly, a financial consultation lasting 20 minutes (each employee completes a Fact Find and submits prior to the consultation) for a complete financial makeover.
  - Secondly, a 20-minute session with a counsellor (a highly trained psychotherapist who will elicit and assess any personal or emotional issues on a fully confidential basis. If further sessions are required, the company may fund same but will never be aware of the nature or reasons.)
  - Thirdly, a review of the employee's finances in total confidence again at the end of the year with a Money Doctor adviser.

- *The Money Doctor* – Ireland's best-selling and most comprehensive finance guide published by Gill & Macmillan – given free of charge to all employees annually. 'John Lowe's finance annual is a superb easy-to-use manual that gives you dozens of ways to retain and grow your money' – Bill Cullen.
- Quarterly newsletter – a personalised email newsletter with all the latest money-saving news and tips.
- Two workplace seminars per annum – one formal (Surviving the Recession: Simple Steps to Transform Your Finances) and one informal (the Sandwich Challenge, on-site in the company canteen for quick one-to-one queries). Further seminars provided if required.
- 24-hour availability – all initial communications, whether by email, letter, fax or voicemail, will be responded to within 3 hours of the next working day.

Independent advisory services include:

- Budget planning: avail of a simple budget template or an elaborate software tool for spending analysis and review.
- Debt management – includes representation to employees' creditors if required; see Money Doctor's EAR.
- Financial product advice: mortgages, loans, credit cards, life and health cover, pensions investments and savings, etc.
- Redundancy, separation and retirement planning.

- Family finance: may involve calling to employees' homes to convene family discussions on the family finances (e.g. living expenses, budgeting, planning for major life events, etc.).

The bottom line

Financial stress in the workplace has proved to be costly to businesses around the world. By providing your employees with the information and resources to make financially beneficial decisions in their lives, you are providing your business the opportunity to reduce costs, increase worker productivity, reduce absenteeism and improve your organisation's bottom line. In today's economy, the cost of obtaining independent financial advice is outside the realm of most employees' resources. The solution offered in The Money Doctor Employee Well-Being Programme provides a cost-effective, financially expedient process to improve your business' bottom line. Now, knowing the potential cost savings available, can you afford *not* to implement this programme in your organisation?

The cost

There is an annual retainer fee payable by the company that is based on the number of employees and site location, but it is equivalent to the price of a cup of coffee per day per employee.

This fee is fully tax-deductible against company profits.

The first three face-to-face sessions with any employee (as detailed above) are free. Thereafter, if further work is required, the cost per hour will be €195 and can be payable by the employee or the company or both. Every hour will be documented and invoiced.

Providence House, Lower
Kilmacud Road, Stillorgan,
Co. Dublin, Ireland

Tel +353 1 278 5555
Fax +353 1 278 5556

Email info@moneydoctor.ie
Web www.moneydoctor.ie

APPENDIX 8
USEFUL ADDRESSES

THE REVENUE COMMISSIONERS

Check www.revenue.ie for contact details for your local Revenue office numbers, addresses and email addresses.

You can also avail of the Revenue On-line Service at: www.ros.ie or at:

Revenue On-line Service Helpdesk
Revenue On-line Service
2nd Floor, Trident House
Blackrock, Co. Dublin

The opening hours of the ROS Helpdesk (1890 20 11 06 or for callers outside the Republic of Ireland + 353 1 7023021) are: Monday to Thursday – 8.30a.m. to 8.30p.m. and Friday – 8.30a.m. to 6.00p.m.

COMPANIES REGISTRATION OFFICE

Email info@cro.ie
Tel. (01) 8045200 LoCall 1890 220 226
Fax: (01) 8045222
DX No. 145001

Companies Registration Office
Parnell House
14 Parnell Square
Dublin 1

THE FINANCIAL REGULATOR (NOW OPERATING AS PART OF THE CENTRAL BANK OF IRELAND)/NATIONAL CONSUMER AGENCY

www.nca.ie
    P.O. Box 9138
    College Green
    Dublin 2
    Tel. (01) 2244000
    Fax: (01) 4104900

THE INSTITUTE OF CHARTERED ACCOUNTANTS IN IRELAND

www.icai.ie
    Chartered Accountants House
    47–49 Pearse St
    Dublin 2
    Tel. (01) 6377200
    Fax. (01) 6680842

THE ASSOCIATION OF CHARTERED CERTIFIED ACCOUNTANTS

www.accaglobal.com
    ACCA
    9 Leeson Park
    Dublin 6
    Tel. (01) 4988900
    Fax: (01) 4963615

THE INSTITUTE OF CERTIFIED PUBLIC ACCOUNTANTS IN IRELAND

www.cpaireland.ie
    17 Harcourt Street
    Dublin 2
    Tel. (01) 4251000
    Fax. (01) 4251001

THE IRISH CREDIT BUREAU

www.icb.ie
   ICB House
   Newstead
   Clonskeagh Road
   Dublin 14
   Tel. (01) 2600388
   Fax: (01) 2600390

LAW SOCIETY OF IRELAND

www.lawsociety.ie
   The Law Society of Ireland
   Blackhall Place
   Dublin 7
   Tel. (01) 6724800
   Fax: (01) 6724801

MABS (MONEY ADVICE BUDGETING SERVICES)

www.mabs.ie

Cork MABS
12 Penrose Wharf
Penrose Quay, Cork
Tel. (021) 4552080
Fax: (021) 4552078
Email: cork@mabs.ie

Dublin MABS
There are numerous MABS offices in Dublin, so to find the one closest to you go to www.mabs.ie/contact_us/contact_us.html.

Galway MABS
The Halls (3rd Floor)
Quay Street
Galway Co. Galway
Tel. (091) 569349
Fax: (091) 569478
Email: galway@mabs.ie

Limerick MABS
Unit 9, Tait Business Centre
Dominic Street
Limerick
Tel. (061) 310620
Freephone: 1800 418088
Fax: (061) 404605
Email: limerick@mabs.ie

Waterford MABS
6b Wallace House
Maritana Gate, Canada Street
Waterford
Tel. (051) 857929
Fax: (051) 841264
Email: waterford@mabs.ie

St Vincent de Paul
www.svp.ie
National office
SVP House
91–92 Sean McDermott Street
Dublin 1
Tel. (01) 8386990
Fax. (01) 8387355

The Samaritans
National Helpline 1850 609090
Dublin Branch (01) 872 7700

APPENDIX 9
IMPORTANT TAX DATES

ANNUAL TAX RETURN

Form 12 is the short version for those whose main source of income is from an employment or pension (other than a company director for whom there is a separate Form 12) and is therefore taxed under PAYE.

Form 11 or Form 11E must be completed each year by self-employed persons or those with income not taxed at source.

To download these forms, go directly to www.revenue.ie/forms

The initial instructions for Form 12 are: 'You are hereby required, under Section 879 Taxes Consolidation Act 1997, by the Inspector of Taxes named above to prepare and deliver, on or before 31 October 2012, a tax return on this prescribed form for the year 1 January 2011 to 31 December 2011.'

You must make a return of income on Form 11 if in the year 2008 you:

* opened a foreign bank account
* acquired a material interest in offshore funds in a member state of the EU, EEA, or the OECD with which Ireland has a double taxation agreement and/or
* invested in a Foreign Life Policy issued from a member state of the EU, EEA, or the OECD with which Ireland has a double taxation agreement.

To assist you in completing this return, each section of the form has been colour coded into the different categories of income, tax credits, allowances and reliefs.

All Revenue forms and information leaflets are available from the Revenue Forms and Leaflets Service at LoCall 1890 30 67 06 (ROI only) or from the Revenue's website www.revenue.ie or from any Revenue office.

PENALTIES

The law provides for penalties for failure to make a return, or the making of a false return, or helping to make a false return, or claiming tax credits, allowances or reliefs which are not due. These penalties include fines up to €126,970, up to double the tax in question, and/or imprisonment.

IMPORTANT TAX DATE DEADLINES

October is an important month in the tax calendar as 31 October is the last day by which an individual taxpayer must 'Pay and File' for the tax year ended on the previous 31 October.

The table below uses October as the example because of its importance, and shows what day in October returns and payments become due.

Some returns are required more than once a year (e.g. every month as in the case of PAYE/PRSI) as indicated in Column 2:

Date	Frequency	Category	Description
14	Monthly	Income tax and PAYE/PRSI	Payment of PAYE/PRSI deductions to 30 September.
14	When applicable	Dividend Withholding Tax	Due date for payment and filing of returns of withholding tax on dividends paid by companies in September 2013.
14	Bi-monthly	VAT	Filing of VAT 3 return together with payment of any VAT due.
14	Monthly	VAT	Filing of Intrastat return for September.
21	Annually	Corporation tax	Company year-end 30 November 2013: First instalment due, minimum 72% of total liability for the year.
21	Annually	Corporation tax	Company year-end 30 April 2013: Second instalment due, bringing cumulative payment to 90% of total liability for the year.

21	Annually	Corporation tax	Company year-end 31 January 2013: Payment of balance of corporation tax and filing of corporation tax return and Form 46G.
28	Annually	Company Secretarial	Filing of Annual Returns dated 30 September 2013.
31*	Annually	Corporation tax	Company year-end 30 April 2013: Close companies with undistributed profits may have to make a distribution by this date to avoid surcharge.
31*	Annually	Company Secretarial	Company year-end 31 January 2013: Final date for holding Annual General Meeting and latest possible Annual Return Date for 2013.
31*	Annually	Capital Gains tax	Filing of return of capital gains tax for 2013. Payment of capital gains tax on disposals from 1 January 2013 to 30 September 2013.
31*	Annually		Income tax and Payment of preliminary income PAYE/PRSI tax for 2013. Payment of income tax balance for 2013. Filing of 2013 tax return.
31*	Annually	Pensions	Payment of retirement annuity premiums, PRSA premiums and personal contributions to occupational pension schemes for tax year 2013 – you must also elect to have these treated as paid in the tax year 2013.
31*	Quarterly	VAT	Filing of VIES return for calendar quarter ending September.

APPENDIX 10
100 TOP MONEY-SAVING TIPS

Are you having trouble making ends meet? Do you run out of money before pay day? Are you extravagant with your money? Do your current financial circumstances require you to do a complete overhaul on your lifestyle and spending? What are the areas that will allow economies in your spending? Almost every item of expenditure should be queried – do you need it and, if so, are there better or cheaper alternatives? Many of the following tips are practical and easy to implement. Some of you will know or have heard them before, but they will give you the impetus to focus on your own finances to start saving money *now* when it matters.

FINANCIAL

1. **Plan a yearly household budget.** Add all your yearly household bills and divide by twelve. That figure is the amount you need to put away each month to meet those bills just to run the home. Any capital or 'luxury' spending must be found outside of this annual budget. You could also adopt a monthly budget if preferred, but in any event you should put at least two hours every month into planning your finances to ensure you are on track with your spending. Remember, if your expenditure exceeds income, you have two choices: earn more or cut costs. You should query EVERY item of expenditure – do you need it and is there a better or cheaper alternative?

2. **Be smart with your surplus cash.** Do not leave surplus money in your current account or low interest-bearing accounts. At least transfer it into your bank's best deposit account, and when you need funds to meet commitments, transfer the money over a couple of days before it is due. If that deposit account is sizeable, negotiate with your bank – their rates are much less than, for example, KBC Bank (3.25% – on demand up to €100,000 or 1 year fixed at 4.15%) and, therefore, they may have the discretion to increase that deposit rate in order to hold on to your business.

3. **Check your bank charges on a regular basis and cut down your banking bills.** There are too many cases of overcharging from *all* the banks to think that *your* bank is not one of them! Sometimes, these charges can be waived at the discretion of the manager – if you don't ask, there'll be no waiving. Try to avoid exceeding your overdraft permission if you have an overdraft, as the surcharges and fees are punitive. You should also operate online bank accounts – they offer better deals, are easier to operate and there's no waiting in queues, as well as saving you time and travel expenses.

4. **Check your mortgage and loan interest rates.** Sometimes we go to great lengths at the initial stages of obtaining a mortgage or loan, trying to ensure the most competitive interest rate at the time. Once taken out, there is a tendency to overlook the maintenance of that loan. You could very easily find out that your lender's original rate or current advertised interest rate bears no resemblance to your own. If you are currently on a variable rate, this is a good time to check if you should switch to a fixed rate; if your lender is uncompetitive, it is also a good time to see whether you should switch to another lender.

5. **Avail of your annual capital gains tax (CGT) exemptions.** The first €1,270 of chargeable gains to an individual arising from the disposal of a capital asset (e.g. shares) is exempt. This is allowable for each tax year but is not transferable between spouses. The rate payable on CGT is 25% over the threshold. For Capital Acquisition Taxes (CAT), remember that the threshold from parent to child (Group A of three groups) is currently €332,084 for each child. The tax rate for CAT is also 25% over the thresholds.

6. **Check your life and health cover.** You could be over-insured. Do a review on all your insurances. Are you getting the best value? What happens if you or your spouse die or become permanently incapacitated? If you took out life cover (with home mortgages it is mandatory) you may have been a smoker at the time. Once you have been smoke-free for 12 months, you could save yourself over 50% of the annual premiums. It is worth checking out.

7. **Health insurance comparison.** With only four health insurers in Ireland (VHI, Aviva, Laya and GloHealth), it is really important that you stay up to date on what is the best deal for you. The Health Insurance Authority does an excellent comparison of all three and updates it. Check out www.hia.ie.

8. **Check your general insurances.** Your home buildings and contents – is your cover competitive? If you have commercial or residential investment property insurance, is that competitive? Do you require any special risk insurance that you 'risked' being without to date – you may not be so 'lucky' next year! – such as public liability, professional indemnity, PC hacker, virus insurance and even insuring for that round of drinks after a hole in one on the golf course.

9. **Avail of any exemptions on income tax liability plus claim any tax reliefs and allowance entitlements up to the last four years.** This includes medical expenses, rent relief, pension relief, bin charges, etc. Text MONEYDOCTOR to 53131 and start the tax refund process (normal SMS rates apply). You may be unwittingly exempt from paying income tax (e.g. an Irish resident artist producing originals that have cultural and artistic merit, income from woodlands, etc.) while you should also ensure, if self-employed and your partner is working in the business, that the full entitlement of income tax exemptions is taken up by your partner. In other words, pay her/him her/his dues tax-free!

10. **Private college fees.** Tax relief at the standard rate is available for approved courses undertaken by a taxpayer or dependents in approved private colleges. The courses must be full-time undergraduate courses of at least two years' duration. Also, postgraduate courses of between one and four years' duration in public colleges and approved private colleges now attract similar tax relief.

11. **Help your parents or be helped by your children.** Covenants are also still popular, with tax relief available for the donor – you. To qualify for tax relief, the payments must be capable of lasting for at least six years while the recipient has to have unused tax credits to make the covenant work. If a person is over 65, their son or daughter can pay them up to **5% of their income** under a *deed of covenant* and the son or daughter will get tax relief on the amount paid. The covenant must be legally documented in order for the person making the payment to receive the tax benefits. Tax at the standard rate (20%) must be deducted and only the net amount paid over. For example, if a daughter gives her mother €1,000 a year, she makes out a covenant and pays €800 to the parent. The mother then gets the other €200 by way of a tax rebate from Revenue while the daughter also gets tax relief of €210. The net cost to the daughter is €590, while the mother gets the benefit of €1,000. The

Revenue regards the €1,000 as the mother's. The daughter has already paid €410 in tax (41%) on the €1,000 and the tax is now being returned. Effectively, €210 goes back to the daughter and €200 to the mother. The person making the covenant should get tax form R185 from his or her local tax office and submit.

12. **Think pensions.** If you are self-employed, a 5% equity-holding director or perhaps in an occupational pension scheme (where pension holders can make further payments through an Additional Voluntary Contribution), you should review your pension requirements. Age thresholds still apply – e.g. at 50 years old, you can invest 30% of your net relevant earnings into a pension plan – while for every euro you invest in the fund, you will save tax at your marginal rate depending on the type of pension. Just remember, if you were retiring now, ask yourself if you could live off the €230.30 per week from the State pension. Less than half the working population have made provisions outside of the State Pension. While in 2010 there were six workers for every person retiring, in 2051, there will be just two. The incentives are still there to start. Apart from the tax relief on premiums – reducing to 20% in 2014 – all growth in the fund is tax-free, plus 25% of the fund can be taken on retirement by way of a tax-free lump sum (now capped at €200,000). It is still worth it.

13. **ARFs and AMRFs.** Recent changes in the pension laws now allow YOU to decide what you want to do with your retirement fund when you have reached the age of retirement. Up to a few years ago, the *only* choice you had was to take out an *annuity* (a fixed-rate deposit account out of which you receive a monthly interest cheque until you die – the rate *never* changes) with a Life Insurance Company. When you die, however, the capital or fund stays with that Life Insurance Company and your estate loses out. For PRSA and AVC pension holders, that has all changed now and the fund can eventually be passed on to your estate through an *Approved Retirement Fund (ARF)*. Three main conditions apply: a) you must either have at least a €18,000 pension before investing your fund in an ARF *or*, if you do not have a pension, b) put €120,000 of your fund into an Approved Minimum Retirement Fund (AMRF) until age 75 *and* c) you then must take 5% of the ARF each year – called *imputed distribution*. The annuity system is still available and has its merits too. Contact your regulated adviser or your preferred pension provider for further details.

14. **Operate a charge card or a prepaid card as opposed to a credit card.**
    You are probably aware that credit card balances are normally charged between 9% and 24% depending on the credit card company. By switching to a charge card (e.g. American Express) you MUST pay off when you receive your statement or it is debited to your bank current account. Another option is *prepaid cards*, where you can only spend what you lodge into the card – better discipline! See *10 reasons why you should have a prepaid card* plus a *special offer* at the end of these tips.

15. **Think about other forms of investment.** For instance, gold, rock 'n' roll memorabilia, philately or forestry investment. Ireland is the least afforested country in the EU with forest cover of 9% as compared with the EU average of 31%. The Irish climate is the most ideal in the Northern Hemisphere for tree-growing due to our mild, wet climate; trees grow three times faster here than elsewhere in Europe. Timber products are also the second largest import into the EU after oil. The EU and the Irish government promote forestry through grants and premia payments. They are keen to reduce agricultural output, of which there is a surplus in the EU, and substitute it with timber-producing forests, for which there is a growing internal EU shortage. The government, through the Department of the Marine and Natural Resources, specifically offers **capital grants** and **tax-free income grants** under certain conditions as encouragement to investors buying appropriate and approved lands for the planting of trees.

16. **Review your investments monthly.** Products are launched every week and you should monitor their performance on a regular basis. Rates change, some investments go out of favour – you have to be vigilant. If there is a better rate or greater potential elsewhere, do not be afraid to move. The money is better in *your* pocket.

17. **Claim all your tax reliefs on residential investment properties.** These include:
    * 75% of annual mortgage interest paid
    * Maintenance and repair costs
    * Service charges (including buildings/block insurance)
    * Property management charges
    * Private Residential Tenancies Board (PRTB) fees
    * 12.5% of furnishing costs for each of the first eight years after purchase (receipts must be maintained).

18. **Working from home.** If you're self-employed, be aware of the ability to reclaim partial costs by working from home, e.g. electricity, heat and telecoms.

19. **Save.** Be aware of the changing deposit interest rates. You should also have between three and six months' annual income in a *Rainy Day Fund* for three reasons:
    - Emergencies (your car breaks down)
    - Sudden loss of income (a partner loses their job)
    - Investment opportunities (buying a rare Arabian oil lamp).

20. **Rent a room relief.** Renting a room in your home is tax-free up to a limit of €10,000 per year – no expenses may be deducted and it is not available between connected parties. One-bedroom apartments do not count!

21. **Loans for the over 60s.** If your home is mortgage-free or perhaps has a very low loan to value and you have little income, avail of these no-interest, no-capital loans to unlock some of that equity in your home and improve the quality of your life. Only when you pass on or move permanently out of your home does the loan crystallise and your executors discharge the loan.

FOOD, DRINK AND HOUSEHOLD ITEMS

22. **Always shop with a pre-written grocery list.** Stick to what is on the list. Men in particular are disastrous for impulse buying.

23. **Check to see what you need before making out a shopping list.** Many shoppers buy items they already have in stock.

24. **Create a daily list for updating.** If you run short of tea, washing-up liquid, kitchen towels, these can be added to your main shopping list.

25. **Look for special sale announcements in your store, newspapers, on radio and on television.** It may be worth your while buying a month's supply of an item you would normally buy if you can avail of a huge discount.

26. **Shop only once a month for your non-perishables.** This means you have to plan for the full month and should not overspend by additional visits to your local convenience store.

27. **Keep your shopping receipts.** You should track your spending and compare prices (a little black book might be just the job or, better still, avail of the FREE **Money Doctor app** to track your precise spending habits (for iPhone and Android; search your app store by typing in **Money Doctor** and downloading).

28. **Shopping at discount stores should not mean that you ignore generic products in the main supermarkets.** Tesco, Dunnes, Superquinn, Supervalu and Centra stores all produce their own generic goods at considerably cheaper prices than the brand names.

29. **Buy direct when you can.** All vegetables and fruit come from the land. If you have access to a local farm, buy directly from them. Apart from saving money, you will benefit from the fresh produce.

30. **Grow your own.** If you have a garden or a 'plot', try growing a few vegetables, or you could try growing your tomatoes in the house!

31. **Buy in bulk.** Economies of scale apply, in particular to non-perishables (tins of beans) and toiletries (24-roll tissue packs). You will need to analyse your consumption to evaluate your bulk needs.

32. **Don't buy bulk unnecessarily.** A half a ton of nails at rock bottom prices might be fine if you are a carpenter. Special offers such as '3 for the price of 2' might not suit your palate.

33. **Use vouchers and cut-outs.** You will be amazed how all those little discounts add up to big savings on your shopping bill; there is no shame in availing of these offers. You may even have a discount offer on the back of your shopping receipt. Watch out for 'double coupon' days too. Look after the pennies and the pounds will look after themselves.

34. **Avail of in-store discounts and special offers.** Simply by visiting your local store, you might come across a 'loss leader' that you might have on your shopping list.

35. **Shop online.** This can be cheaper because impulse buys no longer apply. Delivery charges can be negated by the cost of travelling to your supermarket and parking. Not to mention the latte!

36. **Online discount websites.** Before you shop, you should spend a few minutes checking out some of the discount websites for economies: www.onoffer.ie, www.dealrush.ie, www.finefare.com and www.youririshshop.com to name but five.

37. **Check the date on all your purchases.** No point in arriving home with
     out-of-date food fit for the bin. The same goes with food in stock –
     ensure that you consume foods that have been stored for the longest
     time first and, of course, that they are still safe to eat.

38. **Avoid buying at the check-out and never ask for cash back.** You are
     bombarded with chocolates, batteries, magazines, etc., in that last-ditch
     attempt to lure the money from your wallet at the check-out before you
     leave the shop. Resist the temptation! Receiving cash back only increases
     the cost of your purchases as the cash back is soon frittered away.

39. **Bring your own bags to the store.** There is a 22-cent charge for every
     bag bought at the check-out. You could kill two birds with the one stone
     by buying biodegradable and environmentally-friendly bags.

40. **Buy food with balance in mind.** Food and drink should be based on a
     balanced diet. Eating pizzas and drinking Coca-Cola seven days a week is
     not going to do a whole lot of good for your diet, nor does it do much
     good for your wallet. Plan your meals to reflect this balance and save
     money in the process.

41. **Avoid snacks after shopping.** You have been shopping for an hour and
     you go to the store café for a coffee and a sit down. Go home and put on
     the kettle instead.

42. **Don't buy on an empty stomach.** You often end up buying food simply
     because you are hungry.

43. **Bring your own lunch to work.** Prepare your own roll or baguette and
     refill your water bottle, as long as the water from the tap is fit to drink.
     Water will soon be scarce, so use it wisely.

CARS AND FUEL

44. **Review your car.** Does it need replacing? Could you upgrade the model
     for efficiency purposes (e.g., if it's currently getting 25 miles per gallon/
     40 kilometres per 4.55 litres and you were to change it for a car doing 35
     miles per gallon, you would save 40% on fuel costs).

45. **Change your car to diesel or an electric model.** Apart from the
     environmental support through reduced carbon emissions, you could
     save hundreds of euro by making such a change.

46. **Avoid company cars.** In about 80% of cases, it does not pay to maintain a company car. Benefit in Kind (BIK) on company cars is prohibitive – 30% of the value of the car when first purchased. For example, with a Toyota Avensis diesel at €25,520, for as long as you have this as a company car you will pay BIK each and *every* year of €7,656 or €638 per month, irrespective of the falling value of the car through depreciation. Better to take mileage expenses at €0.6348 per mile.

47. **Buy a classic or vintage car (over 25 years old).** Apart from the style, it would be cheaper to buy, and if you deem this car a company vehicle, the tax payable will be based on the value of the car at the time of purchase! Plus, car tax is minimal, and they are cheaper to insure.

48. **Reduce your dependency on car fuel #1.** Pool your car and share it with others going the same way or working in the same company.

49. **Reduce your dependency on car fuel #2.** Charge your work colleagues a fuel-sharing fee should they have no car and want you to drive them to work each day.

50. **Reduce your dependency on car fuel #3.** Keep your car in top trim with regular car servicing, keeping the correct pressure in your tyres, driving under the speed limit, driving smoothly and carrying no unnecessary weight inside the car.

51. **Check your tyres for wear.** New tyres will be more efficient than the worn tyres that currently adorn your car. If they are over two years old, and under normal annual mileage, your car can be a death trap anyway. Review those tyres!

52. **Shop around for fuel.** Take a note of your local stations and their fuel prices. Sometimes, to grab greater market share, stations will run a discount campaign to drive custom through their business. Look out for fuel discount cards and websites (www.pumps.ie).

53. **Reduce your dependency on cars #1.** If you are a two-car family, review the need for the second car. Work out the practicalities. Would public transport – which is improving all the time – be more appropriate?

54. **Reduce your dependency on cars #2.** Would buying a bicycle be practical? Apart from the obvious exercise angle, the humble bike costs nothing to run and there are even tax breaks for employers and employees alike through the Bike To Work scheme.

55. **Think electric cars.** Hybrid cars are already with us, but the future car will be an all-electric model. Already capable of reaching 120kph with a range of about 40 miles without charging, they can only improve year on year.

56. **Car loans are deterrents.** If you are a person who changes your car every three years and just renew the existing (and expensive) car loan at that point, try saving over a three-year period so that you do not need that car loan.

57. **Car loans.** Shop around if you must take out a car loan. Expect to be charged between 6% (if you have a really solid relationship with your bank) and 15% depending on the institution you approach. Avoid moneylenders like the plague.

58. **Walk.** Good for the body, pocket and your dependency on cars.

59. **Use public transport.** It's actually much more economical than maintaining your own car.

60. **Home oil.** Shop around through the various home heating companies looking for economies. Paying upfront for the year's oil requirements may reap dividends.

61. **Home heating.** Remember to switch off the heating when you're away, even for weekends, and especially at the onset of summer.

62. **Boiler.** If your boiler is more than ten years old, you could consider replacing it with a new condenser boiler which uses energy more efficiently and should repay installation costs within two years.

63. **Insulate your house and your pipes.** You will save hundreds of euro through minimising heat loss.

64. **Avail of energy grants for improving the efficiency of your home.** There are a number available, check out www.seai.ie/grants.

LIFESTYLE AND MISCELLANEOUS NEEDS

65. **Brush up the CV.** Keep your CV updated. You never know the day when you may be looking for a job. The most recession-proof employments can be found in education, healthcare, environment, energy and security. If you are not in these industries, you should brush up your skills: go to night classes or take online courses. Whatever you do, don't stay in a sector that is in decline.

66. **Buy cloth napkins and nappies.** Cloth versions are more economical.

67. **Stick to your annual clothes budget and look after your clothes.** Limit your spending on clothes to a budget rather than impulse buying for that special party. Change into casual clothing after work. Hang up everything rather than leaving things on the floor or throwing them on a chair.

68. **Check out charity clothes shops.** There is no shame in buying clothes from these outlets as, first, you are helping the charity and, second, the clothes, often with designer labels, are far cheaper than buying new.

69. **Use eBay to sell unwanted items.** Watch out for special offers throughout the year, e.g. 50% off normal advertisement placement fees. Great for selling unwanted clothes, electrical and electronic goods, concert tickets, etc.

70. **Buy generic medication.** You will always find brand name medicine more expensive. Ask your doctor to prescribe generic medicine.

71. **Go to your library.** All your magazines, movies and books are there and are free. You can even order online and just collect. The good news for authors is royalties are now being paid, albeit miniscule ones, when books are taken out. Now you know! You can also read newspapers online.

72. **Review your health club.** If you enjoy a membership, ensure that you are getting value. Monitor your weight and fitness. The same applies to golf clubs or any sporting or social membership. IF YOU ARE NOT USING IT, CUT IT OUT.

73. **Entertain at home.** Game nights, movie nights, music soirées. As entertainment outside the home becomes more expensive, the simpler life beckons, but it can also be much more fun and much more social.

74. **Plan your annual gifts.** Family birthdays, Christmas presents, and special friends' gifts you know you will have to buy. Why wait until the week before Christmas to buy them – the most expensive week of the year?

75. **Review your cable and telecoms.** Do you really need the movie channels? If you are a golf buff, are you really going to spend THAT much time on Sky Sports AND Setanta, let alone the Golf Channel?

76. **Subscribe to Skype (www.skype.com)**, especially if you have to make calls to international numbers. With over 310 million subscribers and 15 million users online at one time, the savings are very significant (Skype-to-Skype calls are free from your computer, while Skype to landlines are only 0.017c per minute). If you have chatterbox children, block all outgoing mobile calls – the saving could be significant. You should always check your telecom bill and review the top ten most-called and top ten most-expensive numbers. This can be very revealing!

77. **Check with the ComReg website (www.callcosts.ie).** Shop around for your broadband also. This site gives you all the broadband operators and various associated costs. The new eurotariff legislation on roaming charges means it may be cheaper to phone home than send a text message (which is not covered under the new legislation).

78. **Shop around for your electronic communication handsets.** Mobile phones incorporating MP3 players, internet, email, camera, video and radio are becoming cheaper and more sophisticated by the year. Some of the electronic equipment you now have is either out of date or incorporated into new gizmos. Sell it. Also *use rechargeable batteries –* even placing batteries in the fridge will prolong their life.

79. **Social networking.** Use these websites to your best advantage: Facebook, Twitter, MySpace, LinkedIn, YouTube. Putting your name in front of millions can reap dividends for whatever your purpose.

80. **Friends' holiday homes.** You may find that your friends are under financial pressure and would welcome offers at a discount to rent their foreign holiday homes. A win—win situation for them and you.

81. **Do your own garden and handyman jobs around the house.** You will tone your muscles, become fitter, plus your garden will positively bloom – not to mention attracting the admiring glances from your neighbours!

82. **Take haircuts at longer intervals.** Instead of every six weeks, make it ten weeks. Better still, cut your own hair or ask a friend to do it.

83. **Garage sale.** Rather than storing, hoarding or dumping your prized possessions, sell them from your garage or car boot.

84. **Wheelie bins.** Only leave out your respective bins (general refuse bins, etc.; there is NO charge for the green bin) when they are completely full. Collection charges apply irrespective of weight if you leave the bins out.

85. **Enter competitions.** Newspapers, magazines, radio and TV – someone *has* to win and it could be you. If you're not in, you can't win!

REDUCE YOUR ELECTRICITY BILLS

86. **Review your gas/electricity utility provider.** With the successful 'Big Switch' campaign from Bord Gáis, competition is now intense. ESB is back on the field (they had to wait until 40% of their business had migrated to other providers before they were allowed back in the game) and with Airtricity and Flogas, the consumer has choice. Keep checking.

87. **Changing your bulbs to CFLs.** This will save you up to 20% of your annual bills. They may not look as pretty, but they will put money back in your pocket. Soon they'll be the only kind available.

88. **Only use washing machines and dishwashers with full loads.** Like your dustbin, it will pay you to optimise the load.

89. **Never have the immersion on with your central heating.** The immersion should only be used during the summer or when you do not need your central heating. The immersion is like a kettle – it should be switched off when you have heated the water.

90. **Using your immersion.** Unfortunately, unlike kettles, immersions do not turn off automatically. It only takes about 15 minutes to heat enough water for the sink, and about 45 minutes for a full bath. Leaving the immersion on all day and night eats money. Switch it off when not in use!

91. **Use timers and night timers.** Together with dimmers for light switches. Also for those washing loads at night. Heavy sleepers never hear the din but count the money!

92. **Use nightlights, especially in the bathroom.** They are cheap to run.

93. **Avoid peak time.** Use as much as possible between 5 p.m. and 7 p.m.

94. **Turn off all lights in rooms not being used.** Children should be especially encouraged to turn off lights in their own bedrooms when they leave for school on winter mornings. Minimise lighting where you can. Think of using candles – it's more romantic!

95. **Only boil water in a kettle for your immediate needs.** There is no need to put on a full kettle of water when you only want one cup of tea!

96. **Take short showers.** If bathing, have all the family use the same water,

unless one of them has just returned from a filthy rugby match!

97. **Ensure that your fridge and freezer is full.** If you cannot fill it, place jugs of water inside. It is cheaper to run a full freezer than an empty one.

98. **In summer, use the clothes line to air your washing.** This is cheaper than the expensive tumble dryer. Only use that tumble dryer off-peak and preferably at night time rates.

99. **Switch off all electronic equipment when not in use.** Leaving them in 'stand by' mode uses 20% of the normal output.

THE FINAL TIP

100. **KEEP IN TOUCH WITH THE MONEY DOCTOR (consultation@moneydoctor.ie or call +353 1 278 5555).**
   - Buy *The Money Doctor* finance annual each year.
   - Book a 20-minute *Money Doctor consultation* – only €65 – for independent, experienced, trusted and authorised advice, a once-per-year financial makeover.
   - Download the *Money Doctor app* to track your spending. It's free!
   - Choose the *Money Doctor seminar* for your company (an hour-and-a-half journey through personal finance).
   - As an employer, enquire about our Employee Well-Being Programme.
   - Use social networking to keep in touch with *Money Doctor*:
     - Facebook
     - LinkedIn
     - *Money Doctor* website to subscribe to the newsletter.

John Lowe, Fellow of the Institute of Bankers, is founder and managing director of Money Doctor, regulated by the Financial Regulator and author of the best-selling *The Money Doctor* finance annuals plus *50 Ways to Wealth* (both Gill & Macmillan), is now available for seminars and consultations: email seminars@moneydoctor.ie or consultation@moneydoctor.ie or call **(01) 278 5555**. Follow John on Twitter (@themoneydoc), Facebook and LinkedIn.

APPENDIX 11
THE MONEY DOCTOR'S TIPS FOR THE TOP

In this appendix, I am delighted to introduce five innovative, competitive or leading-edge products and services that I stand by and endorse, and that I feel could be useful in your armoury for better managing and protecting your money.

Please contact me directly if you want further details. These are not in any order:

1. **Standard Life MyFolio Funds**
2. **An Post's www.mybills.ie and BillPay**
3. **Sharewatch stockbroking services**
4. **Independent Trustee Services**
5. **Canada Life's Lifelong Income Benefit investment**

1. STANDARD LIFE'S MYFOLIO FUNDS
MyFolio – which one is for you?

Each person has different investment needs and goals – some for the short term, while others are longer-term. Some are quite conservative when it comes to investment decisions, while others are happy to take a more adventurous approach. It all comes down to finding the right balance between risk and reward.

Standard Life has developed five *MyFolio funds*, which help to make investing *really simple*. All you have to do is choose the fund that matches your risk level.

What are MyFolio funds?

They're a family of multi-asset funds that are risk-based and are managed by a team at Standard Life Investments. These multi-asset funds invest in different assets, including equities, bonds, property and money market instruments (including cash), which helps to spread risk. Each fund is designed to maximise potential returns for your chosen level of risk. They are monitored, reviewed and actively managed by the fund managers.

A choice of five funds: there are five multi-asset funds ranging from the really cautious funds – cash and government bonds (*MyFolio I*) to the more *risky* funds – energy stocks and emerging markets (*MyFolio V*). Bear in mind that if you want growth in your investments, there has to be an element of risk. The higher the risk, the potentially greater the return, but also the potentially greater the loss. Here are the choices:

MyFolio I (lower risk)

This may suit you best if:

- You're conservative with your investments.
- You're prepared to take a small amount of risk to achieve modest or relatively stable returns.

MyFolio II (lower-to-medium risk)

This may suit you best if:

- You're relatively cautious with your investments.
- You want to try to achieve a reasonable return and you're prepared to accept some risk in doing so.

MyFolio III (medium risk)

This may suit you best if:

- You take a balanced view of investment risk.
- You don't seek out risky investments, but don't avoid them either.

MyFolio IV (medium-to-higher risk)

This may suit you best if:

- You're relatively comfortable with investment risk.
- You're aiming for higher long-term returns, and understand that this can also mean sustained periods of poor performance.

MyFolio V (higher risk)

This may suit you best if:

- You're very comfortable with investment risk.
- You aim for high long-term investment returns and do not overly worry about periods of poorer performance in the short-to-medium term.

How MyFolio can help you spread the risk

A golden rule of investing is diversification or 'spreading the risk'. And when you think about it, it's just common sense. Putting all of the money you have to invest in just one company's shares is a really high-risk strategy. Diversification across different investments can help reduce risk.

Multi-asset investing

Diversification isn't just limited to investing across shares of different companies. It can also mean spreading your money across different types of assets, such as shares, bonds, property and investing in a range of countries. Each asset responds differently to changes in investment conditions. Some could go up in value, at the same time as some go down. So, spreading your money across assets can help to smooth out your investment over time. You should keep in mind that even a well-diversified portfolio can still fall in value.

What are the benefits of investing in a MyFolio fund?

Simplify your fund choice:

With so many funds in the market to choose from, choosing the right one can be daunting. With only five funds to choose from, MyFolio funds makes this choice a lot simpler.

Diversification:

These multi-asset funds invest in a broad range of assets. This helps to spread your risk.

Monitored, reviewed and actively managed for you:

The assets in these funds will all perform differently at different times. So, each fund is monitored, reviewed and actively managed by a team at Standard Life Investments. If investment conditions change, they'll make sure your fund still matches your chosen risk profile.

Choice of risk level:

As there are five different risk levels to choose from, if your attitude towards risk or your circumstances change, you can simply switch to another MyFolio fund that offers a higher or lower level of risk.

Ease of access:

These funds are priced daily and are available across a range of our pensions, savings and investment products.

Be aware though that an actively managed fund can fall as well as rise in value and may be worth less than what was paid in. MyFolio funds will not be suitable for you if you do not want to take any risk.

STANDARD LIFE – an A-rated, well-capitalised insurance company you can trust
Pensions and Investments since 1834

It's important to trust the companies you deal with. Standard Life is a leading provider of long-term savings and investments. Headquartered in Edinburgh and operating internationally, they've been in Ireland since 1834 and have helped generations of Irish customers plan for their future.

Global investment expertise

Standard Life Investments manages the *MyFolio funds*. Based in Edinburgh, they are global active fund managers with a talented and experienced team of more than 200 investment professionals.

    For further details contact:

Standard Life
90 St Stephen's Green
Dublin 2

LoCall 1890 252 222
Direct +353 1 639 7070
Web www.standardlife.ie

2. AN POST'S MYBILLS.IE AND BILLPAY SERVICES

www.mybills.ie is a unique, free online service from *An Post* providing a 'one-stop-shop' for paying bills via the Internet from a comprehensive list of over 100 bills (e.g. Electric Ireland, Bord Gáis). Customers can also set up payments to pay an amount automatically off their bills each month.

One of the key principles behind managing your finances is to match your income with your outgoings as best you can.

Spending on utility and household bills is one area that people sometimes overlook when it comes to aligning their income with their expenditure. *An Post's* mybills.ie and **BillPay** services are two hidden gem services that allow you to do just that.

For those who are computer and web savvy, *Mybills.ie* gives you all of the tools needed to ensure that you can pay your household bills *at times and in amounts that suit you*. Crucially though, **the service is 100% free and easy to use**.

Using the website, you can:

Pay bills from your PC: *Mybills.ie* allows you pay over 100 household bills online without the expense of having to physically bring it elsewhere for payment. You can pay one or multiple bills with just one click!

Pay bills in increments: Finding the cash to pay your household bills can be tough – especially in the current financial climate. Using *Mybills.ie*, you can elect to pay a certain amount towards your household bill when it suits you. Why tackle a €200 heating bill when you can pay it in instalments over 3–4 weeks? *Mybills.ie* allows you to avoid the disruption caused to your finances by having to pay large utility bills in one go!

Automatically schedule all payments: The really great thing about *Mybills.ie* is that the site allows you to automate the payment of bills in a way that suits you. Unlike direct debits, these payments can be instantly cancelled or postponed at the push of a button. I know many people who use this feature to schedule multiple utility bill payments week to week to coincide with the arrival of their pay. Using this approach, they greatly limit the potential for a shock to their finances caused by an unpaid or unexpectedly large bill.

Store household bill records: To manage your finances effectively, it's essential that you know exactly what your income and expenditure is month to month. All bills paid through *Mybills.ie* are recorded for you so that you can log in to see how much you paid and when. You can even use some analytical tools to see how your household bill payments have changed over time. Use the history section to see a list of bills that you have paid. You can use the statistics section to get an overview of bills you have paid by biller(s) or/and by date range.

Using *Mybills.ie* is really simple. All that you need to do is to firstly register on the site. They'll send you on some details in the post and then you're ready to go! If you make one change to the payment of your household bills year, I would strongly recommend that you start to pay them through the *Mybills.ie* website and save yourself time *and* money!

Registering with *Mybills.ie* is an easy three-step process:

1. *Personal and log-on details.*
    Mybills.ie requires you to enter in some personal details including your name, postal and email address. Your logon details are what you will use to access your bills next time you visit mybills.ie. As part of your log-on details you must supply a password and a corresponding password hint, which will be used should you forget your password. The concept behind this method of authentication is that you can choose a secret truly known only to you and devise a password hint that will prompt your password if forgotten. If you forget your password you can request your password hint from the system.

2. *Set up biller and payment method*
    You will also need to set up a biller and a payment method.

3. *Registration complete!*
    Here you review your details to ensure that you have entered them correctly. Please note that following registration you will have to wait until you receive your PIN in the post before you can make a payment using a registered payment method.
    For queries, email customersupport@mybills.ie or phone *LoCall* 1890 61 71 71 (lines are open from 9am to 5:30pm, Monday to Friday). When contacting with technical queries, please be able to state which Operating System (e.g. Windows 7, Mac OSX) and which Browser (e.g. Firefox, Chrome, Safari, Internet Explorer, etc.) versions you are using.

For those who are not comfortable with computers, *An Post's* BillPay service continues to offer many of the features listed above.

You can pay practically any household bill at one of over 1,100 post offices nationwide – *free of charge* 6 days per week and at hours to suit your schedule. Again, like *Mybills.ie,* you can pay bills in instalments, though there are low minimum payment amounts associated with some bills.

What's more, by using **BillPay**, you'll be helping to support your local post office – a critical cornerstone of any community that provides a variety of services offering real value and friendly service.

3. SHAREWATCH – the cost-effective way to buy shares

Sharewatch Limited is an Irish Financial Services Company regulated and authorised by the *Central Bank of Ireland.*

Its unique business model and carefully selected partnerships allow *Sharewatch* clients to contract directly with the world's largest brokers and avail of **low-cost** trading, high security, award-winning technology and a complete range of products.

Sharewatch Limited is registered in Dublin, Ireland #286532 and part owned by *Independent News & Media PLC (INM)*, a global international newspaper and communications group with market-leading brands in Ireland, Northern Ireland, South Africa, Australia and New Zealand. Directors are *Peter Byrne* (Managing), *John Crowley* (Secretary) and *Garret Doyle* (Non-executive) representing *Independent News & Media*.

All Trading will be executed, cleared and administered by Forex Capital Markets Limited (FXCM), a company authorised and regulated by the Financial Services Authority. Registration number 217689. FXCM Inc. is a publicly traded company listed on the New York Stock Exchange (NYSE: FXCM). Saxo Capital Markets UK Ltd. London is registered by the Financial Services Authority (Registration Number FC026688). Saxo Bank A/S is a fully licensed and regulated European bank. Saxo Bank A/S is subject to stringent financial reporting requirements under EU directives and specific regulations regarding client handling.

Sharewatch Limited provides a wide range of low-cost trading products and services.

Share trading

Sharewatch Limited offers a multi-market and multi-currency share trading platform. Markets include Ireland, UK, USA, Australia, Canada, Spain, Germany, Netherlands, France and Switzerland.

Bonds

A full list of bond instruments are available for trading. Offline traded bonds are traded on the following commissions: 0.08% with a minimum charge of €80.

CFDs (Contracts For Difference)

CFDs trade a broad range of markets and assets including stocks, indices, commodities, ETFs and Forex, with low margin requirements and on award-winning trading platforms.

Spread betting

Low spreads (better value) offer you thousands of different products including shares, commodities, metals, currencies and indices. Avail of futures contracts as well as rolling daily contracts.

Forex (Foreign exchange)

Extensive range of currencies from an award-winning, easy-to-use FX platform.

Better value

Sharewatch Limited charges €14.95 or 0.3% for trading most global markets online offering *significant* savings when compared to its competitors. For those who prefer telephone trading, fees of just 0.3% (min €50) are extremely attractive and highly competitive. There are NO annual fees.

The www.sharewatch.com Financial Portal provides a whole host of free content including stock quotes, news, graphs and more besides.

Sharewatch

Sharewatch Limited
NSC Campus
Mahon
Cork

Sharewatch Trading
Northern & Shell Building
10, Lower Thames Street
London EC3R 6AD
UK

Sharewatch Saxo Trading
   26th Floor
   40 Bank Street
   London E14 5DA
   UK

   Web www.sharewatch.com
   Tel: LoCall 1890 818 111

4. INDEPENDENT TRUSTEE COMPANY (ITC)
Self-Administered Pension Structures

A **pension trust** is a tax-efficient way of saving money for retirement years. Saving for retirement is an important part of retirement planning for you and your family's future. A **self-administered pension** (or **self-directed trust**) offers you the control over what your pension invests in, therefore tailoring your pension to suit your needs.

It provides a flexible and transparent way of saving for your retirement. Independent Trustee Company, established in 1994, is Ireland's premier trustee company and leading provider of self-administered pensions. They have an excellent range of products ensuring that you are in full control of your investments.

When it comes to self-administered pensions, good governance and structure are key elements to your fund's success. Independent Trustee Company can offer you both.

Their self-administered pension plans provide four key features:

Control	– you sign off on all scheme transactions.
Transparency	– you can view your pension scheme operating account online.
Flexibility	– you decide what investments your scheme makes.
Security	– they hold pension schemes off their balance sheet which means that they don't treat your pension scheme as one of their assets.

ITC provides three main **self-administered pension** products:

SSAPS	(Small Self-Administered Pension Scheme),
PRSA	(Personal Retirement Savings Account) and
ARF	(Approved Retirement Fund) and AMRF (Approved Minimum Retirement Fund).

ITC SSAPS (Small Self-Administered Pension Scheme)

This is a very tax-efficient occupational pension plan and can be set up by a director who is a company owner and paid a salary, or an employee with agreement from the employer.

A **SSAPS** offers additional benefits to the conventional pension schemes provided by life-assurance companies. For example as it is self-administered, it allows you to control your contributions and investments. All the assets in the SSAPS are held in trust on your behalf. Traditionally, a SSAPS has fewer than 12 members, but some providers – such as Independent Trustee Company – provide one-member schemes only.

Under Revenue rules, an approved independent Pensioneer Trustee is appointed to your scheme and they administer it in line with Revenue's rules and regulations. You will or may also act as co-trustee on your SSAPS with the Revenue approved Pensioneer Trustee, such as Independent Trustee Company.

Why choose an ITC SSAPS?

Control – As co-trustee of your SSAPS, you have control over your investment and funding decisions. You do not have to delegate the responsibility to an insurance company fund manager who considers you as one among many policyholders. You create a personal investment plan that fits your appetite for risk, your budget and your retirement target. Your investment choices can be sourced from a wide variety of Irish and international investment providers. You control when to start and stop, increase and decrease contributions to suit your circumstances, rather than according to the terms of an insurance company contract.

Transparency – The ongoing cost of your SSAPS is fully transparent and depends on your investment strategy, which you control. You have online access to the operating bank account. This allows you to track the movement of monies within your SSAPS in real time.

Flexibility – Your needs and circumstances shape the investment strategy and the level and timing of contributions. Your SSAPS is also portable, which means that you can continue to contribute if you change your employer.

Security – Your pension assets are held in trust on your behalf, through a SSAPS. This means that they are completely segregated from ITC's assets, other clients' assets and your company/employer assets. This differs from insurance companies, which hold pension assets on their balance sheet. If your company fails, your SSAPS is secure from claims by creditors.

ITC PRSA (Personal Retirement Savings Account)

A PRSA pension is a portable, tax-efficient pension that offers you control over your investment decisions and the flexibility to make contributions when it suits you. It is designed to help you, the sole member, accumulate wealth for your retirement. You can have a PRSA pension if you are:

- an employee, or
- a director, or
- a self-employed professional, or
- a sole trader.

A PRSA pension can be set up regardless of your current or future employment status. Unlike traditional pension schemes offered by insurance companies, you can choose from a wide variety of investments such as individual properties, land, private equity, publicly quoted shares and cash. Your investment choices can be sourced from a wide variety of domestic and/or international investment providers.

ITC A(M)RF (Approved (Minimum) Retirement Fund)

An ARF is a tax-efficient post-retirement investment fund. An ARF can be set up if you:

- have a Personal Pension Plan or
- have a Personal Retirement Saving Account Plan
- are a member of an employer-sponsored defined contribution pension scheme or
- are a member of an employer-sponsored pension scheme and have made Additional Voluntary Contributions (AVCs).

All your assets in an ITC ARF are held under trust on your behalf. You have control over where your funds are invested and the frequency of income drawdowns.

You can draw a regular income from your ARF to suit your needs. Once you have satisfied the AMRF requirement, there is currently no upper limit to the level of withdrawals that can be made. If you are aged 61 or over and you do not make a withdrawal during the year, you will be obliged to withdraw at least 5% of the fund (called an *imputed distribution*). All withdrawals from your ARF are subject to income tax, PRSI and income and health levies, as appropriate.

On your death, your spouse can step into your shoes and take over the ARF, tax-free. They can continue to manage the ARF investments and make withdrawals from the ARF as they wish. On the death of this spouse, the ARF must be wound up. The assets of the ARF will pass to the estate. Inheritance and/or income tax charges will be applied.

As well as offering control, flexibility, choice and transparency through their pension structures, ITC offers a high-quality professional pension trustee service. ITC is approved by the Revenue Commissioners and the Pensions Board as a Pensioneer Trustee, and are regulated by the central bank of Ireland. ITC is also approved as Trustee Trainers by the Pensions Board and is one of the founding members of the Association of Pensioneer Trustees in Ireland.

For more information:

Independent Trustee Company Limited
Harmony Court
Harmony Row
Dublin 2

Tel: +353 1 6611022
Fax: +353 1 6611024
Web www.independent-trustee.com

5. CANADA LIFE'S LIFELONG INCOME BENEFIT INVESTMENT

When you retire, outside of the State Pension there are basically two systems used to give you income, either from your own savings into a pension fund or your employer's savings into your fund.

After you receive your tax-free lump sum (25% of the pension fund to a maximum of €200,000 or one and a half times your final salary) the two systems are:

Annuity – a guaranteed income for life that is determined at the start of your retirement and can only change if you have factored inflation into the equation. However if there is a residual in the fund when you pass on, the insurance company keeps the balance, not your family or to whomever you bequeathed your estate

Approved retirement fund (ARF) – introduced by the Finance Act 1999, ARFs allow greater control of your retirement fund. You can choose the type of investment – equities, gold, property, etc. – and you have greater control over the fund. The good news is that if you are run over by a bus after 6 years, your estate keeps the fund. But there are a few rules and regulations:

- The first €120,000 must be invested in an Approved Minimum Retirement Fund (AMRF) until aged 75 unless there is a guaranteed minimum annual pension of €18,000 (including state pension). Obviously if your total pension fund is less than €120,000 and no guaranteed pension, you then have just the one choice – an annuity.
- From age 60, if you have elected to retire you MUST withdraw 5% of the fund each year (called imputed distribution). This is fully taxable and subject to PRSI and USC.

You could therefore work out how much of a fund you will need to keep you in the kind of luxury you have become accustomed to in previous years. Then, importantly, choosing the right system to manage your retirement fund is also a serious consideration for you and your family.

While there are other combined options, depending on fund size, there are pros and cons for both systems – if longevity is in your genes or yours is a placid lifestyle, as the annuity monthly payment is FOR LIFE, you might beat the system and the insurance company. With an ARF, at a withdrawal rate of 5% it only takes 10 years to deplete your fund by 50% – and if you retire at aged 60, having less than 50% of your fund to see you to the average male age of c. 81 might leave you a little short.

Canada Life's Guaranteed Lifelong Income Benefit ARF has a unique *lifelong* income benefit. In other words, it has *all* the benefits of an annuity's guaranteed income irrespective of the balance in the fund while enjoying also the benefits of an ARF.

There is nothing worse than outliving your fund, and between product charges, inflation, poor market returns and other possible necessary annual withdrawals, an ordinary ARF could leave you well short of a comfortable retirement. The Canada Life product is a serious option worth consideration as it:

- *Guarantees income for life*
- *Allows access to the fund at any time*
- *Gives a choice of funds to choose from*
- *Provides a minimum payment on death (which is greater than the death benefit applying to a 'normal' ARF)*
- *This death benefit is the higher of*
  - *The fund value at death OR*
  - *The original amount invested minus gross payouts, surrender penalties and administration charges where applicable.*

While it is important to know and avail of the thresholds to maximise your tax relief on pension contributions, important to know that all growth in the fund is tax free and that you can take up to €200,000 or 25%, whichever is the greater, as a tax-free lump sum, it is what you do with the 75% of your hard-earned retirement fund that matters.

By providing both security and flexibility, the **Canada Life Lifelong Approved Retirement Fund** with lifelong income benefit provides a creative and innovative new retirement option, offering you:

- *A secure, predictable, guaranteed income for life in retirement;*
- *Access to your retirement fund when you need it;*
- *A choice of investment options;*
- *The potential for your income to be increased through income 'lock-ins'; and*
- *A minimum payment on death.*

You should note that if you do make a discretionary withdrawal, your guaranteed income will be reduced.

The minimum payment on death is equal to the higher of the current fund value and the premium paid less all withdrawals made (including any surrender penalties, administration charges and tax).

Canada Life, part of the *Great-West Lifeco Inc*, have been operating in Ireland since 1903, are AA rated and very well capitalised. Their Guaranteed Lifelong Income Benefit ARF provides the security of knowing that your full ARF investment will always be paid back to you, between living and dying.

For further details, call LoCall 1850 203 203 or +353 1 210 2000 or write to:

Canada Life
Canada Life House
Temple Road
Blackrock
Co. Dublin
Web www.canadalife.ie

Michael Noonan, Minister for Finance, delivered his second Budget speech on Wednesday, 5 December 2012, while Brendan Howlin, Minister for Public Expenditure and Reform, outlined the cuts in public spending. Described as the toughest ever, it was the third last of the austerity budgets when €3.5 billion was taken out of the economy through a series of benefit cuts (€2.25bn) and tax increases (€1.25bn) against a backdrop of unprecedented deficit challenges in Ireland and worldwide. This Budget still left a 0.3% shortfall on the agreement to bring the deficit to 7.5% of GDP by the end of 2012, as agreed with the Troika. Over the last five years, eight new levies have been introduced, including the universal social charge, the income levy, and the second property charge, most of which have now been absorbed into expanded taxes with different names. Next year the government has to find another €3.1 billion, and in December 2014 a final €2 billion to balance the books and bring us back to where we should have been seven years ago.

Mr Noonan said at the end of his speech:

> When I stood before the house last year on December 6th, the Irish government was locked out of bond markets. Our two-year bonds yields were almost 10%; now they are less than 2%. We have seen a total transformation in only 12 months. Today, markets and foreign lenders are willing once more to lend to Ireland and to Irish businesses. This is essential for our businesses and our economy to continue its path to recovery.

But like most Irish people when faced with seemingly insurmountable hardship, we are good at taking the medicine and getting on with it. While there were several positive initiatives, including a package of tax measures to support the SMEs, help employment and foster business expansion and survival, the synopsis that follows only relates to the personal tax payer.

HIGHLIGHTS

- **Property tax** on all residential property: 0.18% up to €1m, 0.25% over this threshold.
- Three-year **property tax exemption** for first-time buyers.
- **Child benefit** reduced by €10.
- Unearned income will become subject to **PRSI** in 2014.
- DIRT, Capital Gains Tax and Capital Acquisitions Tax rise to 33%.
- VRT rate and motor tax will increase from 1 January 2013, while there is **no increase** in excise duty on petrol or diesel.
- Beer/cider and spirits up by 10 cent, and a bottle of wine up by €1.
- A 20-pack of cigarettes up by 10 cent.
- **No change** to income tax or corporation tax.

LOCAL PROPERTY TAX

Property tax on *all* residential properties will be introduced from 1 July 2013. The main features of the tax will be as follows:

- The Revenue Commissioners will collect the property tax.
- Property owners will be able to choose from a wide range of payment options. These will include direct debit, credit or debit cards, cash payments or 'deduction at source' from salary/occupational pension or certain state payments.
- Tax imposed on market value as assessed by the owner. The initial valuation will be valid up to and including 2016.
- Valuation guidance will be issued by the Revenue Commissioners, or taxpayers can use a competent valuer.
- Property tax will be levied at 0.18% for the first €1 million and 0.25% thereafter.
- Properties with a value of more than €100,000 and less than €1 million will be assessed at the mid-point of valuation bands of €50,000 width. Properties valued in excess of €1 million will be liable at 0.18% on the first €1 million with no banding applied.
- From 1 January 2015, local authorities will have discretion to vary the local property tax rates by +/− 15% of national central rate.

- National central rates to remain unchanged for lifetime of government. Using an example of a property in the €150,000–€200,000 threshold, the half year charge in 2013 will be €157.
- **Voluntary deferral** will be available for property tax for low-income earners. Interest will be charged on deferred amounts at a low rate (4%).
- Exemption from local property taxes for new and newly acquired or previously unoccupied homes acquired before 31 December 2016. Exemption will also apply to first-time buyers for four years and residents in unfinished estates during this period.
- **Non-principal private residence charge** to cease from 1 January 2014, and the **household charge** will cease to have effect from 1 January 2013.

Revenue will strictly enforce the Local Property Tax and they will collect any unpaid Household Charge for 2012. Any arrears that are not paid before 1 July 2013 will be increased to €200 and will be collected through the Local Property Tax system.

INCOME AND OTHER TAXES

Tax Credits and Tax Bands
- No changes to existing rates or bands.

Universal Social Charge
- The reduced rate of USC for those over 70 years of age with an income in excess of €60,000 will be discontinued from 1 January 2013 and the standard rates of USC will apply.
- The standard rate of USC will also apply for medical card holders earning €60,000 and above with effect from 1 January 2013.

PRSI
- Unearned income will become subject to PRSI (currently 4%) in 2014. This means that PRSI will be payable on income generated from wealth such as rental income, investment income, dividends and interest on deposits and savings.

- Where modified PRSI rate payers have income from a trade or profession, such income and any unearned income they have will be made subject to PRSI with effect from 1 January 2013.
- The minimum level of annual contribution from the self-employed will rise from €253 to €500.
- The weekly €127 PRSI allowance for employees will be abolished for all those earning €352 a week.

Deposit Interest Retention (DIRT) Tax

- DIRT will be increased from 30% to 33% for payments made annually or more frequently. DIRT will be increased from 33% to 36% for payments made less frequently than annually. Exit tax on life assurance policies and investment funds are also being increased by 3% to 33% for payments made annually or more frequently, and 33% for payments made less frequently than annually as of 1 January 2013.
- Exit tax on investments over 12 months also increased by 3% from 33% to 36%.
- With PRSI deduction of 4% from 1 January 2014, it now means any interest earned will be subject to a total tax deduction of 37%, for example a 3% gross rate will give you 1.89% NET.

Capital Acquisitions Tax (CAT)

- Up 3% to 33%.
- Thresholds reduced by 10%:
  - Category A (parent to child)   €225,000
  - Category B (nephew/niece, etc.)   €29,887
  - Category C (all others)   €14,587

Capital Gains Tax (CGT)

- Up 3% to 33%.

For Those with Preferential Loans

- Benefit in Kind (BIK) **increase** from 12.5% to 13.5% in the specified interest rate used in calculating the taxable benefit from preferential loans, other than home loans. The specified rate for home loans will be decreased from 5% to 4%.

SOCIAL WELFARE BENEFITS

Child Benefit

- Reduction of €10 for the first child from €140 down to €130 per month.
- Third child benefit is reduced by €18 to €130, while the fourth child and subsequent children benefit is reduced by €20 to €140 each.
- The additional monthly payment for twins and triplets will be maintained.

Jobseeker's Benefit and Allowances

The primary weekly rate of social welfare payment of €188 per week will not be cut, but the duration of Jobseeker's Benefit is to be reduced by 3 months from the current 12 months to 9 months for those with 5 years' PRSI contributions, and from 9 months to 6 months for those with less.

Jobseeker's Allowance for those long-term unemployed remains unchanged, but is still means-tested.

Maternity Benefit

- Maternity Benefit will be treated as taxable income from 1 July 2013 and, as is the case with all social welfare payments, Maternity Benefit will continue to be exempt from the Universal Social Charge.

Other Benefits

- **Back to School Clothing and Footwear Allowance** is reduced by €50 to €100 for children aged 4 to 11 from qualifying families, and by €50 to €200 for children aged 12 to 22 from qualifying families.

Contributory and Non-Contributory Old Age Pensions PLUS all other weekly benefits were left as is.

INDIRECT TAXES, EXCISE AND OTHER DUTIES

Oil & Petrol

- No increase on excise duty for petrol or diesel.

VRT and Motor Tax

- VRT and motor tax across all categories will increase from 1 January 2013. A dual registration period will be introduced in order to incentivise a year-round market.
- Increase of 7.5% on cars registered before 2008.
- Cars emitting between 110g and 120g of carbon dioxide per kilometre of travel will have the annual motor tax bill jump by 25 per cent, from €160 to €200 per month.
- Emission-free cars bought since 2008, or electric cars bought before then, will see their tax fall by almost a quarter to a flat rate of €120 per year.

Alcohol and Tobacco

- Cigarettes up by 10c per pack of 20.
- Roll-your-own tobacco will increase by 50 cent per 25g pack.
- There will be a *pro rata* increase on other tobacco products.
- Beer and cider up by 10c.
- Wine up by €1 per 75cl bottle.

OTHER ITEMS

Pensions

- A provision to allow people to access 30% of Additional Voluntary Contributions (AVCs) to their pensions up until 2016 will be introduced.
- The current €2.3 million Standard Fund Threshold continues for 2013.
- Tax relief on pension contributions will be available to subsidise pension schemes that deliver income of up to €60,000 a year. This will take effect from 1 January 2014.
- The Pension Levy will not be renewed after 2014.

Medical

- **Prescription charges** for medical card holders to be raised from €0.50 to €1.50 per item.
- The monthly prescription charge cap for a family is being increased from €10 to €19.50.
- **Drug Payment Scheme** threshold is being increased from €132 to €144 per month.

- People 70+ with income of €600–€700 per week for a single person and €1,200–€1,400 per week for a couple will see the medical card replaced with a GP-only card.

For Farmers

- The definition of registered farm partnerships will be expanded to add other production partnerships, such as beef, to the 640 milk production partnerships that can already avail of the enhanced 50% rate of stock relief.
- Farmers will get extended rate of stock relief. The general 25% rate and special 100% rate of stock relief, which were due to expire on 31 December 2012, have been extended for a further three years.
- The farmers' flat rate addition will be reduced from 5.2% to 4.8% with effect from 1 January 2013.
- Relief from CGT for disposals of farm land for farm restructuring from January 2013 to December 2015, subject to EU State Aid approval.

Political Cuts

- There will be a 10% cut to the Party Leaders Allowance, including the tax-free payment of €41,000 paid to non-party Oireachtas members (not a big imposition on themselves), and the free envelope allowance will be cut by 50%.
- It is also proposed to abolish unvouched expenses for Oireachtas members.

Student Registration Fees

- The student contribution in higher education will be increased by €250 in each of the years 2013, 2014, 2015. This means fees will rise from €2,250 this year to €3,000 in 2015.

Carbon Tax

- The carbon tax will be extended to solid fuels on a phased basis over two years, starting after this winter period. A rate of €10 per tonne will apply with effect from 1 May 2013, and this rate will increase to €20 per tonne on 1 May 2014.

Introduction of Real Estate Investment Trusts (REITs)

- A new property investment product called REITs is to be launched to allow personal and pension investors invest in 'rental investment property'. The proposed broad outline of a REIT is as follows:
  - ◆ A REIT will be a property investment company listed on the Stock Exchange. Investors will therefore buy shares in the company.
  - ◆ The company will invest, with some limited borrowing, in a diversified pool of rental investment properties.
  - ◆ Income will be paid out annually to investors.
  - ◆ Investors can sell their shares at any time on the Stockmarket. However, the market price could be at a discount to net asset value; there will be no guarantee that the share price will follow the net asset value of the fund.
  - ◆ Investors will pay tax on their returns, probably as a collective investment fund, e.g. private investors may pay exit tax at 33% on income returns and 36% on investment gains, while pension investors will probably get a tax-free return.

The Department of Finance leaflet on REITs states as Benefit for Small Investors:
- The entry cost for a REIT investment is the price of a single share. Small investors can therefore participate in the property market without mortgage borrowings or property transfer costs.
- Small investors can gain access to returns from high-quality investment-grade property assets, which have previously been the preserve of very large investors only.
- As REITs are designed to produce regular income returns to shareholders, they may give a new alternative investment option for retirement savings.

REITS are likely, therefore, to bring a new investment product to the market for private and pension investors.

Movie Investment

- The Film Tax Relief Scheme (known as Section 481) will be extended to 2020.

INDEX